# FORMAL EDUCATION IN AN AMERICAN INDIAN COMMUNITY

# FORMAL EDUCATION IN AN AMERICAN INDIAN COMMUNITY

## Peer Society and the Failure of Minority Education

Murray L. Wax
Rosalie H. Wax
Robert V. Dumont, Jr.

*with the assistance of*

Roselyn Holyrock
Gerald Onefeather

WAVELAND
PRESS, INC.

Prospect Heights, Illinois

For information about this book, write or call:

    Waveland Press, Inc.
    P.O. Box 400
    Prospect Heights, Illinois 60070
    (708) 634-0081

*Cover photo:* Courtesy of the Red Cloud Indian School Archives.

*Formal Education in an American Indian Community* previously appeared as a special supplement to *Social Problems* (the official journal of the Society for the Study of Social Problems), Volume XI, Number 4, Spring 1964.

Originally published 1964.
1989 reissued with changes by Waveland Press, Inc.

ISBN 0-88133-447-2

Printed in the United States of America

7   6   5   4

# Contents

# Tables

# Preface, 1964

## A Guide to the Reader

Those who must skim the pages of reports as they run from crisis to meeting to office are advised to turn to the chapter titled "Summary and Recommendations," which has been written with them in mind. Readers who wish to examine a picture of a contemporary Indian reservation and who are indifferent to the preliminaries of a research investigation are advised to turn to the second chapter, titled "Ecology, Economy, and Educational Achievement," Skeptics and critics will want to read not only the first chapter but also the Appendix before proceeding into the heart of the text.

The focus of this book is not on the Dakota as an isolated people bearing the survivals of an aboriginal culture but on the social processes of the contemporary community of Pine Ridge including, especially, its system of formal education. Having first been written as a research proposal, the first chapter does review the many and often excellent ethnographic studies of the Dakota peoples of the far past and near present. Otherwise, the text provides only the minimal background necessary for understanding how Sioux traditions affect the current situations where "Indians" and "Whites" meet — and avoid — each other and try to educate, guide, manipulate, thwart and live with each other.

The reader who is familiar with the problems of the schools in urban slum communities will be struck, as we were, by the marked parallels between these educational institutions and those of Pine Ridge. In both, scholastic achievement is low and dropout is high, the major loyalties of the children are to their peers, and the children are confronted by teachers who usually see them as the inadequately prepared, uncultured offspring of an alien and ignorant folk. In view of this marked similarity, we hope that our analysis will contribute to an understanding not merely of Indian schools but also of the many urban schools which serve as the reformative, custodial, and constabulary arm of one element of society directed against another.

# Preface, 1989

When I was meeting with a few other specialists on Indian education a few years after the publication of this study, Francis McKinley (a member of the Ute Tribe on the staff of the Far Western Laboratory for Educational Research) suggested that the report should be widely distributed among the Indian tribes. I reminded him that the reviewer for the *American Anthropologist* had deplored the "hysterical" tone of the report. "Now, it's historical!" was McKinley's rejoinder.

The report was historical not only in the context of Indian affairs, but also in educational research. Most educational researchers had been preoccupied with tests and measurements, which were then subjected to mechanical data processing and finally to even more mechanical statistical analysis. At the same time, anthropologists had confined their attention to studying informal education among nonliterate peoples. A subdiscipline called "educational sociology" was housed in Schools of Education, but it lacked disciplinary recognition, and only a handful of sociologists had in fact been observing schools, most often in the context of community (i.e., small town) studies, where the attention was primarily on the school as an agency of socialization in class and caste. The resultant array of research studies did not speak to the genuine concerns of students, parents, and educators.

The present study was a pioneer example of what, over the next quarter century, was to become a significant, albeit numerically minor, current of ethnographic studies of educational institutions. Even in its design, this project was innovative. The details — serious and hilarious — may be found in Rosalie H. Wax's *Doing Fieldwork: Warnings & Advice*, but the outline was simple. We pitched our tent next to a Country Sioux (i.e., rural and traditional) family, and then, when the weather turned cool and I suffered too much illness, we moved into an abandoned schoolhouse which afforded ample opportunities to observe unsupervised children. Members of the research team observed classrooms, mostly at the local school, but also at the other reservation schools (federal, country, and mission). We talked to parents and interviewed them formally; we talked to teachers and other educators, and interviewed *them* formally. We talked with children and did our best at interviewing them. We attended community gatherings, parent teacher meetings, and religious ceremonials. In this way, we intimately observed, and experienced as much as possible, the lives of rural Indians in a reservation community; and, we came to understand much of the distinctive Sioux perception of reality and what it was that they desired for their children. (We also perceived the discrepancies between the views of the Sioux and those of the federally employed educators.) To an anthropologist, this style of participatory research is now taken for granted, but it was novel for educational research. It remains novel for most educational researchers even today, despite the minor vogue of ethnographic studies.

At the present writing, a quarter century later, ethnography is considered by many as a valuable educational research technique. Yet, most ethnographic studies differ significantly from this one. The stated goal of most educational research is imposed from without by the reformist wing of the bureaucracy, who require assistance in making the schools more efficient: teaching more (conventional) subject matter to more pupils at less cost. Ethnography then becomes a component of a larger, tightly structured, research project. In contrast, our team, emerging from the anthropological tradition of Indian Studies, were respectful of Indian culture and critical of the middlebrow culture of the public schools. As is evident from the attached essay of 1971, we were skeptical toward the conventional "Dick-and-Jane" blend of scholastic instruction, especially in the context of the Sioux reservation, while we were ourselves disciples of the higher learning of the Great Tradition.

In my observations and analysis, I pondered what might be authentic as education for the Oglala. Given my heritage, I privately used the metaphor of Hassidic Judaism, whose children — at least the boys — are given a thorough formal education, but not that of the public schools. The same is true for other communities whose religious-ethnic integration is strong (e.g., fundamentalist or sectarian Christianity). This educational pluralism has been one of the distinctive — and, in my mind, powerful — features of the American ethos (although it has recently come under challenge with the movements for desegregation and increased federal supervision of schools). As I looked at the reservation schools, I saw them as preaching a single mythical and homogenized version of America, whereas the Sioux had every right to ask that their children be socialized into their own unique ethos. This is what gave to this report a cutting edge too often lacking in other ethnographic studies, and — to be honest — it is why the reviewer in the *American Anthropologist* perceived our report as "hysterical."

In the initial decade following the research, I thought of our achievement as being the clear and emphatic demonstration of the central role of the peer society in the schools. I was often invited to talk about this project, and I invariably found that my audience (even an anthropological one) tended to adopt an individualistic approach to the classroom, as if it were the arena for the interaction between a teacher and an aggregate of students; when, however, I reminded the audience of their own childhood sensitivity to their classroom peers, they at once understood that, even apart from the reservation schools, teachers usually confront groups or societies of students, rather than "naked" individuals. The reservation had provided a natural experiment in which the solidarity of the peer society was intense, and the resultant confrontation with the teacher dramatic and painful.[1] A parallel case might occur whenever the local community is ethnically (or racially) homogeneous and its children confront a school system that appears alien and intrusive.

These findings provide the inner meaning to the otherwise obscure or debatable ones emanating from such massive statistical studies as "The Coleman Report." This is an additional benefit deriving from the methodological innovativeness of this ethnographic project. Unfortunately, this benefit is perceived by few; for, despite the newly gained respectability of ethnography in educational research, few critics consulted the research about peer societies in an effort to comprehend the school social dynamics that were expressed in Coleman's tables.

The study, then, has had a limited and peculiar history. When the manuscript was ready in 1963 for publication, the then editor of *Social Problems*, Howard S. Becker (himself a pioneer student of formal education), recognized its value and arranged to have it issued as "Monograph Number One" of the journal. It was then reprinted on an ad hoc basis by the Business Office of the Society for the Study of Social Problems, corresponding to its usage as a college text. Somewhere along in the years, perhaps when the Business Office was transferred, the report slipped from the collective memory of the SSSP, perhaps because it had been published as a special monograph rather than as a regular issue of the journal, or perhaps because the specificity of the report's title did not convey its relevance to students of general "social problems." Meanwhile, it was reprinted as part of the 1968 Hearings of the Special Subcommittee on Indian Education (90th Congress), and portions were included in various anthropological readers. The study had already been cited by activists who wanted to place reservation schools under the control of tribal (or other local Indian) control, as in the case of Rough Rock among the Navajo, or Rocky Boy among the Assiniboine.[2]

If, then, a quarter century after its original publication, I had to point to the special virtues of this research study, I would say that at the most fundamental level it is the research design that accords a place of privilege to the local community, and examines the schools from that viewpoint. Rather than being a study of a federal school — with some notice taken of the social environment — it is instead a study of how the local (ethnic) community deals with a school which has been imposed upon it and which demands that the children be given into its care. Given this innovative — and indeed radical — research design, the findings were bound to be novel and to have serious consequences. The sociological analyst might at this point refer to "conflict theory," and it is true that the research design anticipated *cultural* conflict, but what emerged as the major finding was a form of *social* (rather than cultural) conflict, and this appeared directly from our observations, rather than from our theoretical preconceptions.

Many students of applied social-science (be it applied anthropology or sociology) have pessimistically concluded that the impact of most projects is minor and sometimes even contrary to intent. A quarter century after the conclusion of this research, I find that the study did have a positive effect, especially among the Oglala of Pine Ridge, but also generally within Indian education.[3] This does not mean that the tribally controlled school systems are ideal, but only that a set of major and unrecognized problems have been replaced by a set of minor problems of a familiar sort. I would hope, then, that a current generation of readers would find this report of contemporary interest, as well as of historical interest to students of Indian affairs.

Murray L. Wax

# Footnotes

[1] Later, when we worked among the Cherokee of eastern Oklahoma, Dumont observed a parallel solidarity of the peer society (see his and my "The Cherokee School Society and the Intercultural Classroom," *Human Organization*, 18 (Fall 1969):217-226.

[2] Copies of this study were distributed widely among the Oglala who had participated in the study. In addition, Dumont organized a summer school-camp, and his continued presence on Pine Ridge must have acted as a catalyst. In the climate of the times (with the "War on Poverty" of the Lyndon Johnson presidential administration), a movement to place the Loneman School under their control emerged among the local Sioux community. Some of the subsequent events are described in Case Study II of the pamphlet, *Who Should Control Indian Education?*, produced by the Far West Laboratory for Educational Research and Development in 1970.

[3] In the decade following this report, and likely stimulated by its findings, a National Study of American Indian Education was commissioned, and its major findings reported in the book, *To Live on This Earth* by Estelle Fuchs and Robert J. Havighurst (Doubleday, 1972). More detail may be found in the separate reports upon local regions, prepared for the Study. Unhappily, since that time, there has been no major study of Indian education, nor any overall review of the consequences of local control.

# Acknowledgments

This monograph issues from a research project whose major source of financial support was the Cooperative Research Program of the U.S. Office of Education. Supplementary assistance was received from Emory University mainly via its division of Teacher Education. A small grant from the Phelps-Stokes Fund facilitated the drafting of the original research proposal.

The research idea was conceived by the senior authors, Murray and Rosalie Wax, as a result of their experiences with Indian college students participating in the summer Workshops on America Indian Affairs, conducted annually on the campus of the University of Colorado. The research idea developed into a formal project proposal after attendance at an anthropological conference where Everett C. Hughes encouraged the audience to interest themselves in the study of education and to approach the Office of Education for financial assistance.

When the research proposal had been accepted and became Cooperative Research Project 1361, Robert V. Dumont, Jr., was engaged as Research Assistant. Even before the official date the Project was to begin, he moved to Pine Ridge and began his field observations, continuing them for over a year. He now plans to return to that reservation with an educational research and demonstration project. His signal contributions to the collection and interpretation of the data, as well as his devoted interest in the total problem of Indian education and accommodation to the national society, were such as to earn him the status of junior author.

While detailed acknowledgment of the assistance rendered to the Project by the inhabitants of the Pine Ridge Reservation is made in the Appendix, here we wish to note that Mrs. Roselyn HolyRock was a true friend to Rosalie Wax and a valuable field assistant in her own right. Her father, Harry Jumping-Bull, gave sage counsel and assistance, as did numerous other persons, especially Moses TwoBulls, Henry BlackElk, Jr., David Long, Calvin JumpingBull, and Matthew TwoBulls. Another field assistant was Gerald OneFeather, who was especially helpful to the Waxes and Domont during their first few months on Pine Ridge and whose family helped introduce them to significant aspects of Sioux life.

Dr. Philleo Nash, Commissioner of Indian Affairs, was sympathetic to research on Indian problems. Recognizing our wish to conduct our investigation independently of the Bureau, he maintained a helpful but disinterested attitude toward our study, while instructing his staff to assist us in whatever way possible to facilitate our efforts. We thank him and them.

Many employees of the Bureau of Indian Affairs spoke with frankness and concern about educational problems and policies. We benefited by their remarks

xiii

and appreciated their statement, even in those cases where we have not agreed with their suggestions. Since our monograph is critical of existing policies, we felt it would be unwise to mention any particular Bureau employees by name for acknowledgment of assistance. Rather, we thank all those who took the time to speak with us.

Consultants to the Project included Robert K. Thomas, Robert W. Rietz, Everett C. Hughes, Ernest L. Schusky, Tillie Walker, all of whom provided valuable counsel. Thomas, in particular, has instructed us on Indian thought and Indian affairs for many years. Himself having conducted research on Pine Ridge, he was able to advise us on our initial adjustment to the area and introduce us to old friends.

Personnel of the Cooperative Research Branch of the Office of Education impressed us, throughout the process for applying for the funds or conducting the research, with their probity, courteous detachment, and interest in economical and socially beneficial research.

Finally, we wish to thank Howard S. Becker, Editor of *Social Problems*, Frank F. Lee, Business Manager of the Society for the Study of Social Problems, and their staffs for their assistance in bringing this monograph to publication.

Responsibility for the design and direction of the research project and for the final wording of the text of this monograph belongs solely to the undersigned.

Murray and Rosalie Wax

# Chapter I

# PERSPECTIVE AND OBJECTIVES OF THIS RESEARCH

Much of this chapter was written before our field investigation. It was first a proposal for research and then an article.[1] The discussion may be recommended to the reader insofar as he is interested either in the basic orientation, concepts, and hypotheses which we brought with us into the field or in the relationship of this to other studies of American Indians and their educational situation. Because of our desire to mention and review previous studies, the rhetoric of this chapter is the most formally academic of the report.

## SOME HISTORICAL BACKGROUND

If much of the historical interaction between American Indians and Whites (Europeans) has centered about trade, warfare, and the eviction of the Indian peoples f r o m their homelands,[2] an equally constant theme has been education. From the time of the Spanish and French missionaries until the present day, the Whites have been concerned with educating the Indians.[3] Usually, this has implied not simply the imparting of literacy, technical skills, or academic lore, but also the transmutation of his culture and personality—from a heathen into a Christian, from an economic collectivist into an individualist, and, in the case of

the nomadic groups, from a hunter into a settled and diligent farmer.

The Indians were interested in the technological accomplishments of the Whites and quickly accepted a number of them. Their adoption of the domesticated horse, for example, was so thorough that the mounted warrior has become the popular stereotype of the true Indian. We can no more think of the traditional Navaho without his sheep (domesticated in Europe) than of the Pilgrim fathers without maize and pumpkins (domesticated in the Americas). Indians were also attracted to the formal learning of the Whites and, during the period of European exploration and early settlement of this continent, several of the independent tribal units were hospitable to the founding of schools. The Cherokee nation became an outstanding case. It established its own school system, operated a national newspaper, and spread literacy more widely among its people than the neighboring White states did among theirs. Within a short

---

[1] "American Indian Education as a Cultural Transaction," *Teachers College Record*, LXIV (May 1963), pp. 693-704.

[2] William T. Hagan's *American Indians*, Chicago: University of Chicago Press, 1961, is an excellent, brief history of the contact between Indian and White in North America. A recent, illuminating study is Henry E. Fritz, *The Movement for Indian Assimilation: 1860-1890*, Philadelphia: University of Pennsylvania Press, 1963.

[3] Evelyn C. Adams, *American Indian Education,* New York: King's Crown Press, 1946, is a short and colorless history of Indian education, containing an extensive bibliography. Sketches of article length will be found in Hildegard Thompson, "Education among American Indians: Institutional Aspects," *Annals*, CCCXI (May 1957), pp. 95-104; Harold E. Fey and D'Arcy McNickle, *Indians and Other Americans,* New York: Harper, 1959; and Alexander Lesser, *Education and the Future of Tribalism in the United States: The Case of the American Indian,* New York: Phelps-Stokes Fund, 1961. Willard W. Beatty, in his essay "Twenty Years of Indian Education" within the collection, edited by D. A. Baerreis, *The Indian in Modern America,* Madison, Wisc.: State Historical Society, 1956, pp. 16-49, reviews the period of his own activity as an administrator from the late 1920's until the reversal of policy under the Eisenhower administration.

time, a sprinkling of Cherokee were college graduates, so that it and related Indian nations of the south were referred to as "Civilized Tribes." Had they or other tribes then receptive to formal learning been given even another generation in which to absorb, diffuse, and integrate Western knowledge into their cultures, the results might have been surprising. But the lawless and violent frontier, with its hordes greedy for land, advanced too swiftly. Perhaps, also, the very learning of the Cherokee was too gentlemanly for the contest. They might have been better off if their young men had learned the baser arts of metallurgy and chemistry, the manufacture of guns and gunpowder; instead, they learned how to argue and win a case before the United States Supreme Court and then found their cause lost when President Jackson ignored the decree protecting their national rights.

The hunger of the Whites to exploit the resources of the frontier could not be slaked, and as the power of the United States increased relative to its Indian neighbors, it embarked on a final series of efforts designed to exterminate them as separate peoples or assimilate them forcibly into the general population. The Indian Removal actions of the nineteenth century and the Reservation system broke the power of the independent tribes and brought them under severe control. Allotment of reservation lands in severalty usually led to further disorganization and impoverishment.

As the tribes were forced to surrender most of their political independence, so too did they surrender any effective control over the formal education of their children. The White administrators did not merely regard them as incompetent to operate schools, but also felt that contact between Indian parents and their children would corrupt the latter into "Indianness." So, during the latter part of the nineteenth century, children were virtually kidnapped from their homes to be incarcerated in boarding schools where they were subjected to a severe discipline in order to mold them into "Whites." Education was thus transformed from a process over which the Indian had had some control (and which he might have viewed as a device for helping himself and his people) into an instrument of the superordinate White directed punitively at the sense of Indian identity.

Indian communities which have resulted from this process are of several different forms. At one pole are the rather small groups who have lived intimately with White society for generations, possessing little autonomy and actually preserving more outmoded European practices than native Indian ones. At the other pole is a diversity of tribes, relatively autonomous and isolated, which preserve a great many native practices and customs even while selectively adopting many of the technological complexes of the larger society. For many of these people the native language is the primary one within the houshold and the first learned by the child; likewise the native religious orientation continues to regulate the habits of the family and community, even when a veneer of Christianity has been applied. Despite the persistence of native traits, theirs is not the aboriginal culture but a "reservation culture," a distinct and novel form, adapted to their peculiar mode of existence.[4] It is the groups with these "reservation cultures" that constitute what is referred to as the "Indian problem," and it is their community dynamics that we shall now review.

---

[4] John Witthoft, "Eastern Woodlands Community Typology and Acculturation," *Symposium on Cherokee and Iroquois Culture*, eds. W. N. Fenton and J. Gulick, Bureau of American Ethnology, Bulletin, No. 180, Washington D. C.: Smithsonian Institute, 1961.

# INDIAN UNDER-EDUCATION

The problem of who today is an "Indian" confuses the utilizing and interpreting of educational indices. The Bureau of Indian Affairs compiles its statistics with regard to those persons over whose property it has the status of trustee or regarding whom it has legal grounds for assuming at least part of the role of guardian. Courts of law are oriented toward issues of inheritance and tend to grade Indianness in "quanta of blood" according to the registration of forebearers; the courts have been indifferent to the question of "way of life" and have scarcely had to deal with a fraction of the chicanery and evasion of the nineteenth century, when Whites claimed to be Indians and Indians claimed to be Whites in an effort to participate in or withdraw from the reservation system and land allotment.[5]

Even from the official figures for federally recognized tribes, however, it is clear that the education situation is deplorably poor.[6] As of 1950, the median number of school years completed among Indians twenty-five years of age and older was less than six; the comparable figure for the White population was over nine years of schooling. In interpreting the figure for the Indians, we should bear in mind that for a large number education was being offered in a language that was totally or partially foreign, so that much of the effort in the earlier grades was devoted simply to instruction in English (and the routine of the school of an alien culture). Moreover, the

low median level means that a paucity of persons has gained any sort of advanced education, so that Indian communities lack leaders who are broadly educated in the intellectual traditions of the larger society.

Not only do very few Indian youngsters attempt college, but among those who do the drop-out rate is extremely high. When the senior authors (Rosalie and Murray Wax) directed the summer Workshop on American Indian Affairs in 1959 and 1960, some of the reasons for this academic failure were painfully clear. Although the participants were among the best Indian college students in the nation, a fair number were not fluent in English and a large number were inhibited about participating in class discussion; despite their intelligence and originality, many were shockingly provincial and miseducated, as compared to college students at any major university. Even their knowledge of American and Indian history, which one might have expected to have some depth, was of the level of American popular culture.[7] For the moment, we are not concerned with questions of cause or responsibility for this condition but only wish to remind the reader of what he well knows—that merely serving time within school walls is not equivalent to education.

In the past, and still today, the simple fact of tribal geography has contributed to educational difficulties. The large tribal groupings of reservation culture are located in barren and inhospitable areas of the country. Because they are thinly scattered in regions of poor roads, accessibility has been difficult for any administrative purpose, including schooling. (This

---

[5] See, for example, Richard K. Pope, "The Withdrawal of the Kickapoo," *The American Indian*, VIII (1958), pp. 17-27.

[6] U. S. Census Bureau, *Non-White Population by Race*, Washington, D. C.: Government Printing Office, 1953. Kenneth D. Anderson, E. Gordon Collister, and Carl E. Ladd, *The Education Achievement of Indian Children: A Reexamination of the Question, How Well are Indian Children Educated?*, Washington, D. C.: U. S. Bureau of Indian Affairs, 1953.

[7] Rosalie H. Wax, "A brief history and analysis of the workshops on American Indian Affairs conducted for American Indian college students, 1956-1960, together with a study of current attitudes and activities of those students" (Mimeographed, 1961).

has tended to justify the use of boarding schools from an early age onward.)

When we consider the current situation of the education of young Indians, the picture is considerably more complex because of the variation among regions and tribes. Some tribes have had the good fortune to fall heir to wealth recently, in a period when society at large has assisted them to retain it rather than conspiring against them. An outstanding case is the Navaho, who had virtually no exposure to formal education a decade ago; today, all manner of ambitious programs for educating Navaho youth are flourishing. As they are among the largest of tribal units and have a high rate of natural increase, their change in status will have a great effect on over-all Indian statistics; until now, they have often not been included in totals and averages. At the opposite pole are tribes like the Sioux of the Dakotas, who were and are still poor, who were poorly educated and who remain so. Unlike the Navaho, they have been within reach of schools for some time, altho attendance and enrollment remain major problems.[8] Perhaps the most depressing areas— and also the least known—are the remnants of the tribes, once termed "civilized," in eastern Oklahoma and elsewhere. Because the federal government withdrew its trusteeship a half-century ago, while at the same time destroying the tribal government and distributing tribal lands, no formal statistics on the conservative "Fullblood" group have been reliably kept.

In estimating the scope of the Indian educational problem and the efficacy of various programs for education and betterment, it is important to keep in mind the high rate of natural increase of the Indian population and especially of its conservative core.[9] A certain proportion of the young people have been achieving some degree of education, migrating from their home community, even being assimilated into the larger population, without significant effect on the social and educational status of the residue. Any permanent "solution" to the Indian "problem"—any amelioration of the conditions of economic, social, and psychic depression—must reach the vast majority of each community. A number of scholars have argued that the migration of the youthful, energetic, and better educated has actually accentuated difficulties by depriving home communities of persons who might be able to serve as a bridge between the more conservative Indians and the external society. It can also be argued that the effect of boarding schools is pernicious; educating the child away from home makes him unfit for sympathetic and cooperative action with his kith and kin on his return as an adult.

## CROSS-CULTURAL EDUCATION

American Indian education is, of course, but one instance of the widespread phenomenon of cross-cultural education. Some of its problems are not particularly the responsibility of either Indian or White, but arise whenever educators of one cultural tradition confront pupils of another.[10] A key variable in this transaction is the locus of power—the *de facto* control of the educational process—which may lie with the educators, the pupils, or

---

[8] U. S. Bureau of Indian Affairs, *Statistics Concerning Indian Education*, Lawrence, Kans.: Haskell Institute, issued annually.

[9] J. Nixon Hadley, "Demography of the American Indians," *Annals* CCCXI (May 1957), 23-30.

[10] Jules A. Henry, "Cross-Cultural Outline of Education," *Current Anthropology*, I (July 1960), pp 267-305; Murray Wax, "More on Cross-Cultural Education," *Current Anthropology*, II (June 1961), pp. 255-256.

elsewhere entirely. Within Western history, an early instance of the powerful pupil is Philip of Macedon, who hired an Athenian named Aristotle to tutor his heir, a wild but talented lad, and to instruct him in the intellectual accomplishments of a defeated and politically subordinate people. A more equable balance is manifest in the custom of European aristocrats of the past few centuries, who hired alien tutors of good (though poor) families to instruct their children in the languages and customs observed in other civilized lands. The configuration, now so common, in which the pupils stem from a subordinate or socially disadvantaged stock, seems to be part of the movement for public education, which is a recent development within Western civilization.

As an aspect of that movement, our metropolitan public schools have been geared to educating and "Americanizing" the children of impoverished immigrants, whether from foreign countries or from our own native areas where a distinct subculture has maintained itself, as among the Negroes of the Deep South or the Whites of the Middle Southern hills. Even where the ethnic stock of a community is reasonably homogeneous, there are still significant differences in culture and political power among the various classes.[11] Thus, we are accustomed

---

[11] For sociological studies of the school system of a midwestern city, see August B. Hollingshead, *Elmtown's Youth*, New York: Wiley, 1949; W. Lloyd Warner and Associates, *Democracy in Jonesville*, New York: Harper, 1959. For studies of the school system of a modern metropolis—Chicago—see the following dissertations and theses executed in the Department of Sociology, University of Chicago: Howard S. Becker, "Role and Career Problems of the Chicago Public School Teacher" (Ph.D., 1951); Martha Wagenschein, "Reality Shock" (M.A., 1950); John Winget, "Ecological and Socio-cultural Factors in Teacher Inter-School Mobility" (Ph.D., 1951); Harold MacDowell, "The Principal's Role in a Metropolitan School System" (Ph.D., 1954).

to a tripartite educational configuration in which ultimate control rests with a school board derived from the higher reaches of community status and power; day-to-day regulation rests with administrators and teachers of a middle level of status and power; and the parents of the pupils—many of whom represent the lower levels of the community—have little or no voice as to what is taught their children or how it is done. Because we take this configuration so much for granted, it is worthwhile reminding ourselves that, especially in the cross-cultural situation, it is neither natural nor inevitable that the recipients of the education lack control over the school system. This is of some international significance. In the countries that were formerly colonies, the nationalistic drive for independence has also affected the educational institutions: Rather than being the targets of the educational missions of more advanced peoples, these new nations wish to operate their own schools and to utilize foreigners as advisers only.

The goal of the educational process is another issue which also affects that of the locus of control. Traditionally, formal education has had modest or specialized goals, such as furnishing the populace with the rudiments of literacy so that they could read Holy Scriptures or giving them the simple intellective skills basic to the common manual arts; only an elite was given prolonged, intensive training of an abstract sort. With the public education movement, the school has been assigned, or has come to inherit, the task of fully socializing children through adolescence along with the assimilation of children of "deviant" ethnic backgrounds into the common American mould as a corollary responsibility. Where socialization and assimilation are the educational goals (rather than, say, vocational training) the school becomes in effect a challenge to the authority and wisdom of the parent generation. If some degree of control over the educational process remains with the parent group, the conflict may be meliorated. But when the locus of control is elsewhere, then the schoolroom may become the focal point of all manner of tensions, thus complicating the simple transmission of knowledge. On the one hand stand adults who represent a particular, superordinate, civilized tradition; on the other hand sit pupils in whom are to be inculcated the customs, values, and thoughtways different from and antagonistic toward those of their elders.

Both parties to the cross-cultural school exercise selectivity with regard to the content of the educational transaction. From the variety of his own civilized society and its intellectual traditions, the educator selects customs, creeds and knowledge which are moral and proper or the effects of which will, he hopes, be salutary. In this fashion, he tends to draw an unrealistic picture of his society and, if his goal were simply assimilation, he would have ill-prepared his audience for the actualities of life.[12] Conversely, most pupils tend to cling to the customs and values practiced in their homes and to view the subject matters of their curriculum with the detached eye of the practical man: How can this be of any use to us? (It is notorious that the traits most easily adopted in cases of cultural contact are those of immediate utility and gratification; for example, on the American frontier, the Indians quickly learned the use of iron kettles and alcohol and the Whites the use of canoes and tobacco.) Within the edu-

cational situation, most pupils are oriented not toward assimilation and the discarding of native ties, but toward sharing in the material benefits associated with the culture of the teacher.

An additional element in the cross-cultural transaction is the impact of the school as a social institution. The more the school and its educational processes encompass the child, the greater is their impact, if for no other reason than that they thereby isolate him from other associations and relationships. Most Americans have come to take for granted and to regard as normal and wholly desirable a system of formal education that physically separates child from parents for most of the hours of the day and most of the days of the year. Where the child of a primitive society would early have been given responsibilities within his kin group—caring for those younger than himself, garnering food, herding flocks—here he is sorted and segregated by age level, isolated from external responsibilities, and devoted solely to his own educational development. Without entering into the merits and demerits of this system, it is plain that its introduction into Indian society is thoroughly disruptive of traditional patterns of socialization, social control and familial labor.

## RELATED RESEARCH

Despite the fact that variants of the cross-cultural school have occurred in many different lands and over long spans of time, they have rarely been studied empirically. In his lengthly review article for the World Journal of Anthropology, Jules Henry notes this sparsity and comments that "The works of anthropologists tend to stress the repressive and destructive effects on the subordinate group of education by the dominant group."[13] Feeling

---

[12] George M. Foster is the first anthropologist to examine the mechanics of this selective transmission by a study of the Spanish influence upon the Americas in his book, *Culture and Conquest,* New York: Viking Fund, 1960. However, scholars such as Ruth Hill Useem have noted the workings of this process among the Sioux.

[13] *Op. cit.,* p. 284.

that way, most anthropologists up until the recent past have tended to ignore, when they did not condemn, the process of education that brought teachers of the Euro-American civilization into contact with "natives." The principal studies of any sort on the cross-cultural schoolroom that Henry is able to cite are those made by the Committee on Indian Education Research.

Outside of the U. S., one of the anthropologists most interested in this cross-cultural educational process has been Dr. Margaret Read. From her African experiences, she constructs a scheme of six stages to describe the adoption of formal education by a people.[14] These are highly suggestive, but the process seems less troublesome among the people she has studied; at any rate, it would be difficult to fit any American Indian people, except perhaps the Navaho, into her pattern.

Research and writing on American Indian education may be divided into three categories: (1) the studies of the intellectual and emotional development of Indian children sponsored by the Committee on Indian Education Research; (2) the appraisals of the technical adequacy of Indian education sponsored by the Bureau of Indian Affairs and executed by the School of Education, University of Kansas, during the past decade; and (3) other, smaller efforts.

## THE COMMITTEE ON INDIAN EDUCATION RESEARCH

The field work for these studies was performed during the early 1940's. The publications ensuing may be categorized as follows: studies of particular tribal regional groups (Hopi, Sioux, Navaho, Papago),[15] studies comparing the emotional and intellectual development of the children of these Indian groups with each other and with midwestern White children,[16] and studies leading toward practical recommendations on the handling of the educational and administrative problems of a particular people (the Hopi).[17]

The primary objective of these studies was the analysis of the development of the personality of the Indian from birth to adulthood but, in so doing, they had to take note of the experiences within the system of formal education. They found these to be frequently frightening and traumatic: The large, impersonal school, staffed by Whites and operated according to their severe and competitive ethics, was a painfully different kind of world than the warm, permissive kin group of the child's home.

As we designed the present project our interest was not in personality development but in the schoolroom as a focus of community attitudes and conflicts. We surmised that the *cultural disharmony or shock* noted in the various writings sponsored by this committee still was affecting the child's performance in school. Yet we did not believe that the disharmony was crucial in and of itself. Many other folk peoples have reared their children in a warm and relaxed atmosphere and then sent them into the imper-

[14] See the chapter, "Cultural Contacts in Education" in her *Education and Social Change in Tropical Areas,* London: Thomas Nelson, 1955, pp. 96-111.

[15] Laura Thompson and Alice Joseph, *The Hopi Way,* Chicago: University of Chicago Press, 1944; Gordon Macgregor, *Warriors Without Weapons,* Chicago: University of Chicago Press, 1946; Dorothea C. Leighton and Clyde Kluckhohn, *Children of the People,* Cambridge: Harvard University Press, 1947; Alice Joseph, Rosamond Spicer, and Jane Chesky, *The Desert People,* Chicago: University of Chicago Press, 1949.

[16] Robert J. Havighurst and Bernice L. Neugarten, *American Indian and White Children,* Chicago: University of Chicago Press, 1954.

[17] Laura Thompson, *Culture in Crisis,* New York: Harper, 1950.

8

sonal and competitive European or American school; the children may have found the transition uncomfortable and some may have suffered psychic injury, but on the whole they were able to profit from their educational experiences. Indeed, some of the children described in the studies of the Committee on Indian Education Research did come to like school, though how this happened and what kind of thing they learned was tangential to the interests of the authors in personality development.

## UNIVERSITY OF KANSAS STUDIES

The School of Education, University of Kansas, became research consultant to the Indian Service about 1950.[18] In their most recent study, the complete battery of the California Achievement Test was administered to a large population of Indian children attending schools in the region bounded by Montana, Arizona, Oklahoma, and North Dakota. In addition to (federal and mission) schools especially for Indians, public schools with a large population of Indians were included and in those cases the White pupils were also tested. The resulting data were tabulated with regard to a variety of factors: race and school, region, grade in school, and so on. However, the statistical analysis was methodologically primitive.

In her "Foreword" to the volume,

the Chief of the Branch of Education, B.I.A., presents as its most important finding, the relative ranking of race-school groups on the basis of achievement, namely, (1) White pupils in public schools, (2) Indian pupils in public schools, (3) Indian pupils in Federal schools, and (4) Indian pupils in mission schools. She, and the authors as well, note that the same relative ranking of the Indian pupils is obtained for degree of Indian blood and pre-school language (*i.e.,* the groups with higher scholastic achievement had relatively fewer "Fullbloods" and relatively more children from English-speaking homes). Under these circumstances, the rankings become meaningless or even pernicious as a guide to action. The question which concerns an informed critic is in which type of school does the child of conservative Indian parents (reared according to Indian values and speaking an Indian language in the home) do best?[19] A more refined type of statistical analysis might have been able to yield information answering this and related questions; or, alternatively, such analysis would have made clear whether, indeed, this kind of question can be answered.

The more tantalizing finding of this study was one which showed a successive deceleration in the achievement of Indian children, so that, despite any handicaps deriving from home culture and language, they scored slightly above the norm in the Fourth and Fifth Grades but dropped further from the norm with each successive

[18] L. Madison Coombs, Ralph E. Kron, E. Gordon Collister, and Kenneth E. Anderson, *The Indian Child Goes to School: A Study of Interracial Differences,* Washington, D. C.: U. S. Bureau of Indian Affairs, 1958; George A. Dale, *Education for Better Living,* Washington, D. C.: U. S. Bureau of Indian Affairs, 1955; Kenneth E. Anderson, E. Gordon Collister, and Carl E. Ladd, *The Educational Achievement of Indian Children: A Reexamination of the Question, How Well Are Indian Children Educated?,* Washington, D. C.: U. S. Bureau of Indian Affairs, 1953.

[19] The same criticism and concern for educating the linguistically handicapped Fullblood was voiced by Dr. Ben Reifel, "A point that needs qualification is that public school graduates just seem to do better than the others. Most of the Indians who get into public schools are usually Mixedbloods and live near white people." *Indian Education—Goals and Means,* Vermillion, S. D.: Institute of Indian Studies, State University of South Dakota, 1956, p. 16.

grade level.[20]

Another evaluation under this program was that of Dale as to the effectiveness of the educational program for the community of Sioux at Pine Ridge, South Dakota. Studies conducted in 1938-9 had recommended the inauguration of a vocational educational program to prepare Indian children for a technologically superior usage of reservation resources and many steps in that direction had actually been initiated; *e.g.,* the Oglala Community High School maintained breeding sires of pure-bred cattle, horses, and jackasses, some of the elementary schools attempted to introduce the culture of goats and chickens, and so on.

In the early 1950's a survey was conducted of Indians who had attended any of the schools serving Pine Ridge during the decade 1937-47. Fifty-five interviewers were used, most of whom were teachers. A long, highly structured questionnaire, requiring mostly "Yes" and "No" answers was utilized and was usually administered within a school building. While the data are interesting, the greater part cannot be accepted as valid without an independent check. Every significant circumstance of the survey, as executed, was markedly conducive to bias in favor of the schools and their program. Preceding each inquiry about an item in the vocational program, there was an explanation of the item and how it was intended to help the people of the community, and only then did the interview schedule solicit the opinion of the respondent via an "objective-type" question. It would demand a painful degree of honesty and frankness and some temerity to tell a teacher in his own school building (where the respondent is his luncheon guest) that a school program he has explained and justified as for your benefit had been or is unwise.

## OTHER STUDIES OF INDIAN EDUCATION

The foregoing constitutes the major and more ambitious studies of Indian education as of early 1962. In addition, the professional literature contains a fair number of accounts and studies, usually relative to the situation of a particular people or school. Among the best of these is a project still underway, conducted by Elizabeth D. Hoyt.[21] Rather than accepting traditional stereotypes about Indian attudes toward vocation and labor, she has been surveying Indian school children, inquiring about their hopes for life after leaving school. She has found that, as compared to White children of the same age and grade, the Indians have a much less adequate knowledge of vocations, jobs, and the training required for them. Also, these children express a much greater attachment to their families than do their White peers.

Representative of numerous other studies is the one by the President of the Southern State Teachers College in South Dakota.[22] He reviewed the college's thirty-three years of records, covering one hundred twelve Indian students. Of these, fifty-nine had dropped out within the first three quarters. He traced the problem both to inadequate preparation for college and to the psychological attitudes of the In-

---

[20] For a recent interpretation of this finding by Coombs himself see his address, "Implications of the Achievement Level of Indian Students," before the Annual Conference of the Co-ordinating Council for Research in Indian Education, May 1961 (Report duplicated by the Arizona State Department of Public Instruction, Phoenix), pp. 1-7. For our own interpretation of the phenomenon, see below, the section on Intermediate Grades chapter VI.

---

[21] Her article, "An Approach to the Mind of The Young Indian," *Journal of American Indian Education,* I (June 1961), pp. 17-23, summarizes some of her work.

[22] W. W. Ludeman, "The Indian Student in College," *Journal of Educational Sociology,* XXXIII (1960), pp. 333-335.

dian, e.g. "inferiority complex." We label this study "representative," because it is one of many which analyze the problems of Indian education with the use of scholastic achievement data and responses to so-called "objective" tests. There has been a marked reluctance on the part of educational researchers to examine the school situation of Indian pupils in relation to their own life and outside problems. Some justify this procedure with a curious extolling of "objectivity."

Some of the research now being conducted in the Southwest does begin to look past the achievement records and test scores to community attudes and classroom relationships. A notable example is Edward Parmee's study of the San Carlos Apache.[23] As he pointed out:

> Many Apaches object strongly to the fact that they have almost no voice in the planning and operation of their educational school program, of their reservation school program, and yet they are expected to give it their full and complete support. Apaches say that they are continually told that some day they will have to run their own affairs. Yet, they are given few opportunities today to learn how to manage such a program through experience gained by taking part in its present operation. Large numbers of Indian parents on the reservation have only a rather meager background in education and almost no contact with the schools that their children attend. Communication between parent and child on school matters appears to be surprisingly limited. As a result, many aspects of a school program are neither known nor understood by the parents and they are yet required to give it their full support.[24]

## THE SIOUX ON PINE RIDGE

We felt for a number of reasons that the Sioux would be among the peoples most worth studying. Numerically, they are among the largest of the contemporary Indian peoples; their reservation population in the Dakotas is estimated at forty thousand[25] and a good many more are scattered among neighboring towns and cities. Robert A. White estimates that they number five thousand in Rapid City, South Dakota.[26] The only tribal unit of greater size is the Navaho, but that people have been relatively free of government control and educational efforts until relatively recently, whereas the Sioux have been the target of all manner of federal programs of assistance and education for many years, and nonetheless are impoverished. An additional reason for choosing the Sioux is that their reservation life has already been the focus of considerable ethnographic study.

Once the Sioux were selected as the subjects of study, Pine Ridge proved to be the natural locale, as it and Rosebud are the two largest Sioux reservations, and the latter had recently transferred its educational system from federal to county (public) control. While a study and comparison of both educational systems might have been ideal, the resources of the Project did not warrant such an ambitious task.

From previous studies we expected to find Pine Ridge (as other reservations) divided into two basic factions, those known as "Fullbloods" and those known as "Mixedbloods" (or, less politely, "halfbreeds"). As Macgregor pointed out, these "are actually *sociological* rather than *biological* groups,

[23] See his talk, "Social Factors Affecting the Performance of the San Carlos Apache," at the Annual Conference for Research in Indian Education, May 1961 (report duplicated by Arizona State Department of Public Instruction, Phoenix), pp. 22-26.
[24] *Ibid.*, p. 23.

[25] Sol Tax, *et. al.,* Map: *The North American Indians, 1950 Distribution of the Aboriginal Population of Alaska, Canada, and the United States,* Chicago: Department of Anthropology, University of Chicago, 1960.
[26] "The Urban Adjustment of the Dakota Indians in Rapid City, South Dakota: A Progress Report," mimeograph, 1963.

standing primarily for the way of living according to Indian or White patterns rather than the actual degree of Indian blood." At the time of his study, "in spite of the predominance of intermixture with White, more than half of the Pine Ridge Indian population belong to the sociological Fullblood group."[27] Both factions are dissatisfied with the Reservation conditions of poverty, social disorganization, lack of autonomy, and general cultural depression but differ in their views as to the path to betterment.

As Macgregor described them, the conservative (Fullblood) group turn toward the past, and on some level of thought still feel that "the present situation is not here to stay. . . . unwillingness to accept modern life and culture change and the fantasy of an eventual return of the former Indian life are still common to the thinking of many Dakota."[28] As to proposals for current reform, the conservatives are thoroughly skeptical of anything issuing from the Whites or modeled upon them. In their judgment, the White is the alien, the enemy, and the intruder, who has brought the Indian people only misery. "Acting White" is the most stinging epithet in their vocabulary. They are not sure how to improve the lot of their people, but they find only further malaise in most suggestions emanating from the White and his administrative agencies.[29] The result is an apathetic negativism in which the energies of the conservative population are de-

voted to preserving a style of life which represents a sorry amalgam of impoverished White and deteriorated Indian cultures and with which they themselves are impatient. The more the administrators criticize and press for reform, the more the Indians identify their true "Indianness" with the refusal to budge, even if this would improve their condition. (A good proportion of their White neighbors is always happy to agree that the Indian cannot learn and will not change.) Their syndrome of economic impoverishment, isolation from other cultures and blind conservatism is self-reinforcing, and the greater the pressure upon them to change, the more they resist and withdraw.

In contrast, the progressive faction of the community is oriented toward the White society and the acquisition of White customs, values, and manners; their aim is assimilation. Most of them, however, have a limited perception of the nature of the larger American society. Their view of it is based not on direct vision, but on refraction through the dicta and preachments of a highly mixed crew of administrative officers, school teachers, and missionaries. Ordinarily, the sole corrective available to the progressive is actual experience with neighboring White society in the form of small Western towns, usually provincial and often contemptuous of all things "Indian." In any case they are not particularly helpful as preparation for metropolitan areas where a variety of employment and economic possibilities are to be found.

To obviate misunderstanding, we should again mention here that the foregoing is the image of Pine Ridge society that we construed from the studies of previous ethnographers, such as Scudder Mekeel, Gordon Macgregor, Ruth Hill Useem, Vernon D. Malan, E. E. Hagen and L. Schaw. Our own observations have led us to a different picture of the dynamics of con-

---

[27] *Warriors Without Weapons: A Study of the Society and Personality Development of the Pine Ridge Sioux*, Chicago: University of Chicago Press, 1946, p. 25. Our own view of Reservation factions and divisions, based on our field experience, is given in the chapter, "People and Statuses."

[28] *Ibid.*, pp. 26-27.

[29] Cf. E. E. Hagen and Louis C. Schaw, *The Sioux on the Reservations*, "preliminary edition," Cambridge: Center for International Studies, Massachusetts Institute of Technology, 1960, chap. iii, p. 18.

temporary reservation society, as is evident especially in our chapter on "Peoples and Statuses." The difference may in part be one of date of study (as between our study and those of Mekeel, Useem, and Macgregor) or one of focus of research. We have restated this image here because it guided us in our formulation of theories as to the source of the educational difficulties on Indian reservations.

## OBJECTIVES

Given the foregoing review and analyses of the problems of cross-cultural education and of the nature of community life on Indian Reservations, we might then proceed to formulate a reasonable series of objectives for research investigation. We may begin by reviewing the logical possibilities: The relatively low educational achievement of American Indian peoples might be attributable to one or several of the following: (a) schools that were technically inadequate (*i.e.,* poor quality of personnel, facilities, curricula, etc.); (b) children that were poorly prepared for school (*i.e.,* deficient in the skills the White child acquires in the home or nursery school before entry into the primary grades); (c) disturbed or inharmonious relationships within the school and perhaps involving the community as a whole.

With respect to (a), the Merriam Report of 1928 had found much to criticize in the technical adequacy of the educational systems serving Indians. However, since that time, extensive reforms had been instituted in the entire relationship of the federal government to the tribes. In recent years, the Bureau of Indian Affairs has explicitly aimed at making the education of Indians comparable to that of Whites in the same region or state and, while inadequacies might be discovered in the technical competency of current Indian education, these would be most likely to be of the same nature as those of the neighboring public school systems.

With respect to (b), it is certainly true that, among many tribes, the children of conservative ("Fullblood") parents enter school knowing little or no English and lacking knowledge concerning books, calculating, and the world in general that White children of comparable age have attained. (Conversely, the Indian children have learned a great deal in other areas that tend to be neglected by White parents.) Unquestionably, this could be a serious handicap to Indian achievement in the early grades. However, following from our previous discussions, it was our hypothesis that in and of itself this would be less of a handicap than might appear. The cross-cultural and cross-linguistic school has been quite common during the past few centuries. In the U. S., especially during the past century, children have been raised in ethnic enclaves ("Little Italy," "the Ghetto," "Little Poland," etc.) and learned their parents' tongue first. Nonetheless, many of these children have gone on to educational and vocational achievement. It was our opinion that the most important issue would be the attitude of the parents and their children toward the acquisition of this "general American" knowledge. The immigrants had come voluntarily to the U.S. and wanted to be accepted by their fellows as equally American. While they valued their traditional language and culture, they encouraged their children to learn the language and culture of their larger social environment. The conservative Indian had been less enthusiastic.

We were thus brought to (c) and the question of the relationships among the various Indian and White factions within the community and the manner in which these come to a focus within the schoolroom. In social problem cases such as this, there has often been a tendency to study only one of the principals involved in the relationship: just the Indians (they being the problem to the Whites) or just the Whites (they being the problem to the Indian); or in the schoolroom, just the conservative pupils (who are a problem for the educators) or just the White, middle-class teachers (who are a problem for the conservative Indian pupils).[30] In the basic theories which were to constitute our guides for research on Pine Ridge, we attempted to focus equally upon all parties involved. We will begin by listing these theories and then proceed to review each in more detail:

*Theory 1. Cultural Disharmony.* To children reared in conservative Indian fashion, the atmosphere of a normal, American school is painful, incomprehensible, and even immoral; whereas, to teachers of (normal) lower-middle-class American background, the behavior of these students is often undisciplined, lacking in scholastic initiative, and even immoral.

*Theory 2. Lack of Motive/Unappealing Curricula.* The notions of the Indian people themselves as to careers that are possible and desirable are sometimes much at variance with those of the educators. Where this variance exists, dropout of adolescent students is exceedingly likely.

*Theory 3. Preservation of Identity.* To conservative Indians, their identity as Indians is the last and most valuable treasure remaining to them. Insofar as education is presented to them, or perceived by them, as a technique for transmuting their children and their people into "Whites," then it becomes freighted with all manner of emotional complications and is likely to be rejected.

The theory of cultural disharmony has been most convincingly and empirically presented via the studies carried out under the auspices of the Committee on Indian Education Research. Conservative Indian parents do train and discipline their children in quite different ways and concerning quite different areas of life than do White parents.[31] Their children might then experience the ordinary American school as individualistic, competitive, intrusive, and regimented, compared to life in the home circle. Conversely, the inexperienced teacher might find her Indian students to be unresponsive, intractable, discourteous, and lacking in scholastic initiative.[32]

To our knowledge, no study had been made to evaluate the practical effects of the researches and recommendations of the Committee. The

---

[30] Everett C. Hughes and Helen M. Hughes, "North America: Indians and Immigrants" *When Peoples Meet: Racial and Ethnic Frontiers,* New York: Free Press, 1952, pp. 18-31.

[31] Rosalie H. Wax and Robert K. Thomas, "American Indians and White People," *Phylon,* XXII (1961), pp. 305-317.

[32] "The value system of the teachers stems from middle-class white ideals and often clashes with the orientation of the students. Thus teachers stress cleanliness, the ideal sex standards of the whites, honesty, ambition, hard work, saving money, competition and aggressiveness, time-consciousness, proper grammar and English, and from their students expect (although they seldom get) quick responses and immediate conformance to requests. Most of the teachers have little insight into the Sioux child, his cultural background, his dilemmas, and his aspirations. Thus, both student and teacher are quite often frustrated. If the situation becomes unbearable, the student runs away from school. Teachers may solve their difficulties by being transferred or resigning from the service, or displace their frustrations through scolding and nagging." Ruth Hill Useem, *The Aftermath of Defeat,* unpub. Ph.D. dissertation, University of Wisconsin, 1947, pp. 201-2. Anecdotal material on the problems of sympathetic teachers faced with Indian pupils will be found in Marge Page, "Schoolhouse in the Desert," *National Education Association Journal,* XLII (1953), p. 514; Wayne T. Pratt, "Living Beside Us —Worlds Apart," *Childhood Education,* XXXIV (1957), pp. 165-168; Charles F. Jones, "Notes on Indian Education," *Journal of Educational Sociology,* XXVII, pp 16-23; Estelle A. Brown, *Stubborn Fool,* Caldwell, Idaho: Caxton Printers, 1952, is a fascinating account of the problem of cultural difference in the early part of this century.

field work constituting the basis of their studies had been conducted during the early 1940's. The research subsequently sponsored by the Bureau of Indian Affairs had solely concerned the technical adequacy of Indian education. Meanwhile, to further complicate the picture, increasingly large proportions of Indian children have been sent to regular public (as against federal) schools. Accordingly, as part of the proposed research, we intended to look for cultural disharmony between child and school and, where it existed, to evaluate its effect on the scholastic achievement of the child.

The second theory reflected not only the educational problem of the Indian community, but also its depressed economic state. In many cases the land base is inadequate for the type of agricultural use to which the Indians have been putting it, and the resources for capital development are limited. The Bureau of Indian Affairs has attempted to ameliorate the situation by means of programs of vocational education, including instruction in the style of living typical of or approved by middle class persons in the larger American society (e.g., diet, personal hygiene). However, the crucial questions would be how the Indians regard the vocations and the style of existence so presented to them and whether these fit their conception of how Indians would live. If the Indian found these unacceptable, this would be contributory to educational dropout or failure. Thus, as part of this research, we intended to investigate Indian attitudes toward the curricula of the schools and toward the vocations and style of life implied by them.

While there has been much research oriented about the first theory and some about the second, the third theory is unexplored. At the time we formulated these research objectives it had been our experience that the conservative Indian continued to view White society as a threat to his identity and as presenting alien values. He did not wish his children or his people to absorb these values, and insofar as the school was identified with them, he rejected it. Paradoxically, he might admire the wealth and the power of the larger American society and hope that his people may acquire this without sacrificing their values and integrity. To the degree that the school was being presented as a vessel for transmuting Indian children into "Whites"—or that he correctly or incorrectly felt that this was the function of the school—he would be ambivalent about it or reject it wholly. On the other hand, to the degree that the school was perceived as a device by which Indians might acquire the power and skill to defend their way of life, their just rights, and themselves, the conservative Indian would be its eager advocate. He would also be interested in, and would advocate, things that would improve (without challenge) his style of living; he would like to eat and live better within the framework of life as he valued it.

In summary, the three theories under consideration led us toward asking the following research questions:

1. *Cultural Disharmony.* How do Indian young people come to regard educators and the school? How do the educators come to regard their Indian pupils? What productive and unproductive modes of interaction between pupil and educator become established within the school?

2. *Motive/curricula.* What roles do the various factions and groups of the community (conservatives, progressives, elders, youth, educators) visualize education as being able to play in the careers and lives of its Indian young people?

3. *Identity.* What effect do the various factions and groups of the community visualize education as having upon the values and attitudes of the young people as these relate to membership in the Indian community? How do these attitudes influence the young people in their interest in becoming educated?

# Chapter II

# ECOLOGY, ECONOMY, EDUCATIONAL ACHIEVEMENT

## ECOLOGY

Town versus countryside seems to epitomize life on the Pine Ridge Reservation—the town as the symbol of the national U. S. society and the countryside as the home of the tribal Sioux. At the town of Pine Ridge and in lesser number at the consolidated schools located along the paved roads are nuclei of people who secure their income by affiliation with institutions based outside the Reservation: the federal government, the state or county governments, the Roman Catholic or other mission churches. These town-dwellers are "small-town middle-class" in their style of American living: Their basic income is from salaries; they live in clusters of conventional urban houses complete with lawns; and within these homes the only language spoken is English. Most are Whites, but there are also a few Negroes and Indians; by occupation they are government bureaucrats, teachers, hospital personnel, maintenance engineers, etc.

Scattered over the Reservation prairie, loosely grouped into bands along the creeks and roads, are some thousands of Indians. Most live in cabins, some in tents, and a few in solid houses; most lack the conventional "utilities" of middle class existence, such as running water, electricity, telephone or gas. None has a street address, so that finding an individual home requires detailed familiarity with the landscape. Socially, most of these people are rated as "Fullbloods" and according to federal rolls most are more "Indian" than "White." Whatever their genes, most speak the Lakota language[1] within their homes and to each other. In general they are very poor, and few have any connection with the institutions of the larger U.S. society, except the federal government via *The Bureau* (of Indian Affairs).

The simplistic dichotomy of the ru-

ral Indian and the small-town White is not the whole picture. In and near the town of Pine Ridge are further tight clusters of Indian housing. To the outside observer, these denser settlements have an appearance of horrid slum poverty as compared to the homes amid the acres of grassland; yet some of these houses shelter persons who secure some cash income from their labors and most are better built and furnished than the ones on the prairie. It might be thought that the inhabitants of these clusters would be "mixedbloods." In fact, many are legal Fullbloods. Conversely, the Indians who would classify as financially the most successful are the handful of ranchers on the prairie, who are much more White than Indian in every respect: blood quanta, culture, and associations with other persons. In general, those who are called "Fullblood" and "real Indian" are the most impoverished economically, whether they live in the town slum or the prairie cabins, but they seem to dominate the prairie, whereas the towns are the Bureau's.[2]

The rolling hills and the dry climate provide a terrain most adaptable to ranching. Farming is marginal and dependent on irrigation; other natural resources seem minimal, except inso-

[1] The people of Pine Ridge are primarily Oglala Teton (Dakota or Sioux), speaking the "L" dialect of the Dakota language. Hence their tongue is properly termed "Lakota," while the other dialects are known as Dakota and Nakota. As we shall discuss later, large numbers of the Oglala Sioux prefer to speak Lakota, and many have only a limited facility with English.

[2] Compare the situation of French and English in Quebec as described by Everett C. Hughes in *French Canada in Transition*, Chicago: University of Chicago Press, 1943. The French peasant and the English entrepreneur are the polar symbols, but much of the urban working class consists of landless French.

far as the Badlands and neighboring Black Hills are tourist attractions. Without commercial development the region can provide income for only a sparse population. Yet for the Oglala this arid land has become home and they live within it despite their poverty. The surplus commodities, welfare goods, and services provided by governmental and charitable agencies have enabled them to survive and even multiply, while the possibilities of gainful labor have become less over the decades, particularly as local ranching (and neighboring agricultural) enterprises were rationalized and mechanized in their operation.[3] Meanwhile, the major monetary enterprise of the Reservation has come to be the governmental cluster devoted to caring for and instructing the Indians: the Bureau and its schools, the Public Health Service, state welfare and employment services, and the mission churches. To a limited extent these agencies also represent sources of employment for the Indians themselves, but opportunities are far fewer than applicants, and access to employment becomes a valuable privilege and favor. Competition for those jobs is severe and sometimes a matter of bitter and sordid intrigue. Recently, the Wright-McGill Company has established several "factories" for snelling fishhooks, and these currently employ from twenty to two hundred persons depending on the season. While the wage level of these factories is low and the production demands severe, their success is another indicator of the long-pent demand among the Sioux for local employment. As Robert K. Thomas noted of the Cherokee,[4] most Indian men take more easily to wage work than to intensive, family farming.

Concerning these factories, the general judgment of Michael Harrington seems appropriate:

> The industry that comes to these places is not concerned with moral or social uplift. It seeks out rural poverty because it provides a docile labor market. There is income supplementing as a result, but what basically happens is that people who have been living in the depressed areas of agriculture now live part-time in the depressed areas of industry.[5]

The geographic isolation of the Reservation is intensified by its poverty. The thinly scattered population and the rough terrain make it costly to communicate with or travel to the urbanized centers of power and influence of the U. S., and the poverty of the Indians and low standard of living of most of the Whites who reside on or near the Reservation make the lines of communication and commerce relatively narrow. Newspapers, magazines, and books are essentially absent from the life of the adult Indian. Day-old newspapers can be obtained on subscription or from the drugstore in Pine Ridge town, but the market for them is small. The national magazines arrive several days late, which makes them hardly newsworthy or timely. Cheap portable radios are widespread, and many Indians are thereby becoming familiar with those events in the news which are of interest to them. Television is a great attraction but is restricted to the few homes whose owners are wealthy enough to afford electric power, and whenever a major sporting event is being broadcast, these homes are jammed with male guests.

The isolation of the Sioux population is accentuated by linguistic problems.

---

[3] For a recent, thorough analysis of a similar Reservation economy see Carl K. Eicher, *Constraints on Economic Progress on the Rosebud Sioux Indian Reservation*, unpublished Ph.D. dissertation, Harvard University, 1960.

[4] "Eastern Cherokee Acculturation," MS. Compare also the Mohawk adaptation to high steel work, as well as the success of Tama enterprises.

[5] *The Other America:* Poverty in the United States, New York: Macmillan, 1962, p. 48.

Lakota is not only the preferred tongue in most homes but is also the only one used in the vast majority of conversational exchanges. A fair proportion of Fullbloods have only the most rudimentary command of English, and the English that is spoken on the Reservation is really a distinct dialect; we refer to it as "Pine Ridge English." In grammar, sounds, and especially in the meanings given to certain expressions, it differs markedly from the standard dialects of the U. S. Even those Fullbloods who are relatively well educated (having attended some small Western teachers college) tend to speak Pine Ridge dialect.

Because almost all Sioux can scrape up a few words of Pine Ridge English when forced to do so, some of the Whites say that all of them "know English." They are right in the sense that many Indians speak Lakota because they prefer to do so. However, an important reason for this preference is relative mastery. Many Sioux have great difficulty speaking English and cling to the language they handle with ease and competence; moreover, they realize that in comparison with Whites, they make a rather shabby showing in English. On the other hand, when Sioux do use English words, Whites often incorrectly assume that the speaker is thinking in terms of White norms and values. "Enunciating the words of a language does not mean complete understanding."[6] Since the Sioux' lack of fluency in English is associated with so many educational problems, we will return to it again. Here we note that they can get along quite well locally with only an occasional use of English, but that their lack of fluency contributes to their isolation from the greater national society.

Automobiles are now relatively

widespread throughout the Reservation (horses are consistently employed only by ranchhands and old folks). As most of the Sioux population lack the money to maintain—or frequently, even to buy gas, oil, and tires for—their mechanical means of transport, these are far from certain or speedy. Although the roads linking the Day School centers have been paved during the past decade, many roads on the Reservation are not even graveled, and they become difficult or impassable in wet weather. Nevertheless, people do manage to come to the local hamlet or even Pine Ridge town for business (transactions with Bureau and Tribal Offices), shopping, mail, health and welfare services, gossiping and sightseeing. With so few telephones on the Reservation (even few Bureau employees have them in their homes), the auto aids in the spread of information. An auto in reasonable repair also provides transportation off the Reservation—for an excursion to the neighboring towns, an extended trip to participate in social activities at an Indian community elsewhere, or a journey to employment as seasonal agricultural labor.

## THE DOMINATING BUREAU

For decades the Bureau of Indian Affairs has attempted to disassociate itself from its traditional role of an autocracy "for the good of the Indians." Nevertheless, it is this tradition that still dominates the behavior and expectations of the local Bureau officials and staff, the neighboring Whites, and the Indians themselves. For example, when the piercing ceremony of the Sun Dance was revived in 1961 and 1962, many persons—both White and Indian—expected the federal government to intervene and forbid the act of ritual self-torture. The newspaper of the nearest city declared that "The Sun Dance would still be prohibited by the federal government,

---

[6] Ruth Hill Useem, "The Aftermath of Defeat," unpublished Ph.D. dissertation, University of Wisconsin, 1947, pp. 182f., 328.

according to Supt. L. P. Towles [sic] of the Pine Ridge Agency, if it was felt there would be an orgy of bloodletting."[7] Whether or not Superintendent Towle actually made such a statement, the significant thing in the article is the absence of any reference to the religious rights of Indians as citizens; in general, neither Indian nor White referred to the First Amendment to the U. S. Constitution.

To a considerable degree the dominance of "The Bureau" on Pine Ridge is like that of "The Company" in a company town: other centers of power are minimal. Thus the Bureau dominates economically, as the chief employer, purchaser, and consumer of goods and services on the Reservation. Beyond this the Bureau acts as trustee for a large portion of the land on the Reservation and so controls its use and lease. Were we to diagram the nature of communications on the Reservation, we would have to show the Bureau as a membrane, enclosing the area, mediating and filtering the communications between the inner, "country Indian" society and the outer, urbanized, national society. On the other hand, Bureau officials in the upper echelons have at their disposal the most efficient modern means of communication and transportation—including long-distance telephone lines and chartered airplanes.

Many of the decisions which elsewhere in the U. S. are made by locally elected political bodies, and many of the services which elsewhere are distributed by such bodies, are in Pine Ridge performed by the Bureau. Elsewhere local boards govern the school system, build and maintain the road system, handle the water supplies and sewage, utility franchises and the like."[8]

Countervailing powers in the hands of the Sioux to be employed against the Bureau are still rudimentary. The Oglala have a Tribal Council that has a modest range of powers and functions. Culturally a non-Indian form, it is honored by no one. It has been the target of conservative Indian suspicion since its initiation in the early 1930's.[9] On the other side, Agency personnel have tended to regard it as corrupt, inefficient, and lacking in popular support, and they have frequently been able to outmaneuver it by dealing directly with particular Indian factions, or otherwise to manipulate it to their own ends. Nevertheless there is always strong and relatively

---

[7] *Rapid City Daily Journal*, August 1, 1962, p. 5.

[8] Curiously, the difference between these communities and Pine Ridge is seldom one of financing, for an increasingly substantial part of most local enterprises throughout the U. S. is financed by federal monies—with local persons given the responsibility for disbursing funds so long as they appear to keep within the guidelines established by external authority. (Bureau teachers and administrators exhort the Indian populace to improve themselves morally by reducing their dependence on federal monies. Meanwhile many other communities and organizations in the U. S. define progress as securing such federal support for their own interests.)

[9] Despite the fact that an eminent anthropologist and authority on the Sioux assisted in the drafting of the tribal constitution, it suffered a fatal defect in "the failure to recognize the *tiyospaye*, the focal point of all social interaction in the traditional Oglala society, in the establishment of election districts. In addition to the fact that the proposed election districts tended to divide the *tiyospaye* groups, it seems clear that little attention was given to the commonality of interest within a given election district. . . . The communities which were recognized . . . appear to have comprised the schools, post offices, service stations, trader's stores and churches which had been established around the ration distribution warehouses. These communities are communities of Bureau of Indian Affairs officials and teachers, missionaries, and White traders and their employees; they are not Indian communities." Ira H. Grinnell, *The Tribal Government of the Oglala Sioux of Pine Ridge, South Dakota*, M.A. thesis, Department of Government, State University of South Dakota, August 1959, p. 49.

general competition for the paid positions on the Council, and those who denounce it as innately corrupt stand for office at subsequent elections. (In point of fact the Tribal Government appears no worse than the local governments of many isolated and unsophisticated areas in this nation; quite a number of county governments have been regarded as the corrupt operation of the "courthouse gang" and accused of being indifferent to communal wellbeing. Perhaps the Tribal Government really suffers from being such small potatoes compared to the mighty Bureau.)

Another check on the Bureau is provided by the handful of Indians who have become knowledgeable about the mechanics of the national government and can carry their complaints to their congressman or even to one of the national Indian interest associations. These individuals are not always the wisest in the community nor the most typical, but, as they learn how to twist the lion's tail, they may often receive popular support, even from those who deeply mistrust them.

Bureau personnel, being affiliated with the institution that dominates the Reservation, tend to assume the positions of highest social status and to set the styles of local, fashionable consumption. While most Indian adults receive a tiny income in money, federal employees are paid at levels appropriate to national standards. Compared to the ubiquitous Reservation poverty they are positively wealthy. Accordingly, the Bureau personnel tend to constitute an upper class (or upper caste), personifying the socially desirable styles of housing, eating, and clothing. By way of the school system, they strive to inculcate these same standards into the impoverished and "uncivilized" Indian populace.

These who occupy Bureau or other offices on Pine Ridge tend to mask and justify their superior status with the ideology of assimilation and uplift of the Indians. Many think of themselves as devoting their lives to the betterment of this "uncivilized" people. However, most Indians respond, not by an eager acceptance or a stubborn rejection of the ideological sermons of these officials (or teachers), but much more pragmatically—to the actual and tangible dominance of the local Agency and the superordination of its employees. Since federal salaries and working conditions seem princely to country Indians, they are disinclined to regard these employees as dedicated.[10] (In contrast, the Jesuit fathers, who live a simple life and teach in dilapidated quarters, are respected even by non-Catholics.)

## CASH AND ITS USES

It is arguable that the Sioux (and the government) would have been better off if they had agreed to adopt an isolated, subsistence economy along the patterns of the EuroAmerican pioneers or the contemporary Amish. However, when such a program was tried (most recently during the Depression), neither the land nor the people were suited to it: The western prairies lack the moisture of eastern farmlands, and the Plains warriors and their descendants contemned farming.[11] Meantime, the

[10] "White bureaucratic positions—such as clerks, teachers, and other 'white collar' jobs are considered 'easy' types of work. Although the teacher, for example, tries to instill in the population the value of hard work, the population is more impressed by the actions than the words of that teacher and his position is not considered as 'hard work'." Useem, *op. cit.,* p. 134.

[11] Despite the disasters that have resulted from attempts to farm the Dakota short grass prairies, the reluctance of the Sioux to attempt to farm provides a convenient ideological weapon for their critics. As recently as July 4, 1963, the *Shannon County News* contained an account of a statement by Representative Dave Martin of Kearney accusing the Indians of lacking initiative because they do not attempt to farm Pine Ridge. (The B. I. A. has been outstanding in its concern for proper care of the soil.)

Bureau views its role as one of inculcating into the Indians that cluster of virtues which W. Lloyd Warner has identified as "lower-middle-class"; industry, cleanliness, thrift, sobriety, and family (rather than kin) loyalty.[12] Once trained in this secularized version of the Protestant ethos, and equipped with some modest education and skills, the Indians were to be urged to migrate from the Reservation and become assimilated into the national society. Most Bureau folk are not aware that they are preaching this ethic to a folk who do not share their conception of human character as a phenomenon that may (and ought to) be molded and changed. Nor are they aware that most Indians tend to interpret their words as meaning that "White people" think Indians are innately lazy, dirty and drunken. Since this is distressing and embarrassing all around, many Sioux conclude that the best policy is to stay away from White people as much as possible.

While we ourselves had time to gain only a modest familiarity with Sioux values and ideas, we became convinced that they are almost never understood or appreciated by Bureau personnel or by most White neighbors. For example, many White folk characterize the Indian as irresponsible in money matters, and it is true that most sums of cash, large or small, are usually spent in a few days. Some persons associate this behavior with the ancient hunting economy, where personal property was minimal. We believe that this kind of genetic explanation is no longer wholly satisfactory; the Sioux have been accustomed to money for a long time and none living today really know what a buffalo hunt was like in the days when the herds covered the Western plains. The facts are rather that the Sioux have become adjusted to a rather complex economy in which money plays a special, supplementary role. Country Indians live on their own land and so pay no rent; since their homes lack utilities, they pay no charges for electricity or water. In winter, they may wish to purchase kerosene for fuel, but they can get by with wood that is available for the cutting. As for food, the government furnishes the tribe with commodities judged surplus, and so most families obtain a bare minimum diet; children obtain lunch and snacks at school. Medical care is provided by the Public Health Service. Clothing can sometimes be obtained from charitable organizations or at nominal cost at rummage sales. If a young man is clever and persistent, he can sometimes kill a deer; or if a man is willing to run the risk, he can rustle a calf. Judged by national standards, the life of the country Indian is uncomfortable and even squalid, but it does give plenty of leisure and freedom.

In this kind of life, money is truly an aspect of an auxiliary economy, unconnected with brute subsistence. Money provides luxuries such as better food, toys for the children, new and stylish clothes, gasoline and car repairs, and recreations such as movies and alcohol. One kind of parallel would be the trading stamps of the housewife; from the rational view of the *economic man,* these are an idiocy, but for the housewife they are a currency different than the money which is her subsistence income, and accordingly she can "spend" them as she pleases, even while she must husband her cash and feel accountable for how it is spent.[13]

But despite this and other idiosyn-

---

[12] Ruth Hill Useem speaks here of the "dominant group," the Whites, presenting an idealized version of their own culture to the subordinate group. She illustrates with a discussion of marriage: "Monogamy is the ideal in the white culture and the attempt among Indian Service personnel and missionaries is to introduce this ideal rather than the actual marriage behavior of whites which includes divorce, annulment, sanctioned ways of getting around monogamy, etc." *op. cit.,* p. 99.

cratic views about money, labor, leisure, and virtue, the Sioux are becoming increasingly involved with the national economy. Fundamentally, they are venturesome, and they are attracted by the material goods of modern society. So, today, the automobile has almost displaced the horse on the Reservation. The vehicle may be aged, battered, and incapable of speeds over thirty miles an hour; still it is there, and because it is, its possessor has become obligated to a search for cash to purchase gasoline and oil and repairs. Moreover, the search for cash involves the individual (or family) in a continually widening sequence of transactions with the national society. For example, even low paid employment in federal offices obligates the individual to assume a more conventionally "lower middle class" style of living and dressing, so that the individual is further committed to involvement with the market economy. Moreover, schoolchildren, especially adolescents in high school, are highly conscious of the status significance of clothes and are influenced by national standards of consumption and fashion as these filter into the Reservation by way of teachers and the children of Bureau employees. Girls pressure their parents for more modish garments, rather than "rummage" castoffs that

---

[13] Compare Conrad C. Reining's analysis of "The Role of Money in Zande Economy," *American Anthropologist,* Vol. 61 (1959), pp. 39-43, in which he points out that "Contrary to all expectations, including those of the Azande, increased cash income has not resulted in corresponding expenditures for imported goods. The Azande themselves assume that they would simply buy more European goods if they had more money and thereby become more like Europeans. Instead, there seems to be a distinct tendency to substitute money for goods and services required for social obligations. . . . it has become a preferred form of gift to relatives and friends." The Azande feel that money "should not be used to live on, but that it may be used for social purposes."

are cheap in price. On cold mornings, the observer can see Indian girls shivering in cotton frocks, rather than be clad in the warm woolen castoffs that would be available from the rummage stores but would be eccentric in design.

Impoverished as most Sioux are, their life is a continual struggle to obtain the vital elements of existence, while at the same time preserving the regard of family and kin. When superadded to this, comes the burden of maintaining a "middle class" front, life becomes a sequence of financial and emotional crises and the responsible adult becomes a more or less perpetual scrounger. A Reservation cabin located a mile from a paved road can be a pleasant place (especially in warm months) and with even one wage earner, an extended family group can manage to coexist, providing middle class niceties be ignored. Yet, without running water and other facilities, the cabin, shack, or tent constitutes a poor base for the child or adult who is pressured socially to come to work or to town immaculate in person, modish in dress, and promptly at an early hour of the morn. Moreover, the sight of good clothes, substantial house, and new car triggers demands from the wide circle of impoverished kin who feel, with good reason, that these items are less important than their own more traditional and elemental wants.

## BACKWOODS ARISTOCRATS

In response to this conflict between the values of middle class U. S. and traditional Sioux living, the Fullbloods have developed an ideology as to their place in the world that is more akin to that of royalty in exile than that of the colonial or backwoods peoples they otherwise resemble. In this view, they are the original owners of a vast continental estate that they exchanged with the Whites for certain rights and dues guaranteed in perpetuity by treaty. The Whites and their govern-

TABLE 1

RESIDENT POPULATION OF PINE RIDGE RESERVATION COMPARED WITH
SOUTH DAKOTA AND THE UNITED STATES*

| | Sex | | | Percent distributions | South Dakota 1950 | United States 1950 |
|---|---|---|---|---|---|---|
| Age | Male | Female | Total | Pine Ridge 1956 | | |
| 19 and under | 1,800 | 1,823 | 3,623 | 49.0 | 37.0 | 33.9 |
| 20-34 | 769 | 714 | 1,483 | 20.1 | 22.1 | 23.3 |
| 35-44 | 370 | 327 | 697 | 9.4 | 12.4 | 14.3 |
| 45-59 | 418 | 409 | 827 | 11.2 | 15.7 | 16.3 |
| 60 and over | 389 | 321 | 710 | 9.6 | 12.7 | 12.2 |
| No report | 21 | 31 | 52 | 0.7 | ....... | ....... |
| Totals | 3,767 | 3,625 | 7,392 | 100.0 | 99.9 | 100.0 |

*Source: Malan and Schusky, *The Dakota Indian Community*

ment have profited by this transfer of land but have continually sought to wriggle out of its terms and provisions; nonetheless, the Sioux have a moral and legal claim to all manner of services and benefits in perpetuity. In this view, the Bureau is an agency supposed to serve the Indians, not to "administer" them for the convenience of the White people. Denunciations of the performance of the Bureau are common; the criticism is not accompanied by any suggestions that the Bureau be eliminated or its responsibilities altered, but rather the tone is one which implies that the agency is a slovenly, inept and expensive servant, who cannot be discharged because its services are essential. The blame for the failure of the Bureau to act as it should is directed primarily against the Mixedbloods: it is they (say the Fullbloods) who have connived to liquidate the land, terminate the federal responsibilities, monopolize all the Bureau jobs; likewise, it is they who are responsible for the frequent instances of violence and alcoholism.

It is worthy of note that the Sioux argument refers not to the actual terms of a particular historical treaty, but to their conception of it. It is also worthy of note that most governmental proposals for improving the Reservation situation are presented in a format contrary to this "treaty philosophy" and

so begin by antagonizing the conservatives among the Sioux.

In the light of this ideology a number of aspects of Sioux life acquire a clearer meaning. An outside reformer might be inclined to feel that the Sioux were merely slow in learning languages, as in generally adapting to the ways of the modern world. However, for the people themselves, Lakota is not merely the tongue of one's home and family, but also a strategic device which excludes the Mixedbloods and the Whites and defines the Fullblood. Likewise, traditional ceremonials are performed, not merely for their original meaning within the context of Plains equestrian life, but also as an occasion for asserting the solidarity of the genuine Sioux against all others, and particularly against the Mixedbloods who feel that these rites are heathen, barbarous and shameful.

## BASIC FIGURES: POPULATION, INCOME, AND EDUCATION

The demographic data of this section are taken from the 1958 and 1960 census of the Bureau of Indian Affairs; the tabulations are as presented by Malan and Schusky and by the Nekota Redevelopment Commission.[14] The first Table shows the age and sex distribution of the population on the

## TABLE 2
ANNUAL CASH INCOME OF RESIDENT
PINE RIDGE FAMILY HEADS*

| Annual income | Families No. | Percent |
|---|---|---|
| 0 - 499 | 776 | 29.8 |
| 500 - 999 | 750 | 28.8 |
| 1,000 - 1,499 | 393 | 15.1 |
| 1,500 - 1,999 | 200 | 7.7 |
| 2,000 - 5,000 | 363 | 13.9 |
| Over 5,000 | 63 | 2.4 |
| No report | 61 | 2.3 |
| Totals | 2,606 | 100.0 |

*Source: Malan and Schusky, *The Dakota Indian Community.*

Reservation. This and the more detailed population pyramid constructed by Malan and Schusky (not reproduced here) reveal that, as compared to South Dakota and the U. S. generally, the Reservation population has a larger ratio of children and a smaller ratio of adults in middle age. A process of out-migration is affecting South Dakota as a whole and Indian Reservations in particular. (Clark Johnson noted this phenomenon in the Fort Thompson community and felt that the absence of younger adults accentuated the political predominance of the older Indians, who were relatively more conservative and less well educated.)

Table 2 shows annual cash income. Clearly, it is minute for over half

the families. Comparing Pine Ridge with the State generally in 1950, Malan and Schusky note that the under $1,000-per-year class contained 15 percent of the general South Dakota families of 1950, and it may be presumed that in the six year interval the South Dakotans had become more prosperous. (It is reasonable to expect much of that 15 percent consists of Indians on and off the Reservations.) The disproportion on the high side of the ledger is equally marked, with 16 percent of South Dakota families (1950) having incomes of over $5,000 as against 2 percent of Pine Ridge.

Table 3 and Table 4 list occupations and employment. Over half of the family heads on Pine Ridge had no employment, whereas in South Dakota

## TABLE 3
OCCUPATIONS OF RESIDENT PINE
RIDGE FAMILY HEADS*

| Occupations | Positions held No. | Percent |
|---|---|---|
| Agricultural workers | 557 | 21.4 |
| Unskilled | 136 | 5.2 |
| Federal employees | 129 | 5.0 |
| Armed forces | 120 | 4.6 |
| Skilled and semi-skilled | 101 | 3.9 |
| Service workers | 44 | 1.7 |
| Professional and managerial | 28 | 1.1 |
| Tribal employees | 26 | 1.0 |
| Not working | 1,379 | 52.9 |
| No report | 73 | 2.8 |
| Totals | 2,606 | 100.0 |

## TABLE 4
COMPARISON OF PINE RIDGE AND
SOUTH DAKOTA OCCUPATIONS*

| Occupations | Pine Ridge % | South Dakota % |
|---|---|---|
| Professional and managerial | 1.1 | 15.9 |
| Clerical | .5 | 13.3 |
| Service | 1.7 | 7.6 |
| Government employees | 5.0 | 10.8 |
| Unemployed | 52.9 | 2.7 |

*Source: Malan and Schusky, *The Dakota Indian Community.*

[14] Vernon D. Malan and Ernest L. Schusky, *The Dakota Indian Community:* An analysis of the non-ranching population of the Pine Ridge Reservation, "Rural Sociology Department, Agricultural Experiment Station Bulletin," No. 505 (Brookings, S. D.: South Dakota State College, not dated, issued 1962), pp. 4-11; Nekota Redevelopment Commission, "Provisional Overall Economic Development Program" (Pine Ridge, S. D.; n.d., 1962?). Also pertinent for the issue of acculturation is Ernest L. Schusky, "Contemporary Migration and Cultural Change in Two Dakota Reservations," *Plains Anthropologist*, VII, 17 (1962), 178-183.

TABLE 5
INDIAN ENROLLMENT AND DROPOUT BY GRADES
FEDERAL SCHOOLS, PINE RIDGE*

| Grades | 1962-63 Enrolled | 1956-61-Average Enrolled | Dropout |
|---|---|---|---|
| One | 203 | 214 | |
| Two | 170 | 195 | |
| Three | 198 | 202 | |
| Four | 168 | 182 | |
| Five | 194 | 171 | |
| Six | 199 | 154 | |
| Seven | 134 | 141 | |
| Eight | 132 | 140 | |
| Total One-Eight | 1,398 | 1,399 | 102 |
| Nine | 143 | 106 | 41 |
| Ten | 101 | 65 | 14 |
| Eleven | 49 | 56 | 15 |
| Twelve | 44 | 48 | 16 |
| (Graduates) | (30) | (34) | |
| Total Nine-Twelve | 337 | 275 | 86 |
| Total One-Twelve | 1,735 | 1,674 | |

*Source: Office of Reservation Principal, Pine Ridge Agency.

generally the figure for 1950 was less than 3 percent.

Of especial interest in the present context is the analysis of the age and education of the Pine Ridge population. If the adult population is separated into those aged twenty to forty-five and those over that age, then it is clear that the younger adults have had a fair exposure to formal education. The median years of education completed for the younger group is 8.8 and, as Malan and Schusky note, this compares very favorably with the median of 8.9 for all persons twenty-five years of age and over in South Dakota (1950). These authors comment:

> Often it is contended that many of the Indian problems would disappear if the Indians "became educated." This premise is widely accepted by the Indians themselves, and many of the Pine Ridge respondents in this study expressed this belief.[15]

This quotation serves to recall that originally the "Indian problem" was regarded as one of cultural assimilation, whereas today the concern is the economic misery and social inferiority of the Indian. If assimilation in the narrow sense were the goal, then an Eighth Grade education might be sufficient, especially if this corresponded to the level of education of the general population of that region of the country. However, if the Indian is now expected to compete in the national society and its urban centers, he is still at a significant disadvantage, for the median years of schooling completed by those in the age group twenty-five to forty-four of the general U.S. population was in 1950 already over eleven and a half. In terms of years of schooling completed the Sioux is now on a level with his South Dakota neighbors, but both are at a significant disadvantage when they migrate—as they have been doing—to urban centers.

Another consideration is the quality of Reservation education. While we, ourselves, have much to say on this question deriving from our observa-

---

[15] *Ibid.*, p. 7.

tions of classrooms and our conversations with the personnel involved, it is appropriate here to mention the results of standardized tests of educational achievement. In May 1958, an (*ad hoc*) Committee on Raising Standards of the Branch of Education, Pine Ridge Agency, issued a Report summarizing the results of a recent program of testing. These were dismaying. On every measuring device used, the Oglala Community School ranked toward the bottom ten per cent of the U.S. On the School and College Ability Test, the Oglala Community High School had a percentile rank of eleven. On the Batson Test (University of South Dakota, High School Achievement), its median percentile rank was nine. On the Iowa Test of Educational Development percentile ranks for grades nine to twelve were consistently below ten on all tests within the battery. Seniors at the Oglala Community High School had a median score below that of all other schools in the state, including public schools, mission schools, and other federal schools.[16]

The implication of such extremely low scores becomes even stronger when they are placed in the context of the pattern of school dropouts (Table 5). In comparison with Reservation youngsters of the same age range, high school students and, especially, high school seniors are a highly selected group. While the shifting Reservation population (resulting from migration and the birth rate) makes exact calculation of dropout rates difficult,[17] nonetheless, current figures would indicate that about half of those who enter the primary grades drop out before entering high school, and that of these high school entrants only about a third graduate. In short, the high school graduates are an elite group, comprising about a sixth of the population of their age; many of these are children of Bureau employees, and a number are non-Indian. Clearly if this elite performs so poorly on achievement tests, the state of their Reservation contemporaries must indeed be extremely low.

In the past decade a number of changes have been made in the curricula of the federal schools on Pine Ridge. In particular, the vocational agriculture program was finally dismantled, and the high school program oriented almost exclusively in an academic direction. Courses in a foreign language (Spanish) were added during 1962-63, and the chemistry course is being shifted from a practical, vocational orientation to an academic, scientific one. Such a shift in curriculum should improve the showing of those students who are able to maintain a satisfactory rate of progress through the four years. On the other hand there remains the problem of those students who find difficulty in scholastic work; the new and more difficult academic program may cause them to drop out even earlier. This dilemma is faced by all public schools.

Educational achievement tests are now being administered to children in the Pine Ridge schools. Unfortunately the data offered to us by the school administration would have required

---

[16] John Artichoker's comment of 1956 appears excessively cautious, "As far as the academic end of it is concerned, I don't see why there should be anything lacking because the government schools are supposed to follow the state course of study. I sometimes wonder, though, if the teachers haven't taught at too low a level, so that when the youngsters reach the twelfth grade they might be just a little bit behind other people." Speech on "What We Need to Know About Indian Education" before the Second Annual Conference on Indian Affairs, published in *Indian Education— Goals and Means,* Vermillion, S. D.: Institute of Indian Studies, State University of South Dakota, 1956, p. 12.

[17] A cohort analysis was attempted by our staff, but owing to shifting population and absence of centralized, accurate records, it could not be carried to completion.

## TABLE 6
### AGE, SEX, AND EDUCATIONAL ACHIEVEMENT; OGLALA
### SIOUX, PINE RIDGE RESERVATION, JUNE 1960*

| RESERVATION POPULATION | Under 15 | 15-18 | Age Groups 19-35 | 36-65 | Over 65 | Total |
|---|---|---|---|---|---|---|
| Males | 1526 | 383 | 1070 | 996 | 308 | 4,283 |
| Females | 1605 | 388 | 1127 | 1024 | 261 | 4,405 |
| No report on sex | .... | .... | .... | .... | 1 | 1 |
| TOTALS—each age group (Male and Female) | 3131 | 771 | 2197 | 2020 | 570 | 8,689 |
| AVERAGE GRADE COMPLETED (By each age group) | | | | | | |
| Male | 1.66 | 7.35 | 8.62 | 7.57 | 5.07 | |
| Female | 1.59 | 7.68 | 8.65 | 7.54 | 5.33 | |
| FULLY EMPLOYABLE | | | | | | |
| Males | 1518 | 380 | 1030 | 973 | 306 | |
| Females | 1601 | 384 | 1109 | 1023 | 259 | |
| TOTALS—each age group (Male and Female) | 3119 | 764 | 2139 | 1996 | 565 | |

*Source: Aberdeen Area Office, Bureau of Indian Affairs.

a more careful analysis than we had time or qualifications to undertake. It is especially necessary to distinguish between the scholastic performance of the children enrolled in the federal schools and the scholastic performance of Oglala Sioux children, generally. The federal schools on Pine Ridge are now serving a substantial number of non-Indian children; in 1962-63 these included 222 pupils of the Shannon County (public) school system[18] and a number of children of federal employees. It might be anticipated that these non-Indian children are among the better pupils in the schools and that their presence would markedly bias any overall scores of educational achievement. In addition, the Oglala Community School is now serving other Indians besides the Sioux, and the general impression seems to be that these visitors are also better students than the local children. On the other side, there is the problem of poor attendance and dropout in the advanced grades. If children are to be considered as enrolled in school, then they must be included in the testing; otherwise, the circumstance of their failure to be present on the day of testing will bias the test scores upward. All in all, it might be advisable for regular evaluations of scholastic achievement to be made by an agency independent of the Bureau and skilled in the interpretation of tests and the statistical analysis of data. Such evaluations should be contracted for on a long term basis, so that a consistent battery of tests be used year after year and so that the testing agency be free of any pressures to bias test results in one direction or another, depending upon current political considerations.

* * *

For readers interested in further demographic details, several additional tables on Pine Ridge and adjacent counties of South Dakota and Nebraska are appended.

[18] South Dakota Department of Public Instruction and the Educational Research and Service Center, State University of South Dakota. "Survey Report, Shannon County School District," mimeographed, March 1963, p. 10.

## TABLE 7

### PINE RIDGE RESERVATION AND ADJACENT COUNTIES*

Comparative Data, 1956

| Pine Ridge Reservation, S.D. | Population 1950 | Per Sq. Mi. | Increase '40 to '50 % | Urban % | Non-White % | 65 yrs. and over % | Median Age | Median School years completed (25 yrs. old +) |
|---|---|---|---|---|---|---|---|---|
| Shannon County | 5,669 | 3 | 5.6 | .... | 84.3 | 5.8 | 20.9 | 8.1 |
| Washabaugh County | 1,551 | 2 | −21.7 | .... | 58.7 | 5.4 | 22.5 | 8.5 |
| Bennett County | 3,396 | 3 | −14.7 | .... | 27.4 | 6.3 | 24.8 | 8.8 |
| Adjacent South Dakota | | | | | | | | |
| Fall River County | 10,439 | 6 | 29.1 | 48.2 | 3.9 | 9.7 | 33.0 | 9.5 |
| Jackson County | 1,768 | 2 | − 9.6 | .... | 2.7 | 9.9 | 29.4 | 8.9 |
| Adjacent Nebraska | | | | | | | | |
| Sheridan County | 9,539 | 4 | − 3.3 | .... | 3.0 | 8.6 | 28.7 | 10.1 |
| Dawes County | 9,708 | 7 | − 4.1 | 48.3 | 2.0 | 9.9 | 29.8 | 10.8 |
| Cherry County | 8,397 | 1 | −12.9 | 32.2 | 1.4 | 7.7 | 27.9 | 9.5 |
| South Dakota, total | 652,740 | 9 | 1.5 | 33.2 | 3.7 | 8.5 | 28.6 | 8.9 |
| Nebraska, total | 1,325,510 | 17 | 0.7 | 46.9 | 1.8 | 9.8 | 31.0 | 10.1 |

* Source: U. S. Bureau of the Census, *County and City Data Book, 1956,* Washington, D.C.: U.S. Government Printing Office, 1957.

## TABLE 7—*Continued*

| Pine Ridge Reservation, S.D. | Dwelling Units,1950 With running water private bath, etc. % | Vital Statistics, 1954 Live Births | Deaths | Marriages |
|---|---|---|---|---|
| Shannon County | 10.4 | 244 | 76 | 6 |
| Washabaugh County | 7.5 | 50 | 10 | .... |
| Bennett County | 18.4 | 92 | 27 | 39 |
| Adjacent South Dakota Fall River County | 47.0 | 270 | 154 | 116 |
| Jackson County | 15.8 | 40 | 19 | 31 |
| Adjacent Nebraska Sheridan County | 48.7 | 262 | 93 | 68 |
| Dawes County | 56.3 | 220 | 110 | 76 |
| Cherry County | 48.1 | 190 | 73 | 63 |
| South Dakota, total | 38.0 | 18,166 | 5,766 | 6,102 |
| Nebraska, total | 56.5 | 33,852 | 12,870 | 11,307 |

## TABLE 7—*Continued*

| Pine Ridge Reservation, S. D. | Employers reporting under OASI, 1953 Reporting units Jan.-Mar. | Employees mid-Mar. | Taxable payrolls Jan.-Mar. $1,000 | Urban Places Name | Population 1950 |
|---|---|---|---|---|---|
| Shannon County | 13 | 81 | 43 | .... | .... |
| Washabaugh County | 1 | .... | .... | .... | .... |
| Bennett County | 41 | 140 | 70 | .... | .... |
| Adjacent South Dakota Fall River County | 193 | 885 | 504 | Hot Springs | 5,030 |
| Jackson County | 35 | 112 | 55 | .... | .... |
| Adjacent Nebraska Sheridan County | 216 | 848 | 449 | Valentine | 2,700 |
| Dawes County | 257 | 1,157 | 632 | Chadron | 4,687 |
| Cherry County | 164 | 687 | 393 | .... | .... |
| South Dakota, total | 12,684 | 77,641 | 50.819 | (omitted) | |
| Nebraska, total | 28,152 | 237,364 | 170,346 | (omitted) | |

# Chapter III

# PEOPLES AND STATUSES: BLOOD, COLOR, CUSTOM, AND SOCIAL ACCEPTANCE

Historically, Pine Ridge came into existence as one of the areas to which the wild Indians of the Sioux nation were to be restricted. Outnumbered and outgunned, suffering the loss of the game which had been their staff of life, they were nonetheless a nuisance, capable of raids upon settlers and travelers and of embarrassing the army squadrons sent to discipline them. Confined to a reservation which was solely theirs and was supplied with food, instruction, and agricultural implements, the Oglala Sioux might become civilized or, at any rate, less troublesome.

Even at the time when the Reserve of land was created, there must have been some question as to who or what was an "Indian." French traders, Yankee explorers and troopers had been breeding with the Sioux for years—even centuries—and in some cases the progeny had been given at least some of the training of their male forebears. The social category of "halfbreed" was well recognized, but it was likely regarded as temporary. Most White people anticipated that Indian culture and identity would vanish, through epidemics, social disintegration, or assimilation. The Redman, when subjected to civilization, would melt into the White and become "American" like everyone else.

Today there are probably more people claiming Indian identity than ever before, and, on the Pine Ridge Reservation, such terms as *Indian, Whiteman, Mixedbloods,* or *Fullbloods* are heard on every hand. At the same time, the question of who is an Indian, or more precisely, who is what kind of an Indian, becomes increasingly vague and elusive. The meaning of *Indian* alters according to social context (who is speaking of whom), status, wealth, physical appearance, style of life, and location of residence. The meanings of such terms as *Mixedblood* and *Fullblood* are even more elusive. Clearly, the residents of the Reservation believe there is a basic and obvious distinction between "Mixedblood" and "Fullblood," and so too do most scholars, following the sociological polarity (and factionalism) Gordon Macgregor described a generation ago between the "white assimilated" and the "unassimilated . . . who live in the shadow of their former Indian culture."[1] Yet, as we shall observe in this chapter, no simple sociological, cultural, or biological realities correspond to any of these basic terms (Indian, White, Mixedblood, Fullblood). Distinctions can be made and are made, but the social and political consequences of these distinctions are perhaps more significant than the original logic of classification.

We would like to suggest that this seeming confusion and disagreement about definitions of identity is, in itself, an extremely significant datum. On the one hand, it reflects the social distance maintained both between Bureau personnel and Indians and among the various groups of Indians. Differences of meaning develop in each enclave and tend, in part through sheer absence of communication, to persist. On another level, the various and variable definitions are related to a bitter covert conflict, in which certain groups

---

[1] *Warriors Without Weapons*, p. 23f. The same distinction between "sociological fullbloods" and "sociological mixedbloods" was used quite recently by E. E. Hagen and Louis C. Schaw, *The Sioux on the Reservations*: The American Colonial Problem, "preliminary edition," Cambridge, Mass.: M.I.T. Center for International Studies, May 1960, p. VI-5; however, those authors actually spent little time in field work and based their presentation mostly on previous research, especially that of Macgregor.

strive to project a set of negative images upon other groups. Thus most Bureau personnel think of Indians as strange and inferior beings who enjoy living in a state of incredible deprivation and filth; in this sense, Mixed-bloods who live like Bureau personnel are not really "Indian." Those who consider themselves "really" Indians try to evade this (Bureau) definition and, in the process, create new notions of "Indianness" (some of which would amaze their grandsires), to wit: Mixed-bloods are amoral alcoholics given to running amok, they are grafters and embezzlers and, worst of all, they are snobs; "real" Indians are stable, unassuming, honest, friendly and pious.

It is not necessary to point out that this situation is rife with distress and anxiety. Many Sioux desperately want to know where they stand with respect to the White man and to the future. Others, who are beginning to suspect where they do now stand, are thoroughly shaken and do not know where to turn. Some, we suspect, would just as soon not know where they stand. But insofar as some of these people continue to struggle, even if feebly, against the idea that to be Indian is to be inferior, they will bewilder the inquirer with inconsistent and elusive views about Indianness.

We believe that some familiarity with and appreciation of this disorderly and confusing situation is essential to even a modest understanding of the dynamics of Pine Ridge life. Since inconsistency is a prime characteristic of the data, we have arranged them in arbitrary fashion, using categories with which the social scientist is at home.

## PHENOTYPES AND BLOOD QUANTA

The observer on Pine Ridge can often recognize casts of feature and styles of pigmentation that are distinctively *Indian*. At the ceremonial gatherings, where men appear in dance regalia, the facial resemblance between some of them and the paintings and photographs of their ancestors is marked. The observer also encounters many persons on the Reservation who are classified as "Indian," and who so classify themselves, but who in their features and pigmentation are pronouncedly, or even entirely, "European." Thus, even at first encounter with the population of Pine Ridge, the peculiarities of "Indianness" are evident.

Anglo-Saxon principles of heirship have been applied to "Indianness" and thus created a "legalistic genetics" in which the individual is characterized by his "blood quanta." The federal government maintains a tribal roster in which each person is characterized by "eighths" (i.e. great-grandparents), so that "8/8" signifies wholly "full-blood" and "4/8" the exact "halfbreed." As this characterization presupposes an absolutely accurate census and controlled records of marriage and birth, it represents something of a legal fiction. Sioux and European had interbred for a century or more before the conditions of Reservation life and tribal rosters. Be that as it may, many governmental and charitable programs state a minimum blood quantum (usually a quarter) for eligibility, and court decisions as to share in tribal properties are phrased according to Anglo-Saxon notions of blood inheritance.[2]

While being a *legal* Indian had marked disadvantages a generation and

[2] "Senator Dirksen once wrote to the Secretary of the Interior and asked a simple question: What is an Indian? He got a six page reply, and when he was through reading it he still didn't know. Some legislation deals with the fullblood, the half, and the quarter. Some deals with less than that. . . ." Speech of Senator Francis Case on "Pending Legislation in Congress Affecting Indians" before the Second Annual Conference on Indian Affairs, reprinted in *Indian Education—Goals and Means,* Vermillion, S. D.: Institute of Indian Studies, State University of South Dakota, 1956, p. 2.

more ago, it has few or none today. Meantime, legal identity as a Sioux has become a ticket to the lottery of the Indian Claims Commission: Who knows what benefits might ensue? *Looking* Indian may have disadvantages: In Western towns Fullblood Indians are regarded with some suspicion as drunks, brawlers, and thieves; while in the urban centers, persons of dark Indian pigmentation can easily be taken for Negro.

Because of the various programs of assistance available to those who are classed as "Indian," and because of the possibility of such bonanzas as the favorable settlement of the Black Hills claim, people who otherwise would prefer to pass as totally White are nonetheless moved to emphasize their Indian identity and even to maintain residence on Pine Ridge. Many other competent, legal Mixedbloods might leave the reservation and get along comfortably either as Indians or Whites, were they not so narrowly provincial in their range of experience and so strongly oriented toward life as Bureau employees. Here, of course, their legal identity as an Indian brings them preferment in employment over Whites, while their superior "know-how" and knowledge of English brings them preferment over Fullbloods. Still other Mixedbloods have been accepted as *de facto* Fullbloods by the communities in which they reside. Usually they have accomplished this by marrying Fullbloods, taking up residence with their in-laws, and following the rural or "conservative" Indian style of life.

Fearful lest the actual and potential financial benefits of "true Indianness" be dispersed so widely that the "legitimate" claimants would lose their proper share, many of those who can lay legal or other claims to "Fullbloodedness" make vigorous efforts to validate definitions which exclude the "lesser bloods" from eligibility for programs of assistance. The high point of such disputations is reached whenever the Black Hills Claim is mentioned and councils of high standing (and no standing whatsoever) can palaver for hours as to who should be eligible for what share of this envisioned fortune.

Reservation inhabitants are usually quite knowledgeable about the legal-genetic "Indianness" of other families in the community. Sometimes, they will use this as a basis for contemptuous remarks in either direction—against those who are more or less legally Indian. This leads to interesting and ironic complications. Thus, a young man of our acquaintance claimed Fullblood status despite the fact that his mother was genetically a mixedblood. He consistently spoke ill of Mixedbloods, though his wife was genetically less than half Indian. His mother, who claimed and generally was given *de facto* Fullblood status was once, in our presence, insulted by some persons of unimpeachable Fullblood status. "Those are *real* Fullbloods," she told us, caustically, "They walk right over you." Later, however, she tried to convince us that these persons had been rude to her because she was associating with "hated White men," namely, us. On other occasions uncomplimentary accusations will be phrased simply in terms of the genetics of the family line and the presumptive immorality of its womenfolk:

> When there was that fort over there a long time ago, some of the Indian girls went down there to work. Nine months later all came back with babies—White man's babies—that's where all the Mixedbloods come from. I got up and said that at the Tribal Council meeting, and it sure made them Mixedbloods mad, but it's the truth.

Ironically, Mixedbloods use the same type of tale as an attack on the morality of the traditional Fullblood: Fullbloods sold their women to the Whiteman, ergo, morals of Whites and their partial descendents are superior.

The older generation of Whites on the Western plains, and especially the older ranchers, tend to believe in the superior virtue of the pure bloodline (as against the racial mixture). They have found confirmation of their view in the behavior of the older Fullblood Indians, whose ethos was markedly similar to that of the rancher. Cowboys and Indians shared many of the same habits and admired much the same type of hero. Older Whites of this sort deplore the present condition of the Indian and the corruption of aboriginal (circa 1930) virtues.

The more modern Whites tend to judge Indians by the extent of their adoption of the secularized Protestant ethos. They condemn them for being drunk, disorderly, and extravagant, and they grudgingly tolerate those who are diligent, clean, and reliable. If they think racially, they tend to feel that the more the admixture of White blood, the better the product.

For those interested in the legal-genetic composition of Pine Ridge, we reproduce a recent tabulation of blood quanta and age. It will be noted that, while the ratio of completely "full" (eight-eighths) bloods is declining, the proportion of those who are predominantly Indian (three-fourths and over) is reasonably stable, ranging from sixty to seventy percent of each age group. The actualities denoted by the Table are a contrast to the belief of some Sioux, and of even some federal teachers, to the effect that as a distinct people the Sioux are genetically vanishing (or dissolving). If the Sioux are in fact tending to lose their genetic identity through interbreeding, the process is by no means rapid.

## PATRONYMICS

WhirlwindHorse, TwoBulls, PoorBear, JumpingBull, WeaselBear, are some of the typical surnames on Pine Ridge. Those and many similar names denote an unbroken paternal lineage of Indianness; they are "fullblood" names. In contrast, names such as Merrival, Roubideaux, Clifford, Apple, and Mesteth, while equally prevalent on the Reservation and of respectable vintage, indicate that somewhere in the past a White man married into the Teton Dakota people. Among the contemporary Oglala, persons who bear a name of this latter sort are not considered quite as "Fullblood" as others who bear a properly "Indian" name, regardless of genetic composition or style of living.[3]

Robert K. Thomas suggests that there is a plausible historical rationale to this contemporary differentiation. The Whites who early intermarried among the Dakota were traders. They were not nomadic with their wife's people but settled down and established trading posts or forts; while their children imbibed Indianness from their mothers, they never shared in the roaming life of their peers. That such children were marginalmen and middlemen is shown in the Lakota term designating "Mixedblood," *iyeska,* which literally means "interpreter."

The ambivalence of the Sioux about their contemporary situation is manifested in their handling of surnames. Some have shortened their names, so that they are not particularly distinguishable as "Indian" names. The usual pattern of contraction is to eliminate all but the first word of the name, so that a name, say, of the order of

---

3 "People in Dzitas, especially older people, divide their neighbors into two groups: *vecinos* and *indios*. A *vecino* is anyone with a Spanish surname. An *indio* is anyone with a Maya surname. . . . No matter how poor or how dark-skinned a man or woman may be, or how humble his occupation, if he has a Spanish surname it is proof that he is not an Indian, that he is a descendant of Spaniards, and that *indios* should recognize that he is better than they." Robert Redfield, "Race and Class in Yucatan" as cited in Edgar T. Thompson and Everett C. Hughes, *Race: Individual and Collective Behavior,* Glencoe: Free Press, 1958, p. 42.

## TABLE 8

### Blood Quanta by Age Groups*
### in per cent**

| Fraction Indian Blood | All Ages | Age Groups, in Years | | | | | | | | |
|---|---|---|---|---|---|---|---|---|---|---|
| | | 0-5 | 5-9 | 10-14 | 15-19 | 20-24 | 25-34 | 35-44 | 45-64 | 65+ |
| Less than ¼ | 7.6 | 7.5 | 7.2 | 6.1 | 9.6 | 5.5 | 5.2 | 3.9 | 2.9 | 2.5 |
| ¼ to ½ | 10.9 | 16.4 | 15.5 | 15.5 | 16.8 | 14.0 | 9.6 | 14.3 | 12.8 | 12.9 |
| ½ to ¾ | 15.4 | 16.4 | 16.0 | 13.7 | 13.4 | 12.2 | 14.7 | 14.0 | 12.7 | 18.9 |
| ¾ to Full | 21.4 | 34.6 | 37.3 | 34.8 | 29.9 | 30.3 | 29.1 | 19.7 | 17.9 | 9.0 |
| Full | 44.8 | 25.1 | 23.9 | 29.9 | 30.3 | 37.9 | 41.4 | 48.0 | 53.7 | 56.7 |
| | 100.0 | 100.0 | 100.0 | 100.0 | 100.0 | 100.0 | 100.0 | 100.0 | 100.0 | 100.0 |

* *Source:* Aberdeen Area Office, Bureau of Indian Affairs, as reproduced in *The Sioux on the Reservation,* by E. E. Hagen and Louis C. Schaw, "preliminary edition"; Cambridge, Mass.: Center for International Studies, M. I. T., 1960, p. 2-3.
** *Note:* In computing the percentages, individuals were omitted for whom no report was obtained. There were 215 such individuals, or 3.0 per cent of the total, at Pine Ridge. Percentages in some columns will not add to the total of 100.0, because of rounding.

"BlueEyeHawk" becomes s i m p l y, "Blue." Since some of these Indian surnames do run to five or even a dozen words (of the order, say, of "Ran-Among-the-enemy-and-stole-their-flag"), the desire to abbreviate can sometimes simply reflect despair at struggling with bureaucratic schedules designed for surnames of a few syllables in length. However, some of this contraction reflects uneasiness at being identified as "Indian." A person with a name like "Blue" has more control over the circumstances where he acknowledges being "Indian" (just as a person with a name like "Wax" has a different kind of experience being a Jew than a person with a name like "Cohen" or "Shapiro.") One teacher told us of a boy whose formal registration was under a "White" name but who used an "Indian" name in his classwork.

## SOCIAL STATUS: LO!
## THE POOR INDIAN

The social gulf between the Bureau employee in his "suburban" house and the conservative Indian in his cabin on the prairie is enormous. The width of the gulf is scarcely altered by the pigmentation of the employee—white, black, or red—or the nature of his employer or job. Likewise, it is not altered by the linguistic abilities or sophistication of the country Indian.

As a general rule, the polar differences between the two groups may be characterized as follows: The Bureau employee speaks English and knows no Lakota; the country Indian speaks Lakota by preference, and if he speaks English it will be Pine Ridge dialect (with many violations of the rules of so-called "Good English"). The family of the Bureau employee has a steady income from one or even several salaries; the country Indian has a minuscule monetary income from lease money. The Bureau employee participates in the ceremonial life of the government and greater urban society; the country Indian participates in the ceremonial life of Pine Ridge and other Indian Reservations. It is almost unnecessary to state that the two groups lead almost wholly separate social lives, rarely mingling with each other, except within an institutional context. Some exceptions occur, and they are significant; some marginal positions are created, notably the school bus drivers and cooks, who usually maintain ties with the Indians out in the community, while earning incomes and living in a style that places them between the teachers and the folks in the community.

Other persons get assimilated socially into one or the other group, depending mostly on their economic status. Impoverished persons of Spanish-speaking derivation will associate with the country Indians; successful ranchers, employees of the state government, and local traders will associate with the Bureau employees.

Clearly, we deal here with a situation of social class or, to the extent that the participants involved feel that there is a biological or ethnic origin to the system of stratification, we might more aptly speak of *caste*. To the country Indian the Bureau employee is either a "Whiteman" or a "Mixedblood"; while to the Bureau employee the country Indian is simply "the Indian."[4] As a result, both groups tend to convert the forms of achievement within urban society into marks of biological and cultural identity: Generally, the man who is educated and rich is White; the man who is uneducated and poor is Indian. Again, for both groups, the traditions and cultural achievements of the Sioux or of Indians generally are reduced to the style of life of the contemporary and impoverished Sioux in his cabin,

while the rich diversity of urban United States or of Western civilization is reduced to the style of life of the Bureau employee and his limited intellectual horizons.

Thus, "Indian" and "Bureau employee" become correlatives, and the existence of the Indian becomes both the reason for existence of the Bureau employee and the bane of that existence. Psychiatrically-oriented scholars like Hagen and Schaw speak of the Sioux as being "hostilely dependent" upon the Bureau;[5] it is equally true that the Bureau employee is hostilely dependent upon the Sioux. For whereever and to what degree the Sioux take control of their own affairs and operate them successfully, then to that degree is the role of the Bureau superfluous. The double standard of morality utilized by Bureau personnel is a significant index to this hostile dependency: As these employees deplore Sioux drunkenness, idleness, tribal politics, etc., the outside observer would think that the rest of the U. S. was inhabited exclusively by people who worked hard for the sheer joy of working, who never became drunk, and whose local governments were embodiments of civic virtue and efficiency. The immoralities and inefficiencies of the Sioux are real, sometimes dramatic—alternately comic and tragic—but they are less different from the rest of our nation than some federal employees can bear to realize.[6]

The poverty and lack of formal education of the "country Indian" afford a substantial basis to the Bureau employee for his feelings of superiority and justified superordination. Many Sioux live in conditions which respectable persons of the urban lower-middle class would regard as subhuman—lacking running water, central heating, and privacy. Since many Bureau employees themselves were reared in

---

[4] Usage varies among Indians who are themselves Bureau Employees. They rarely say "we Indians" before Indians, lest some aggressive Fullblood challenge them. They will use the expression before Whites only if forced to do so, as when, for example, they are obligated to represent "the Indian" at a conference. On the other hand, when such persons spoke to members of our study they always implicitly made clear that they considered themselves Indians while, at the same time, they always differentiated themselves from "residual families," "backward folks," or, if no words came, by an inclination of the head toward the heart of the reservation and the word, "them."

[5] *The Sioux on the Reservations, op. cit.*, p. VI-8 *et passim.*

rural Western surroundings, they tend not to object to the absence of the facilities so much as to the disorder, dirt, and *sang-froid* of the Indians living amid them. For the Bureau employee must feel as if he has risen morally above his own natal state, while many Sioux act as if they did not care about the very things for which the Bureau employees work so hard; the menfolk, especially, spend hours visibly doing nothing—unashamedly enjoying their leisure. Bureau employees feel that if Indians could only be educated, disciplined, and accustomed to regular work, the "Indian problem" would be solved, but it is plain from their talk that they regard this as an almost utopian goal.

This definition of *Indian* is covertly circular and therefore self-reinforcing: for, if to be "Indian" is to be poor and ignorant, then, implicitly, the successful man is no longer "really" Indian. The following remarks of a Bureau employee, who regards himself as a social and political liberal, exhibit this conceptualization clearly. He began to tell us about a talk he had had with X, a man who is legally Fullblood and has reached a respectably high position in the Pine Ridge Agency:

> The other day I heard X say, "How would you like to get up every morning with the feeling that you belong to an inferior people?" But I feel you have to make allowances for X. After all, so few Indians have been successful.

_____

6 Judging by the following excerpt from a review of a book about colonial India, the British civil service of that period shared much in attitude with the contemporary personnel of the B.I.A. For the author of the book "reports his initial shock, upon his return to Britain from India, to discover Englishmen committing all sorts of crimes and misdemeanors. 'I had to learn that what I had thought was the way Indians behaved was really the way people behaved.'" Review by Lewis A. Coser of *Prospero's Magic: Some Thoughts on Class and Race* by Philip Mason, *American Sociological Review*, XXVIII, 4 [Aug. 1963] 655-6.

We took issue with the last statement and began to name notable and highly successful Indians. "Were they Indians?" asked our friend, and then added: "But they weren't real Indians —not like *these* people."

While many points might be made about this interchange, we were struck by the rigidity of this liberal person's negative conception of the Indian. He seemed quite unable to associate wealth, status, or prestige, with Indianness. We had on many previous occasions noted that Indians whose work brings them into frequent contact with Bureau employees tend to adopt this negative imagery of their ethnicity.

The country Indian is well aware of his negative status within the greater social system of Pine Ridge. To protect his self-esteem he has developed a number of devices, most of which serve to isolate him from painful contact with Bureau personnel. One of those is avoiding face-to-face contacts with Bureau personnel—"going to Pine Ridge really makes me nervous."7 For if the Indian accepted the Bureau's perspective, he would have to acknowledge his own status as lower class. Contrariwise, by emphasizing or exaggerating his true Indianness and alienness, he can insist that the Bureau world and its perspective are not valid. Rather, the Bureau is a corrupt and inefficient device of the Whites, which should serve the Indians but in fact does a poor job of it. (This tendency to regard the Bureau as entirely corrupt not only works an injustice on those employees who are doing a good job, but also creates a miasma of confusion in which the

_____

7 Sometimes we wonder whether the country Indians' disposition to use the country stores, or, if they had the means, to travel fifty or a hundred miles off the reservation for shopping or medical needs, may not also, in part, be a device to avoid encountering the "Mixedbloods" and the "White people who look down on you."

genuine corruption and incompetence —and the B.I.A. has its share—become obscured from vision.)

In addition to those protective devices, the country Indian possesses a self-conception that is, so far as we comprehend it, quite disassociated from the world of the Bureau. Or, one might put it this way. For the Indian (be he town or country dweller) there are two social worlds: in one, the world where Bureau employees and Indians meet, the Indian is seen as inferior; in the other, the "real" Indian world, the Bureau has no place and the individual is respected, or laughed at, in accordance with the extent to which his behavior meets Indian standards. In the latter world, occupational status counts for little and family status for a great deal; no one is "inferior" in the middle-class American sense, but instead is unlucky, crazy, or spoilt by parents or grandparents, or he does not respect other people. No one "improves" or "betters" himself in the Western sense; if one man or woman is respected more than another, it is because he has "acted" more friendly, generous, considerate and modest. Good repute is not attained; it is tentatively and cautiously given. One is rated, not by one's current status, wealth, or admirable behavior, but by every remembered deed of one's past life. In consequence, very few persons indeed are uniformly approved by all acquaintances or relatives.

It should be noted that there is one aspect of the country Indian's point of view that makes the image projected by the Bureau particularly intolerable. This is the Indian's axiomatic notion that an individual's nature, self, or being is a constant: The essence of what one is does not change through the course of one's life. Thus, when an official or a teacher indicates that he thinks that Indians are loathsomely dirty or immoral, the country Indian who accepts this may see himself as irrevocably damned.

A highly relevant aspect of the country Indian's social perspective is his attitude toward association. Should a White person or a "Mixedblood" be willing to associate with him on the basis of parity (social equivalence), then they are ready to identify him as "Indian." Thus Ben Reifel, who is biologically a halfbreed and who bears the Protestant ethic of his Germanic forebears like a flaming torch, is widely regarded as an "Indian," because even though he was Superintendent of Pine Ridge Agency, he would attend community ceremonials and would dance, and when country Indians came to see him he would discuss their problems sympathetically in Lakota. Other individuals, even those whose genes are wholly "White" will also be referred to as "Indian," when they demonstrate a willingness to associate with the country folk on the basis of social parity.[8] Identical principles operate in social relations between Indian groups. Thus when we approached communities notorious even among Indians for their retiring ways—"they don't talk to nobody"— we were successful only if we took along an interpreter who, though an outsider, often went to these folks' social affairs and always bespoke them well.

The social dynamics described in this section deserve emphasis, because the policy of the Pine Ridge school system is to stress the separation between teacher and community. Insofar as teachers and officials continue to keep their social distance from the community, they continually reinforce the notion that they hold themselves superior to the country Indians. The impact of this policy on the occasional teacher who comes from a country "Fullblood" Indian family can be dis-

---

[8] See the discussion of "Education and the Good Man" in the chapter on "How the Conservative 'Country Indian' Feels about School and Education."

tressing to see: Sioux will not be hired to teach in a school if they have strong family ties in its area, the theory being that their kind will drag them down. In order to be hired as teachers, they have first to establish a marked social distance between themselves and the families of their pupils. The result is that some of the loneliest individuals we met were teachers of relatively Fullblood background.

## CULTURE:
## THE TRADITIONAL INDIAN

At first blush, the *cultural* would seem the natural basis for a definition of Indianness: An Indian is one who follows an Indian style of life. Yet, as we shall see, there are complexities and paradoxes. The definition would be most useful if, as in the case of legalistic genetics, a linear scale could be created such that the observer could say of a person (or group) that he lived in a fashion that was 8/8th's Indian, or 5/8th's, or perhaps only 1/32. Many apostles of Indian assimilation (and even cultural anthropologists) have talked as if such a scale were possible. However, scholars such as Robert K. Thomas and Harriet Kupferer have noted that the "White culture" which presumptively stands as the opposite pole of the "Indian-White" scale is not a unitary thing, but is stratified into distinct subcultures, by class and ethnicity. Thus, some Indians have been assimilating or adapting to an urban middle class life, while others have been adapting toward a rural lower class one.[9] To the analysis of these scholars, one may add the general finding of accultura-

[9] Literature on the Eastern Cherokee has been most sophisticated here. See in particular, Robert K. Thomas, "Eastern Cherokee Acculturation," MS, 1958; Harriet J. Kupferer, "Health Practices and Education Aspirations as Indicators of Acculturation and Social Class among the Eastern Cherokee," *Social Forces*, XLI (Dec. 1962), pp. 154-163.

tion studies—that the process is highly selective. Thus, country Indians on Pine Ridge often live in log cabins resembling those of Lincoln's day, while cooking on the kerosene ranges that were common a half-century ago, and listening to popular music from a transistorized radio. On the other hand, Indians are aware of modern innovations in housekeeping and many desire them—adoption depends more on income than on a culturally-motivated resistance.

Further, complicating any attempt to create a scale of Indian-White acculturation is the fact that the Indian life of a century ago has vanished and is in many respects better known to ethnohistorians and antiquarians than it is to the un-self-conscious country Indians of the Reservation prairie. (Indeed, the question of what should be taken as the authentically "aboriginal culture" is endlessly regressive, given the dramatic changes in Sioux life from pre-Colombian days to the Reservation.) Meantime, quasi-educated Indian nationalists devise fantastically purified and rationalized versions of traditional Sioux existence, somewhat on the order of George Washington and the cherry tree.

While it may be taken for granted that the aggregate of cultures on the contemporary Reservation is significantly different from the Indian cultures of a century ago, what must be emphasized is that the changes are not simply ones of acculturation toward European "White" models. The result is that the sophisticated purist or antiquarian may exhibit traits that are more purely Indian aboriginal than those exhibited by the country Indians today. For example, an ethnohistorian denounced the dance costumes of the contemporary Sioux as "inferior" and "inauthentic." Certainly, they are being made with new materials, but they demonstrate an exciting esthetic that is by no stretch of the imagination Anglo-Saxon, European or generalized

38

"American." The costumes are indisputably *Indian,* if generalized or pow-wow Indian, and thus serve to remind the observer that the Redman and the White have always freely adapted traits from each other. Meantime, it remains true that the ethnohistorians can produce costumes more traditional in materials and design than do contemporary "Fullbloods."

The foregoing enables us to comprehend that what is perceived as culturally *Indian* may depend on the interests of the perceiver. For the ethno-historians the *Indian* is identified with Plains culture of a half century and more ago, and the contemporary is regarded as deteriorated. From the quite different perspective of the Bureau employee, the (culturally defined) *Indian* is intrinsically impoverished and uneducated. While (as we shall discuss later) for many Sioux, the truly *Indian* is defined by the behavior of the more isolated and rural bands (e.g. White River or Slim Buttes folk, many of whose habits are not really traditional Dakota). Correspondingly, as we have noted, there is even greater variability in the notion of what is culturally *White* (or generally American).[10]

---

[10] Accordingly, we have not utilized the characterizations of Sioux communities as "traditional," "transitional," and "transpositional," proposed by Vernon D. Malan, *The Dakota Indian Family: Community Studies on the Pine Ridge Reservation,* "Rural Sociology Department, Agricultural Experiment Station Bulletin," No. 470, Brookings, S. D.: South Dakota State College, May 1958. Malan thinks of this triad as forming a typology along the axis of *cultural transition,* which he defines as "a general process embracing all of the readjustments of a minority ethnic group such as the Dakota Indians as they shift from their traditional ways of living to the practices of the dominant society" (p. 1). Both in this statement and the design of the work as a whole there is the assumption of a simple, linear process of transition, in which the tremendous variety of living patterns of the contemporary U. S. are compressed into "the practices of the dominant society."

## CULTURE: ETHOS AND POVERTY

In the ideology of most Bureau personnel the poverty of the Indian is rooted in a traditional absence of discipline and disregard of time, exemplified in the coteries of menfolk idling daylong at the main highway intersection of Pine Ridge town and in the traditionally Indian disregard for the morrow. As a high Agency official described the matter to Bureau employees:

A Congressman comes or a social worker from outside comes and visits one of these Sioux households and says, "My God! There's no food in the house!"

Of course not, they're eaten for today. Why worry about tomorrow? Why worry about eating for tomorrow, they live for today.

Later, the same high Agency official remarked:

The people that work for Wright-McGill have to punch a time clock. This is the greatest thing that has ever happened on this Reservation—in the morning you can see people running to punch that time clock! This is real progress!

For members of the Project staff the success of these factories is an ironical commentary on the Bureau ideology, inasmuch as the factories are operated on the principles and wage-scales of sweatshops. Nonetheless, their success in recruiting labor and obtaining high production testifies to a pent desire among Indians for employment within their home area. This, though it was not perceived, was in fact evident from the successful Indian adaptation to seasonal agricultural labor, especially the potato-picking of the Plains region, which paid poorly, but often provided the laboring family with enough "spuds" to see them through the harsh winter.

Clearly, writing about *the culture of the contemporary Sioux* is hazardous.

If one avoids the mistaken identification with the aboriginal and historical Indian, one is then likely to fall into the trap of identifying Indianness with rural poverty and low social status. Many of the practices of the country Indian are not so much essential patterns of his Indian culture as they are conditional upon his poverty. This differentiation tends to be obscured because most missionaries and Bureau employees dealing with the Indians have been imbued with the (secularized) Protestant ethic and have argued that Indian poverty was a necessary consequence of the absence of that ethic. Since the core of Plains Indian culture has been an ethos that is distinctly different from the Protestant, it seemed to follow from their arguments that only by surrendering his culture could the Indian become successful. If he remained poor, it was because he had rejected the Protestant ethic.

In their stress upon the distinctive nature of Sioux values and ethos, Bureau personnel are in company with many anthropological students of American Indians, including ourselves. Where we differ—both with the Bureau and with some of the preceding students of the Sioux—is in the exact characterization of this ethos and in the judgment which is rendered, accordingly, upon the possibilities of Sioux adjustment to the greater national society. We cannot pretend here to depict adequately either the ethos of the contemporary Sioux or of the American Indians generally and must instead refer the interested reader elsewhere.[11] However, it may be worthwhile to note some of the distortions that have crept both into anthropological writings and into the speech of some Bureau personnel. For example, it is said that Indian children are treated with such excessive permissiveness and indulgence that they are never subject to any discipline. Yet the same observers who assert this will comment on how well Indian children behave in a significant variety of social situations. Again, it is said that Indians are indifferent to property, when observers have repeatedly noted their painstaking care with certain kinds of property in certain situations.

Returning then to the official comment with which we opened this discussion, we may ask whether in fact coming to work on time at a factory represents a change in Sioux values and ethos? Or whether, on the contrary, it is possible for individuals to bear a distinctively Sioux ethos and yet be efficient and reliable workers in a modern factory? Judged by the response of the Indian community of Pine Ridge, working in the Wright-McGill factory is wholly compatible with "Fullblood" identity as a Sioux. Judged by the official comment, those who perform such work have to that extent become "un-Indian."

## THE GEOGRAPHY OF INDIANNESS

We have previously noted the basic Reservation contrast between town and country: on the one hand, the cabins and tents scattered over the prairie and clustering along the creek banks in local communities of kith and kin (*tiyospaye*); on the other hand, the miniature urbanized areas centering

11 Discussions of American Indian ethos and values may be found in the following: Jaime de Angulo, "Indians in Overalls," *Hudson Review Anthology,* ed. Frederick Morgan, New York: Vintage Books, Random House, 1961, pp. 3-60; Dorothy D. Lee, *Freedom and Culture,* Englewood Cliffs, N. J.: Spectrum Books, Prentice Hall, 1959; Robert K. Thomas, "Cherokee Values and World View," mimeographed, 1962; Clyde Kluckhohm, "The Philosophy of the Navaho Indians," *Ideological Differences and World Order,* ed. F. S. C. Northrop, New Haven: Yale University Press, 1949; Murray Wax, "The Notions of Nature, Man, and Time of a Hunting People," *Southern Folklore Quarterly,* XXVI (1962), pp. 175-186.

about the little complexes of federal buildings, especially Pine Ridge town itself. While town and country both contain people of all degrees of Indian blood, the Sioux town-dwellers do tend generally to have more savvy about handling Bureau officials, to be more fluent in English, and to be generally more knowledgeable about the greater national society. Depending on whether the speaker is Indian or White and upon his context, the townsman refers to the country folk as the more conservative, "old-fashioned," "backward," or "residual" Indians.

Place of residence is significant in another sense. People who live upon the prairie are living on land which is "theirs." Actually, it is not theirs in an absolute sense, as it is land which is held in trust for them by the federal government and leased to ranchers (who are usually far wealthier and less "Indian" than they); also, others —among their kin—may own a share of the land. But they do have proprietary rights to the land, and they pay no rent for their occupancy. Some of these rural Indians own sizable tracts of land and derive fair incomes as rentiers; others have small shares in small tracts and derive only a meager income from their status as owners.

Selling land is not easy, because consent of the federal government must first be obtained, and multiple heirship adds further complexities. Yet the fact that the sale will bring a large sum of money is an inducement to impoverished folk some of whom are due for an unpleasant surprise when they find that the monetary proceeds are being held in trust and so are still inaccessible. At various times the federal government has tried to terminate the Reservation situation and has then facilitated the removal of Indian land from trust and onto the market. Accordingly, there are now to be found a fair number of landless Sioux, many of whom now reside in the vicinity of Pine Ridge town.

The Oglala Sioux Tribal Council has enacted a tax on the monies that the landowning Indians obtain from their leases. Like taxes everywhere, it is resented. The landed Indians of the country regard the tax as a device of the Pine Ridge (town) "Mixedbloods," who pay no taxes, because they sold their land. In their stereotype the town Indian is regarded either as a clever type who is craftily monopolizing governmental jobs and privileges (while evading his share of tribal taxation) or as an impoverished and homeless pauper who foolishly sold his land and spent the proceeds; this stereotype is complemented with that of the "Fullblood" landowner who wisely refused to sell his land or renounce his birthright and now finds himself saddled with supporting a body of worthless, self-seeking renegades.

This kind of accusation by country Indians against the towndwellers is significant in revealing another of the social polarities of Reservation life. For in terms of blood quanta the towndwellers are likely to be as much Indian as the rural folk; indeed some of the country *tiyospaye* are highly mixed both in blood quanta and customs.[12] Nonetheless, most residents of Pine Ridge (both Indian and White) regard the country Indian as somehow embodying the traits which are truly *Indian,* and by this logic the more isolated and rural the community the

---

[12] Some of the great variation among the Indian communities of Pine Ridge is revealed in chapter iii of Vernon D. Malan and Ernest L. Schusky, *The Dakota Indian Community:* an analysis of the non-ranching population of the Pine Ridge Reservation, "Rural Sociology Department, Agricultural Experiment Station Bulletin," No. 505, Brookings, S. D.: South Dakota State College; not dated, issued 1962. We found the status of Calico Hall especially significant, because this "exurb" of Pine Ridge town is largely fullblood in membership and ceremonial life, yet is relatively well educated and enjoys relatively high earned income per family (i.e., annual median earned income per family of $785.).

more truly *Indian*.

Thus people of the Oglala Jr. Community (a larger and less isolated country community) will speak of the small bands at Slim Buttes or White River as "real Fullbloods," characterizing them with a set of traits which are partially aboriginal and partially the reflection of Protestant sermonizing and other acculturative influences. Thus, the "Fullbloods" of Oglala assert that the "real Fullbloods" maintain ancient "respect" practices, such as parent-in-law avoidance, and that some of them still do the best beadwork and work the best buckskin. Moreover, they acknowledge that the most able and revered medicinemen come from such "stand-offish" communities. On the other hand, the less retiring Oglala folk shake their heads sadly or laugh over such "old-fashioned" traits as refusing to talk to anybody "even to Indians," hiding children who are dying of tuberculosis from the authorities, excessive modesty in dress (women wearing high-necked, long-sleeved, shapeless garments), and excessive strictness with unmarried girls (who are not permitted to go to baseball games or school movies and yet manage to get into trouble). It should be remembered that these commentators on the notable or odd behavior of the "real shy" people are themselves called dumb and dirty Indians by some of the "metropolitan" Indian folk of Pine Ridge.

The members of these isolated bands seem to be the only folk on the reservation who are not anxious or concerned about Indianness. Since many of them speak no English at all, they may not be aware that there is such a notion. In the several discussions we had with these folk, they made it clear that their major concern is maintaining and asserting the existence of their own tiny community of fifteen or twenty families, which they find threatened by a number of recent changes. Like other isolated ethnic communities, such as the Amish, these small country bands are upset by the process of school consolidation, which removes their children from their "own" little country, one-room affair to a large and more modern edifice where they are thrown together with children from a variety of communities. Elders of the far rural communities of Slim Buttes and White River feel that their children suffer by comparison with the better dressed children of the neighboring Oglala Jr. region. When these rural Indians use the term, "Mixedblood," they refer, not to the town dwellers of Pine Ridge, but to the (country) folk of the Oglala Jr. region, who (so they feel) laugh at their old-fashioned ways, while themselves leading sexually dissolute lives and living well from Aid-to-Dependent-Children funds.

## THE FOCUS OF THIS STUDY

The present study is focused upon the elementary Day Schools of the Pine Ridge Reservation, the rural folk—the country Indians—who send their children to these schools, and the teachers who labor in them. Insofar as some of the country Indian children go on after graduation to become boarding scholars at the Oglala Community High School of Pine Ridge town, this latter school enters these pages.

As may be evident from the discussion of this chapter, these country Indians are relatively conservative in their Indianness, isolated and unfamiliar with the ways of the national society. To them Pine Ridge town is an urban center. On the other hand, they are far from homogeneous in their cultural characteristics: some speak Lakota among themselves; some speak both languages; and some only English. Some are legally quite Fullblooded; others only marginally so. Some are destitute, and some are merely poor. Yet all are Oglala Sioux.

# Chapter IV

# HOW THE CONSERVATIVE "COUNTRY INDIAN" FEELS ABOUT SCHOOL AND EDUCATION

## WHAT DOES A CHILD GAIN BY ATTENDING?

Many Indian parents state that going to school is "good," much as most White parents state that going to Sunday school is "good." They hope that their children will derive some benefit from attending. Parents may coax, bribe, or "get after" [scold] children who are reluctant, but, after all, going to school is not a moral imperative.

When youngsters have good or even fair attendance records, parents may remark with pleasure that "my kids like to go to school"; the implication being that their children, for their own private reasons, enjoy this experience. A few parents confess that they dangle rewards before their children: "I told all four of them that the one that had perfect attendance, I'd get him a transistor radio or a Polaroid camera" (Oct. 5). Parents of children whose attendance record is poor offer various matter-of-fact excuses: The child is not strong; other kids pick on him; he is shy because his clothes are not stylish. Parents of notorious truants conceal their discomfort behind polite laughter and recite a humorous tale of chasing their son half a mile to the school bus, brandishing a broomstick at this hooky-player. Elder kin of such a child will shake their heads in sober disapproval, and the child's maternal grandmother may remark sternly that she ought to "talk to" [lecture] her daughter "about that boy"; but the next moment the whole family will dissolve into laughter as some notable exploit of playing hooky is told or retold.

This easygoing atmosphere is immediately dissipated if the White interlocutor asks, "What has your child learned in school that you like?" or "Has your child learned anything in school that made you happy?" Such questions seem to touch on areas hitherto unconsidered. Taking thought, the parent may mention any of a great variety of skills: cooking, sewing, playing basketball, helping with the housework, reciting prayers, being mannerly at the table, or, occasionally, learning English; or she may name some object made in school and brought home for domestic approbation. If the child has been awarded a Certificate for Perfect Attendance, this will be mentioned. However, the acquisition of such scholastic skills as reading, writing, and arithmetic, or habits of concentration and application is rarely mentioned spontaneously. Indeed, most parents do not seem to be aware that competence in these areas is essential to performance in even the upper levels of the primary grades. Or, perhaps, it would be more just and more accurate to note that, as they themselves completed the Eighth Grade (or less) with only rudimentary scholastic skills,[1] they find even the most modest accomplishments of their offspring impressive and gratifying.

Most conservative adults are convinced that completing a higher education (usually defined as graduating from high school) opens the road to acquiring a good job (defined as paying around fifty to seventy-five dollars a week). A few cynics point out that Mixedbloods who are relatively less educated gain preferment for the good jobs at the Bureau over Fullbloods who are better educated, or they remark that neither educated nor un-

---

[1] Most country Indians who "completed" the Eighth Grade fifteen or twenty years ago impress one as having but little formal education. Those who read or write above the level of the Fourth or Fifth Grade are unusual persons.

educated people can obtain employment today. However, most adults assert that a high school diploma, followed perhaps by a year or two of vocational training, guarantees a life of well paid employment:

> The ones that goes to school, they're the ones that have good jobs. The ones that don't go to school, they're the ones that have a hard time now (elderly male head of clan, Sept. 28).

On the basis of limited experience, this view is reasonable. For the most part, the coveted jobs on the Reservation are held by persons with the training just described. Yet, between the sincere, sometimes passionate, wish that one's children might finish high school—and so achieve economic well-being—and the gratification of this wish, there seems to exist only a great unknown—the educational process.[2] The Sioux parent defines his role in this mystery just as the Bureau has: It is limited almost entirely to urging his children toward perfect attendance. The most that the concerned parent can do is to push his child into the alien world of the school every day, exhorting him to listen and learn.[3]

To the question, "What kind of job do you want your kids to have when they grow up and finish school?" every parent, without exception, declined to answer. "That's up to them," "They haven't told me yet," or "They will decide what they want to be, and I'll help them if I can," were typical responses. These reflect, not parental

ignorance or indifference, but rather what the Sioux call, "respecting other people"; that is, refraining from interference with what is another's way of life.[4] When children have expressed a wish to prepare for a particular career, parents were happy to pass this information on to us. However, the Indian child's conception of the ways in which he might earn a livelihood is in any case extremely limited—nursing and secretarial work for girls, ranching or the Armed Forces for boys.

The alien and profitable skills that may be acquired through education—and, perhaps, the prestige and comfort accruing to parents of steadily employed offspring—are highly valued, and the child who *desires* to attend school will usually receive whatever moral and financial support his immediate family and kin can provide. In fairness to the Sioux, this point should be over-emphasized, since most educators and observers have emphasized the opposite, accusing the Sioux of spoiling their children, giving them anything they covet, and—worst of all —not forcing them to attend school when they don't wish to go. From the educator's perspective, these critical observations do have some truth, but it is equally true, or even more so, that the same "indulgent" and "permissive" Sioux will reduce themselves from their usual penury to downright want, will beg, borrow, and enter into the most complicated intrigues, in

[2] Interviewer: In what way is going to school going to help your children get a good job?
Indian mother (with absolute conviction): Just by going through high school! A high school diploma really helps you get work on the Reservation or any place else (September 25).
[3] As the schools have changed phenomenally in the last twenty to thirty years, the parent's own scholastic experiences are of little help to him in counseling his children. Many parents over twenty-five spontaneously mention this transformation.

[4] Writing about "Apache Parents and Vocational Choice," *Journal of American Indian Education*, II, 2 (Jan. 1963), pp. 1-8, Louis C. Bernardoni points to a similar operation of non-interference between parent and children. Of the forty-six families in his sample, all but three Apache parents "held the attitude that it would be impolite to pry into their son's vocational plans until he brought up the subject, and the boys did not usually plan to bring up the subject until necessary." Cf. also David P. Ausubel, *Maori Youth*, Wellington, N. Z.: Price Milburn, 1961, pp. 63-67.

order to get the money to help a child that asks that he or she be sent to school. Usually, young people leaving the Reservation to enter a trade school or college are honored by feasts and give-aways by their country Indian kin. At one elaborate community fair (at which no White teachers were present) we witnessed a long train of decorated cars and horses parading in honor of a young man who was shortly to begin a course of study at "college" (which proved to be a modest trade school). The young man himself was decked in the regalia of a chieftain and sat in dignified splendor atop one of the leading cars. We asked an Indian bystander, "Suppose he flunks out after this big celebration, how will folks feel?" "Oh that won't matter," said the Indian, "they do this for him because he's trying."

The high regard Sioux have for education was manifest in their responses to the questions asked of the Rosebud people in 1947, "Which three of these persons would you honor the most?" The respondents were given nine alternative categories to choose among, including: old person advisor, educated person, tribal leader, good speaker, smart person, descendant of famous person, rich person, medicine man, brave person. The category of person included in the triad of choices of most respondents was "educated person," being mentioned by seventy to eighty percent of the persons in each of the five "blood groupings" of the authoress.[5]

Thus, in marked contrast to certain other ethnic groups where parents are hostile to book-learning, the Sioux parents tend to regard all education with a benign if muzzy favor. When their children enjoy school, they are pleased and proud; when they hate school, they may for various reasons ask them to go; but Sioux parents are

not going to tell their children that they ought to like school.

## COMPLAINTS ABOUT THE SCHOOL

Most conservative parents do not consider themselves competent to criticize either the formal or the informal functions of the school. Academic matters are defined as the province of the teacher. For example, when asked, "Do you think the teachers are doing a good job teaching your child reading and arithmetic?" most parents say, "Yes," or, "I guess so." When asked, "What makes you say that?" they reply, "They are teachers so they must be doing a good job," or, "The kids bring me their report cards and they have passing grades," which is to say that, if the child is passing, the teacher must be teaching him properly.

A blunt query like, "Have your children ever learned anything at school that you don't like?" leaves most parents quite baffled. Clearly, this is a novel possibility. A response can be elicited with the more carefully phrased, "Did any of your kids change the way they acted after they went to school?" Mothers remember an outbreak of using "bad words" or "answering right back" in the first grades, but they absolve the school from blame because "they learn it from other kids." One especially perceptive mother confessed that she was distressed, not only by the bad words, but by the *fancy words:*

> It's like a different language. I'll say to him, "What are you saying to me?" It looks like the kids are way ahead of you these days. When I went to school, they made us behave. Now they learn them a lot different.

Few parents, however, seem to take seriously the profanity or sassiness of their offspring, and a number laugh or say that their kids were "crazy like that" before they went to school. Grandparents, especially, make this ob-

[5] Ruth Hill Useem, *op. cit.,* Table 3, p. 125.

servation with a jocose pride. Indeed, the same parents who deplore the "bad words" used by their own little boys will chuckle over the dilemma of a more demanding parent:

> He always said he wouldn't let his boys be sassy. That's why he sent them to Mission [Catholic parochial school]. But now they are just as sassy as the other kids. "I don't know what's coming with them!" he says. (Sept. 26).

In any case, the parental complaint is not that the children learn such expressions, but that they dare to use them before and to their parents. "I tell him, 'Don't you let your father hear you talk like that.'"

But whereas parents make very few personal complaints about the schools, they voluntarily and vociferously transmit the complaints of their children. The overwhelming number of these grievances involve being "picked on" or abused by "other kids." This abuse varies from mild to gross physical assault and from tolerable to unendurable teasing. From the indignant recitatives of their parents, one gathers that almost no child gets through the elementary school without several severe beatings and that merciless teasing is an almost daily occurrence. The following stories are typical rather than extraordinary:

> Sophia (Seventh Grader) complained to me that her back hurt, and I looked and found a piece of pencil lead sticking in her back. She said that two girls were quarreling at her. When she was reading in class [reading aloud while standing], one of them walked behind her and poked her with her pencil. (Sophia's mother then complained to the teacher, but the girls threatened to get even with Sophia, who then refused to go to school because she was afraid [Nov. 26].)
>
> Seraphina (Ninth Grader) came home from school with her face all bloody and her blouse all torn up. A girl had laid for her off the school ground and beat her up. She was afraid to go back to school (Sept. 27).
>
> Absalom (notorious truant, thirteen years old and in the Fourth Grade) is

having a hard time. All the little kids pick on him and make fun of him—even on the bus they all pick on him and throw spitballs with rubberbands at him. My daughter feels sorry for him. She feels like taking up for him, because he doesn't do anything to help himself (Nov. 26).

> My niece (Ninth Grader) dropped out of school. She said the Mixedblood girls called her a "Dumb Squaw" and kept laughing and laughing at her because she wore out-of-style clothes (Jan. 14).
>
> My son (Ninth Grader) was in love with Cornelia (a classmate) an he wrote her a love letter. Cornelia showed the letter to all the other kids—what my boy wrote her. They all laughed and teased him whenever they weren't in class, at lunch, all the time! He couldn't stand this, so he quit school.

The reader should note that these parents, and the other parents who told us stories of youthful torment, were deeply concerned not only because of the sufferings of their children but because they are convinced that this physical and verbal torture drives their children out of school. Perhaps the full irony can be appreciated only by the research investigator: Over and over, teachers and administrators have stated that their major problem is making Indian parents aware of the crucial importance of regular attendance. Meanwhile, they deny or make light of the quarreling and teasing of the peer group of Indian school children and accuse parents of harassing them or seeking to make the schools responsible for the occurrence of this mischief. Yet, in point of fact, many parents are thoroughly convinced of the importance of attendance. As they see it—but find difficult to formalize to an outsider, such as a school official —the major problem is the creation of a school environment that will not frighten or shame their children into truancy or "giving up."

Another frequent complaint transmitted by the parents is the children's feeling of inferiority and inadequacy with regard to their clothing:

> Some parents don't have as much

money as other parents that can dress their children real nice. But as long as they keep them clean, that should be enough! Still, the children tease those that are dressed in poor clothes. Things like that the children shouldn't do to each other (Oct. 23).

My girls tell me that the other girls make fun of them. They tell them that they wear rummage clothes. But I say, as long as the clothes are clean and presentable, they have nothing to worry about (Oct. 9).

With those Mixedbloods, now, the boarding school is just like a fashion school! If the girls don't wear the newest kind of style, they make it hard for a person (Oct. 10).

In the excerpt that follows, the complaint of the grandmother triggers a similar comment from another person who happened to be present:

Grandmother: My daughter's little boy —she bought him a pair of pants with elastic on the top. He said some of the others made fun of this. He wouldn't wear the pants because he was afraid that the others would make fun of him.

Visitor: I bought my little boy pants like that, too. He said the other kids said they were girl's jeans, and he won't wear them; he wouldn't even let me put them on him! (Oct. 23)

When parents complain about clothing, they direct their disapproval not at the society of urban (White) America that sanctions invidious distinctions in everyday dress, and only occasionally at the schools where teachers (consciously and unconsciously) favor the children who are better dressed. Instead, they express their resentment at the immediate aggressors, the ruthless peers who tease their offspring.

Another complaint is that the teachers do not maintain order and, in consequence, the children do not learn:

They don't teach them anything! They learn just bad words! There's so many of them going there that none of the kids don't learn much. They just fool around and get crazy [wild, unruly]. They have respect for nobody. . . . The teachers should watch so that the kids don't get picked on, but they don't. . . . The other kids even make fun of the way our kids are dressed (Dec. 1).

I don't think they learn anything but just fighting when they get to school. I'd like for them to teach them to have respect for other people. It seems that they don't teach them the right things nowadays (Oct. 10).

I don't like it that they write notes to each other instead of learning (Oct. 18).

My kids *like* to go to school—that's because they just play there and lazy around. They don't teach them no manners (Oct. 17).

Other complaints were numerically insignificant. Occasionally children complain of "mean" teachers, which means teachers who nag, reprove or strike them, although it seems evident that the children find humiliation before their classmates much harder to bear than brute chastisement. Also, this year a number of small children complained about losing teachers to whom they had become attached.[6] Children sometimes complained to members of this Project about difficulty with certain subjects, and boarding scholars sometimes complained about the hardships of the "work detail," but these were matters rarely mentioned to us by the parents themselves.

## WHAT CAN INDIAN PARENTS DO?

To the question, "What can a parent do if a child learns something at school that the parent doesn't like?" more than half the parents say, "Nothing." Their response does not change if one asks, "What can a parent do if something happens to their kids at school that they don't like?" We must emphasize that "Nothing" is said not ruefully or resentfully, but in a matter-of-fact tone such as one might use in

---

[6] Because of a large enrollment, difficulties in recruiting teachers, and the withdrawal of some new teachers after their shocked encounter with Indian pupils, some classes in the elementary grades were subjected to three or even four different teachers during the first few months of the school year.

answering such a question as, "What could you do about it if someone shot you through the head?" About a third of the parents state that in the event of a serious abuse they "would write to the Principal," but we surmise that even this mild form of protest is employed only on rare occasion.

Only one mother, the wife of a sophisticated Indian intellectual, remarked that such matters ought to be discussed at P.T.A. meetings, but she implied that they never were. Since she herself is a grandmother, she feels that her daughters ought to be the ones to speak up on such matters, but she seems to have little expectation that they will do so because "they are too shy." Most of the mothers interviewed had not been to any P.T.A. meetings during the recent past. Two who had attended a few meetings at the Day School of their district some time ago remarked that the Principal (who had just retired) had told them that subjects like the children's fighting or needing clothes should not be brought up at P.T.A. meetings.[7]

To explain why Indian parents do not react to their children's difficulties as would parents of the urban White middle class—e.g., long conferences with teacher, discussions at P.T.A., pressure on school board, and so on —would involve a separate and lengthy essay on differences in situation, finances, experience, personality structure, and view of the world. It would be more illuminating and more practical to describe what the parents actually do.

## WHAT INDIAN PARENTS DO

The overwhelming majority of complaints by Indian children are directed against other Indian children (rather than against teachers or school conditions). Since this is so, each major complaint becomes a notable matter of community discussion; it is "talked about" by the ladies of the community, and the parties involved rarely evade some degree of censure. Faced with this observant and vocal audience, even conscientious mothers hesitate to approach school authorities unless theirs is a strong case:

> If you keep going and talking to the teachers, then the parents will talk about you. They say, "Oh, you're just trying to go and complain over little things like that all the time" (Sept. 25).

The overzealous mother who "charges down to the school" at every childish tale is "talked about" as much as her opposite, the indifferent mother whose children are troublemakers and truants and "who doesn't really care and just sends her kids to school every day and forgets about them."

The human interest of these community problems is enhanced by their embodying a moral dilemma, one faced by all parents who live under a system of compulsory attendance at school. A Sioux parent is morally obligated and sentimentally moved to defend or "take up for" his child. He is also confronted by a law that says he must send his child to school, and he often feels this to be a moral compulsion. When his child refuses to go to school because of being beaten or teased, the parent's choice may be bitter: The parent may force him to go, but such force is a violation of traditional Sioux norms (according to which each person makes his own choices), or he may acquiesce to the truancy and thus lay himself open to legal punishment. The very conservative parents, residing far out in the country, usually select the latter alternative and, even today, they sometimes hide a frightened child for weeks or months. (When a family is willing to move itself or its children among the neighboring States and Reservations frequently enough, it can some-

---

[7] A P.T.A. meeting is described at the end of Chapter 6.

times keep a child out of school for years. However, this pattern is rare, perhaps because there are too many economic advantages to a fixed residence.) Mothers who have been made desperately aggressive by a threat to their children and their schooling will sometimes quarrel with or even beat up the mothers of the children whom they hold responsible for the plight of their young. Today, neither this violence nor the conniving at truancy meets with the wholehearted approval of the Indian community.

Within the code of Indian morality, the proper thing is not to punish the childish aggressors or their families but to restore harmony, so that the timid children will be willing to go back to school. Thus, the parent who behaves in a seemly manner will strive to place the duty of correcting the "mean" child upon his teacher or Principal or, failing that, upon the child's kin and family. The latter device is most efficient when the parents of the quarreling children belong to the same local community: When a responsible parent visits an equally responsible parent who is a neighbor and related through some chain of kinship and courteously requests him to "correct" his children, then the erring youngster may be dealt with severely. However, with the recent consolidation of the school system, a child often quarrels with members of rather distant local communities, upon whom it is difficult to exert moral pressure. And, when children attend the school in Pine Ridge town (O.C.S.), they may quarrel with schoolmates from broken homes who have no responsible relatives. Finally, it should be mentioned that each local community (tiyospaye) has its own set of inner conflicts, so that while these neighbors and kinfolk should be willing to reconcile their differences and restore harmony, the process of adjustment may be reflected in much tension and squabbling at the children's level. While this is so, it is quite clear that the most savage and irreconcilable teasing and brawling occur between children of different local communities and that fights of children from the same tiyospaye tend to be milder and temporary.

When a parent cannot restore tranquility through the inter-connections of neighborhood and kinship, he may, if knowledgeable, attempt to place the responsibility upon the teacher or Principal. What happens then seems to vary a great deal. Most of the teachers and school personnel are unsympathetic to such complaints and have assured us that Indian children do not tease or "pick on" each other in any but a "normal, healthy" way. Most of them may be telling the truth as they see it, because the children are usually careful to assault each other out of eyesight of the teacher and to tease in Lakota (given sly children and unobservant White teachers, beatings and teasing can and do occur even during class hours).

Principals generally tend to be more sympathetic. However, their efforts may be very limited because most of them have few ties with and little knowledge of their community. If a pupil becomes marked either as a troublemaker or as a truant, the Principal may try to have the child sent to the special school in Pierre designed for children from broken homes (but evidently used as a reform school). For example, in one case a girl complained of assault by another girl off the school grounds. The Principal is reported as having said that he could not control the assailant and the fighting finally ended when the girl in question was sent to Pierre.

The following case illustrates many of the points made above: The great anxiety of the mother that her girl remain in school; the unsympathetic attitude of the teacher; the relative impotence of a sympathetic Principal; the desire of Indian parents, not that erring girls be punished, but that they stop the harmful behavior; and parental sensitivity to the value that the Indian community places upon amity or tranquility.[8]

The lady speaking is one of the more respectable matrons of her community, the mother of seven children. Her daughter, Sophia, is her third child, thirteen years old and in the 7th grade. The narration of her daughter's troubles was prefaced by some comments about the most notorious truant of the community, a lad named Absalom:

I really ought to talk to [lecture] Absalom's mother some time, because Absalom is having such a hard time. He has played hooky so much that now he is thirteen years old and only in the fourth grade. All the little kids pick on him and make fun of him—even on the bus they all pick on him and throw spitballs with rubber bands at him. My daughter, Sophia, feels sorry for him; she feels like taking up for him, because he doesn't do anything to help himself.

Some of the other girls have been picking on Sophia at [day] school. Sophia complained to me that her back hurt, and I looked and found a piece of pencil lead sticking in her back. She said that two other girls were quarreling at her. When she was reading [aloud, standing], one of them walked behind her and poked her with her pencil.

I talked to her teacher, Mrs. Gruber. Then Sophia didn't want to go to school for three, four days. She'd leave in the morning, but when I came back at noon from Pine Ridge (town), she'd be home. She just took her brothers to the bus and then came back. At first she wouldn't say anything, but I got after her, and then she said that those girls were still being mean to her and that Mrs. Gruber had scolded her and said, "Sophia, why are you making trouble like this between the girls?"

Then, I went to school to see Mr. Walker, the Principal. He called in both the other girls and Mrs. Gruber. He also had them bring him all the girls' records. Then, he said (here respondent's voice became stern): "I see here by records that you have made trouble many times. Your records are not good. If we are not able to handle girls like you here, there is a place I can send you, if you don't behave."

Those two girls—they could not say one word to Mr. Walker. One of them began to cry. Then Mrs. Gruber said (here respondent's voice turns to a simper). "Oh, my dear Sophia, have these other girls been mean to you?" She tried to sound real nice to Sophia.

Then, I went to see Mrs. Dancing-Fox [mother of one of the offending girls; the DancingFox family is not a member of the *tiyospaye* of the respondent]. I told her that I always tried to correct [admonish] my daughter, and that Mark [husband] talks to our girls and corrects them every evening. I told her that this kind of quarreling between girls might lead to hard feelings and quarrelings between families and that would not be a good thing.

But that Carole DancingFox, she still wants to make trouble. At the show last week she got together with the Throws-Him girls, and they laid for Sophia after the show. They said bad things to her, and they knocked her down, and her glasses flew away and the part by the ear got broke, and she had a big cut under her eye. One of them must have kicked her.

I wanted to go to see Mr. Penttila [highest educational authority on the Reservation], but Mark said I shouldn't do it. He said this might really make hard feelings between the families. Then he went and talked to Mrs. ThrowsHim and explained that we didn't want any hard feelings, but that, if this kind of fighting keeps on, it will maybe lead to quarreling between the families. Now, my daughter has to go without glasses until December, when we get our lease money (Nov. 26).

## THE MATTER OF CLOTHING

When a child complains about his clothing, this touches his parents on a vulnerable spot. Sioux parents, and especially grandparents, spend large portions of their meager incomes giving their children the things that attract and please them. White observ-

---

[8] The case also illustrates two points of more general interest: First, mature Sioux men strive more openly for communal good feelings than do the women; second, most Indian quarrels (like most squabbles within a little community) are inconclusive. The desired state of community amity alternates with the undesirable state of more or less violent aggression.

ers sometimes criticize Indian parents as "indulgent," when they happen to observe an Indian shack in which a child is playing with a toy that must cost over ten dollars. However, Indian elders value the child's pleasure and do not perceive a moral virtue in denying the child those things for which they may have the money.

When a child complains about being picked on, his parents are stimulated to strike out against some external target, usually the family of the offender, but when the child complains that he is being teased about his clothing, the parents usually blame themselves and do what they can to clothe him more suitably. Of course, the variations are great. If the child has no immediate kin and has been farmed out to distant relatives, his lack of clothing may be real and he may have no one to listen sympathetically to his plight. Or, if his family is unstable, the little money that comes into it may be spent on liquor. To some extent, the children who are most affected by the sartorial standards of their peers are also most helpless about it, having no parents to aid them. It may be that children feel driven to wheedle better clothes off their parents in order to demonstrate to their peers (and themselves) that they do have elders who care intensely about their welfare. However this may be, in the present chapter our interest is in the parents, rather than in the dynamics of the peer group.

When a child is in the elementary grades, most parents tend to be as accommodating as their slender resources allow. If a child refuses to wear a new coat "because the other kids tease him," or "because all the other kids are wearing half-coats this year," many parents will buy him a new coat as soon as they can obtain the cash.

In the course of interviews, some parents remarked defensively that they told their children that "your clothes don't matter so long as they are clean."

Yet in each of these cases, we observed or learned that these particular parents do not dress their children in "neat but sturdy" clothes but instead do all they can to get them the apparel which is stylish among the school peers. Extremely poor parents (e. g., those who send their children to boarding school so that they can eat) do not pay so much heed to the norms of peer clothing—they usually have more elemental matters to worry about. Yet, one very poor mother explained that it was easier to care for boys because, if they did not grow too fast, they could wear the same jeans for three years, whereas girls unfortunately needed clothing more often.

Some teachers have told us that they praise children with clean clothing (which on the dusty Reservation usually means *new* clothing), and we are inclined to believe that many do this. The children seize upon this sanction to torment any schoolmate wearing worn, imperfect, or odd garments. We were surprised to learn how demanding were the sartorial standards of even the early grades:

My boy (Third Grade) doesn't want to wear his jeans. They kind of lost their color—they're kind of light blue like. He says, "That's faded; that's old; they'll laugh at me! I can't wear that." And even his socks, if just a little piece is tore off on the heel or someplace, he says, "Look what's happened. I'm not going to wear those."
I said, "My Goodness, nobody would notice." And he said, "Sure they will. They notice everything. They'll make fun of me. You're not going to school so you don't know how it is at school." Oh, he puts up a big fuss.
My girls (Fourth and Fifth Grade), they have to change anklets every day because when they go (to school) if they don't change anklets they'll say: "Gee, you're lazy, look at your anklets. Where did you get your gray anklets?" She says they really make fun like that. If I wash their anklets they say they want them clean, like new, really white. They say: "Can't you ever wash the anklets white?" And oh, I get mad at them. And they say: "Can't you iron better? Our dresses are wrinkled and

we can't wear them." Oh they get me mad.

We (family) don't want them to dress in a faded dress or jeans because they really make fun of each other. So we have a hard time. We practically go broke. And they have to have new shoes every month (April 25).

In many school districts it seems that some of the parental concern about clothes is translated into a kind of fanatical concern with cleanliness and whiteness like the stereotyped figures of washday soapland. Ideally, Sioux children change their clothes daily, and these are then subjected to an intensive treatment with the hottest water and strongest detergents by mothers who seem to spend a disproportionate share of their time either at the rental laundry or over a wash pail at home.

## HIGH SCHOOL CLOTHING

When students leave the relatively countrified Day School and enter the high school in Pine Ridge town, they find themselves living in a community where the standards of dress are quite different from those of their local communities. In the country, even relatively affluent persons dress in work clothes day in and day out. Men and boys wear practical and sturdy wranglers' outfits. Married women, even those in their twenties, dress in the shapeless rummage clothes or homemade dresses which their mothers and mothers-in-law consider modest and decorous. In sharp contrast, most of the Bureau personnel (White and Indian) of the town of Pine Ridge dress with a middle class propriety of Western timbre.

Within the high school, the norms of dress are high: Girls wear tailored blouses and skirts or modest frocks and sweaters; boys wear conservative sports ensembles. The effect is startlingly proper, and the garments are expensive and not particularly practical to the climate and terrain of Pine Ridge, with its mud and dust and ex-

tremes of temperature. (But then urbanized styles of dress always have a weird impracticality.) To our knowledge, the school administration does not enforce these styles of clothing; rather it confines itself to the usual genteelisms such as banning slacks (the most sensible and modest garment for young ladies in cold or windy weather and therefore not to be tolerated). The administration does require a middle-class style of dress of its teachers, and the women, especially, do dress well and as if they devoted time and money to the task. However, it would be fallacious to regard the teachers' dress as providing more than a setting for the norms of proper apparel, for these are defined and ruthlessly enforced by the peer culture.[9]

The purchase of these ready-made outfits puts a heavy and often unanticipated strain on the means of country families. Moreover, the strain is unrelenting, for even after a nice outfit has been purchased, the poor girl from the country finds that she is still being outdressed and outgroomed by her town rivals, and the ears of sympathetic parents are filled with complaints about those Mixedblood girls.

Inadequate clothing is the most common reason given by both parents and daughters for the dropout of the latter from high school. Clearly, in some cases this is offered as a more presentable reason for dropping out than the more immediate and embarrassing ones of poor scholarship or "getting into trouble"; yet, there is no doubt that many parents believe that if their girls had modish new clothes they would remain in school and graduate. Our observations suggest, instead, that inadequate clothing is but the most obvious of a complex of difficulties suffered by the country girl of conservative family. She is handi-

[9] Country Indians wear extravagant finery or dance regalia only on very special occasions. Their ordinary dress is drab and practical.

capped both in the official side of the school and in the unofficial, informal side. Coming from a semi-literate family that speaks a lower status version of English, associating with peers of similar background, and attending an elementary school of meager scholastic impact, she enters high school at a marked disadvantage to the children from the families of Bureau employees. Even if these latter are not studious, they have a natural facility with "proper English" and are likely to be well grounded in reading and arithmetic. To the peer culture she is a hick, untutored in the "sophisticated" ways of Pine Ridge town. Accordingly, she finds herself baffled in her studies, lonely and snubbed out of class, and generally bewildered by the atmosphere of the high school. At this point she decides that, had she only the proper clothes, everything would be all right. Usually, she cannot obtain them and so she quits and for the rest of her life she will say that she might have finished high school and so gotten a good job if her parents had given her the clothes she needed:

A lot of the children of the government workers dressed better. The children who didn't have no clothes felt ashamed. My father and mother wanted me to go to school. But, I had only old clothing. I went, but I soon ran out of clothes. And, at school, they said I had to have certain clothing. I wrote my parents and told them what to order. Instead of sending the order off, they sent me dress goods and old shoes and stockings, and I didn't have no time to sew or anything in high school. (Respondent dropped out in 9th grade, Sept. 27)

The next account by a sixteen-year-old girl tells us a great deal more about the complex situation of the girl who drops out of high school. It shows how a conservative girl may come gradually to realize that proper clothing "is not enough." It also shows how the problem of clothing is often handled among the extended family of conservative Indians.

Anna Louise is a quiet and shy girl with a pretty face and figure; she looks like a Mixedblood, although she was raised by a conservative family. Her father and mother, now divorced, were both from country families, but his was quite conservative while hers was relatively progressive and comfortably prosperous. (Her mother's brother is a college graduate.) Her story comes to us via her maternal aunt, partly from an interview, which the aunt tried to conduct in English but in which her niece would talk only Lakota, and partly by way of the recall by the aunt of incidents involving the maternal family of the girl. Anna Louise speaks:

When I went to high school, I just had the old clothes I had at the Day School, and the first day of school, when I went into the classroom, I looked at the other girls and then I looked at myself. My clothes were just faded and out of style, and I was embarrassed. Everybody was sizing me up, and I felt I was a freak. I sure didn't feel good.

I told my (paternal) grandmother, and she said, "Just White people wear White clothes, and you're an Indian." She didn't want me to wear a half-skirt and blouse. She wanted me to wear long dresses like an Indian.

So, I wrote to my Dad and asked for some money, so I could buy some clothes, but he didn't answer me. So, I got so mad I quit school (9th grade).

Then I went to Montana, where my sister was working. She's a nurse. She bought me new clothes, and I went to the (public) high school there. But I was way behind, because public school was too hard for me compared to government school. My report cards were really poor, so I quit, because I couldn't keep up with my grade.

Then, I went to work baby-sitting[10] for my sister. I saved all my money, and I bought myself clothes, and I came back and started again here (high school in Pine Ridge).

_____

[10] "Babysitting" is a Pine Ridge euphemism for light housework (the family worked for will, of course, have small children).

Here the aunt continues the thread of the narrative:

Once my niece wanted to go to the formal dance given at the high school for the students. But they had to wear a formal, and she asked her father to give her the money. He never even answered. Then we (maternal relatives of the girl) thought we would all chip in and get her the formal. I thought it would cost maybe $4.75, but when I looked in the Ward's catalog, gee, I saw they cost seventeen dollars!

Then, my mother said, "Oh, those are not formals. Those are what you call bride gowns—what White girls wear when they get married. I will get her something."

So my mother went to Rapid City, and she bought a whole box of rummage clothes. We all looked through it, and we found an old, blue formal. We all thought it looked real nice and that Anna Louise would be happy to wear it. But she looked at it and said she didn't want to wear it.

Then, Martin came home from college for vacation and we told him. He said, "Oh, you Indians are sure awful. She can't wear that kind of old-fashioned dress!" He was working then, and he gave us ten dollars, and we all chipped in some more, and we went to Chadron and we got her a formal for seventeen dollars. My mother said, "Be sure you don't get her a white one, because that's what they wear for weddings. So we got her a red one. Anna Louise thought it was real nice, and she said, "How did you know I wanted a red one?"

Anna Louise continues:

I was getting along good, until I started having trouble with civics and social studies.[11] No matter how hard I try to learn, it's too hard to catch on. When I have trouble with my problems, and I ask the teachers, they tell me to learn it from my book. What's the use of going to school when the teacher can't help you with your lessons?

Then, I can't get along with the Mixedbloods, especially the girls. One (Mixedblood) boy kept asking me to go to the show, but one of the Mixedblood girls didn't like that. She kept after me, called

me names, like "big squaw" and things like that.

I complained and we were taken to the Principal's Office. Then the Mixedblood said I was just jealous of her because she was a cheerleader, and she said to the Principal, "She's just a dumb squaw." The Principal got after her (i.e., scolded her), but afterwards she and the other Mixedblood girls kept making fun and laughing at me. They even made fun of me in class. Every place I go, they'll be making fun of me and picking on me. So, I just quit.

Aunt:

Are you going back to Montana so you can get out of going to school?

Anna Louise:

I'll still go to school there. It was the girls I didn't like.

Later, the aunt said to us, "I think she'll go back; she's only sixteen years old." We would tend to agree. The prognosis for Anna Louise is good as compared to the many other country girls who have been subjected to the torments of Reservation high school. Moreover, Anna Louise comes from an unusually stubborn family. Her sister (now residing in Montana) went back to high school and finished it when she was in her early twenties, married and with children.

This is our most detailed account of what parents (or, in most country families, elders) do about the problem of clothing. It is also the fullest statement by a dropout as to why high school girls from country families play truant or leave school. Clearly, clothes and lack of money to buy them are only part of the story. Giving a country girl a new and fashionable wardrobe would be like giving a poor flower girl an aristocratic English accent—both too much and too little.

## UNDISCIPLINED BEHAVIOR IN CLASS

Parents are not exaggerating when they assert that in some classes the children do little but fool around.[12] Since they virtually never visit the

---

[11] Many country-bred students complain of having trouble with high school social studies. The teacher responsible for these classes is notorious for her hostility to the ways of country Indians.

classes, one can only assume that they are told about this situation by their children. It is interesting that the most vociferous and accurate complaints on this subject come from very conservative parents who connive at their offspring's truancy. May one assume that these children feel so secure in their family relations that they are among the few who dare to tell their parents what goes on in school? (We ourselves have questioned notorious bullies with excellent attendance records. They tell us that they like school and their teacher very much.)

It should be emphasized that most Indian parents have no inkling of how effectively the children's peer groups have been able to sabotage the scholastic process. Indeed, it is possible that if and when their offspring comment at home about what goes on in class the parents think they are bragging and exaggerating: "All kids are like that." But on the several occasions on which we asked Indian parents of our acquaintance to visit classes and report to us, they came back so shocked and upset that they could not at first give a coherent account of what they had observed.

What the majority of conservative Indian parents would do if they became aware that in some classes their children are not learning anything of a scholastic nature we cannot say. Perhaps their unquestioning faith that "teachers must be doing a good job because they are teachers" constitutes a mental block that may be dislodged only by a good deal of concrete evidence.

To date, we can report only on a few. A relatively well educated and wealthy man, who has been a member of the Tribal Council, is aware of the situation. He sends his children to public school and to a high school off the reservation. The oldest will enter a university next year. On the other end of the educational scale are some of the backwoods conservative families, "real Fullbloods," who point out accurately that the classes are overcrowded, that children are not kept in order or properly instructed, and that their own children are abused by the others. As they make these remarks they add pointedly (though not, perhaps, with entire accuracy), that none of these evils existed when they had their own small day school in their own small community. These parents too are taking action in their own fashion. For as they tell us what they think is wrong with the schools, their remarks are usually overheard by one or two youngsters of school age who are clearly staying away from school with the assistance of their elders.

Students of culture and personality may find it interesting that a well-educated Indian who can afford to send his children to college expresses disapproval of a school situation in the same way as some of the most "shy" and "residual" Fullbloods: Both quietly remove their children from the situation.

## THE INDIAN NOTION OF COMPETITION

A minority of parents, mostly Mixedblood, criticize the federal schools because "the schools don't teach the children *competition*." Since so much of the ethnographic literature has emphasized the non-competitiveness of Indians, we were intrigued by this usage and so we asked what they meant by "competition." Soon it became clear that they were not using the term with the meaning usually given it by Whites, *i.e.*, as rivalry or "wringing success from somebody's failure,"[13]

_____
12 See section on middle elementary grades, Chapter 7.

13 Jules Henry, "American Schoolrooms: learning the nightmare," *Columbia University Forum*, VI, 2 (1963), p. 27. This is a selection from his forthcoming book, *Culture Against Man*.

but rather as an attitude toward scholastic work. The teacher who exacts performance of demanding tasks and who exhibits excellence so that his pupils are impelled to strive, is teaching *competition*. Some respondents characterized "competition" as a kind of practical aspiration: "If they (Indian youth) see that the boy who finished gets a good job, they will feel like doing the same thing."

The idea that *competition* centers about a learning relationship between teacher and pupils and not about a contest among pupils was most clearly expressed by an intelligent and relatively affluent Indian rancher, himself a graduate of high school:

> The teachers in the bureau schools are lax. When I was going to school, when we were assigned twenty problems, we knew that if we did ten we could still get a B. Students don't learn much that way. . . . I would always finish early in the study period and then just fool around. But in the public schools, if you're told to do so many problems you do them. . . . When I was in school, in the Fifth Grade I think, I had a teacher who influenced all my further studying. She wasn't exactly mean but she made us work very hard. When she said to do fifty problems, we did fifty problems and no fooling around! She gave me a sense of sticking with a difficult task until it's finished that has stayed with me the rest of my life.
>
> Another thing would help here if we had more teachers from this reservation. When a child sits in class and sees a teacher up there who has made it, it gives him something to hit for.

Though we observed many classes and interviewed many pupils of elementary and high school levels, we found no evidence that the younger generation of country Indians sees class room learning as an area of rivalry. If one learns easily, the proper thing is to help those who do not. There are situations where rivalry holds full sway. Usually these involve contests between the folk of the community and some other group who are or can be regarded as outsiders. Thus, the youthful Sioux are transfigured when they are matched with outsiders in basketball tournaments or dancing contests. The choral group of the high school performs poorly singing for their peers in the local auditorium, but their instructor reported that in performances off the Reservation they "sang their heads off." Moreover, the White person who tried to compete with Indian matrons in the handgame would likely return home with an empty purse. Ironically, the sole situation on the Reservation where middle-class American competition holds sway is among the pupils of high school concerning clothing.

## EDUCATION AND THE GOOD MAN

Most country Indians have accepted the extremely narrow definition of the word, "education," presented to them by government and missionary teachers: Primarily, education means attending school so that one may get a remunerative job. Any job that pays fairly well is a good one. Status, as the White middle-class worker sees it, plays almost no role at all either in education or in occupational choice. Indeed, most country Indians do not seem to have the slightest inkling of what job status means to the White Man. "Why does a man like Kennedy who already has eleven million dollars want to take the job of being President?"[14]

Education, thus narrowly defined as an acquired set of tools and techniques, bears no relationship to being a respected person or a "good Sioux." For a man is considered a "good Sioux"

---

[14] This point has been discussed with insight by Paule Verdet in her unpublished study of Indians in St. Louis and Chicago. A summary was included in *Reference Materials Compiled for the American Indian Chicago Conference*, mimeo, Chicago: Department of Anthropology, University of Chicago, 1961, pp. 44-61.

only because of the way he acts. "There are lots of Fullbloods living out here (deep in reservation) who can only do farm labor. But they are acting far better than those that have an education."

The two types of behavior most frequently mentioned in descriptions of good men are "helping people" and "talking to people." Such men are usually pictured as wise, considerate, experienced, and past their first youth: "You could talk to him and he'll understand you." "He'll help you if he can, but he won't talk about it."

From many such descriptions one gathers that the good man is one who will always take the time to listen soberly and respectfully to a person who needs advice or aid. If he is able to do so, he will help.[15] "Talking to people" has a symbolic significance beyond the simple act of a cordial greeting. It is an overt declaration of equivalence or parity, for, by talking to people one demonstrates that one is not placing oneself above them. Thus, an old woman praises a "good Sioux": "He is always so happy to see his relatives, he goes right up to them and talks. And he always talks to us." (Oct. 26)

Indeed, talking to people in friendly fashion is one way of expressing one's identity as a Sioux and, for some people, as an Indian. For example, on one occasion an interviewer asked a Fullblood lady whether her daughter, who had married a Whiteman and lived off the reservation "had lost some of her being a Sioux." The lady said:

No. I don't think so. She still talks Indian and she talks to people (Indians) she meets. She knows them even when she forgets their names. And her husband talks too. He is just as much an Indian as she is, even though he is a Whiteman.

Becoming an educated man and a good Sioux are also implicitly seen as two distinct processes. In fact, it would be more accurate to say that among the Sioux one does not really *become* a good man. Instead, after many years of acting with unostentatious friendliness, generosity, wisdom, and humility, many people begin to regard one as a good man. The educated man, on the other hand, is one who through resolution, endurance, and a mysterious ability called "being smart" has achieved mastery of certain alien and esoteric skills. Still, all respondents incline to the opinion that a man can be both educated (in the narrow sense) and a good Sioux, and almost all find amusing the idea that too much education might hurt a Sioux. As one lady explained: "Too much education—it doesn't do people harm—an Indian or anybody." The one sharp and rather frequent criticism made of the occasional youth who, after obtaining some college education, returns to the reservation "to drink and run around" is not that his education has ruined him but that "he has an education but he doesn't use it."[16]

As we will show, many administrators and teachers envisage the Indian child either as an unsocialized being—

<hr>

[15] In his discussion of "Cherokee Values and World View" (MS, rev., 1962), Robert K. Thomas presents an almost identical definition of what the Cherokee consider a good man—generous of his time and his food. See also the discussion based largely on Thomas' research in John Gulick, *Cherokees at the Crossroads,* Chapel Hill, N. C.: Institute for Research in Social Science, 1960. (Our questions were not designed to obtain a full picture of the ideal man; rather, we were trying to find out whether the Sioux related formal education and virtue.)

[16] In hundreds of discussions with Indians, White administrators, and teachers we found only three individuals who defined education as a way of life and a good in itself. These were Indians in their fifties and sixties who, though they had not gone beyond the seventh or eighth grades, were voracious readers—true intellectuals.

a kind of vessel empty of all culture —or as a being already trained to bad (Indian) habits which it is the teacher's obligation to replace with good (middle-class American) habits. Since so much of school policy reflects this view, we had anticipated that at least some of the conservative Indian parents would object to current educational practices on the grounds that these were turning their children into Whitemen.

We were able to find no evidence in support of this hypothesis. When we asked questions designed to elicit attitudes on this subject, we obtained the information discussed above: Namely, education harms no one, but on the other hand, it has almost nothing to do with being a good person. Conservative or country Indian parents do not seem to be aware that their offspring are regarded as unsocialized, amoral, or backward by their teachers. That a child could be educated to the point where he would become critical of his kin or attempt to disassociate himself from them is still beyond their comprehension.[17] In justice, it should be added that most of our parental informants had not experienced any gross alienation through education. Few country children graduate from high school. Those who drop out find it difficult to express their motivations even to their close kin. The very few who have graduated from college in the past decade participate actively in Indian social affairs whenever they are on the reservation, despite the fact that many officers of the Bureau disapprove of "mixing in the community." These young men are not, of course, Bureau employees.

---

[17] This does not mean that the country Indian is not aware of and does not resent and shrink from the fact that Bureau employees, many other White men and "stuck-up" Mixedbloods regard Indians as people who behave in crude, ludicrous, dirty and ignorant ways. Nor does it mean that the Indian children are not intimidated and shamed when and if they become aware of the image their teacher holds of them.

# Chapter V

# SCHOOLS, IDEOLOGIES, AND TEACHERS

## BUREAUCRATIC ORGANIZATION

### Cabins and Compounds

As the Bureau is predominant on the Reservation, so is its school system predominant within the Bureau itself, consuming the most money and employing the most personnel of any of the various Branches. Ecologically and architecturally the Day School campuses are focal points of the landscape. The school buildings are the largest and most expensive structures on the Reservation, and each is bordered by a compound of housing built in similar style. In a region where most Indian homes are primitive cabins, the school buildings and the homes of the school employees are distinguished by the usual conveniences and appurtenances of modern urban life: electricity, central heating, running hot and cold water, and the like. In most cases, school teachers and administrators enjoy homes built according to the styles of modern suburbia (although a few teachers are still "making do" with trailers), and the contrast between the home of the country Indian and the school campus to which he sends his children could hardly be more extreme.

A generation ago the Reservation was dotted with one-room school houses; appended to each was a modest farm-style dwelling for the teacher and his family. Within the school the teacher might be responsible for about two dozen pupils and a half-dozen grade levels. He gave some formal instruction and some supervised practice in vocational agriculture; meanwhile, his wife supervised the domestic routine of the school, including the cleaning and feeding of the children and the training of the girls in domestic arts. Isolated by the poor roads of this barren and rolling terrain, the teacher was forced into intimacy with the people of the local community. While in some cases his position within the school and the Bureau gave him the support to play the role of petty tyrant, in general he shared, or at least was familiar with, the social and ceremonial life of his neighbors. Like some veterans of that era, now serving in higher administrative positions within the Bureau, he might become fluent in Lakota and develop country Indian friendships on the Reservation. Even if he were unsympathetic or hostile to his pupils and their parents, he inevitably learned more about them than almost any Bureau teacher does today.

These one-room schools and their quarters were crude but sturdy—neglected and unoccupied, some still stand on the Reservation—and were built on a level with much of Plains rural living at that time. Especially during the years of drought and depression, the standards and styles of living of Indian and teacher were not far different from each other. Even today, driving through the Western Plains, whether on or off Reservations, the observer may note functioning schools of the same size, style, and vintage. On Pine Ridge Reservation, a few are present as public schools, operated by the county and designed for children who are not eligible for enrollment in the more elaborate federal structures of the same area.[1] Throughout much of the

_____
[1] The relationships between the federal and the (county) public school systems of the Pine Ridge area may be characterized as one of reluctant and suspicious cooperation. In a nutshell, many of the White parents fear their children would be contaminated by association in school with Indian children, and many Sioux parents feel that they might lose rights under "The Treaty" if the federal and public school systems were fused.

West, the one-room school is still the norm, although its place is being challenged by consolidation.

Within the past generation, a great deal of money has been devoted to replacing these one-room schools with consolidated schools and, relatedly, to providing modern housing for school employees and paved roads for school buses. These modern facilities constitute a significant symbol of the current problems of Sioux education. Typically, Bureau administrators regard this construction as being *for* the Indians and refer ceremonially to the schools as being *theirs*. In a basic sense, this is so: Most of the pupils in these schools are Indians and most of the Indians on the Reservation send their children to these schools. But in many other and equally basic senses the schools are the Bureau's (and thereby *not* the Indians'). Consolidation was the Bureau's idea and was achieved by Bureau personnel without more than perfunctory consultation with the local populace, some sectors of which still bitterly resent the abolition of their local, small Day Schools. Responsibility for the operation of the schools rests not with a locally elected school board, but with the various officials of the Bureau. Some school officials see their careers and vocations in terms of the successful operation of a particular school, and, while this is unobjectionable or even commendable, it emphasizes that in an important sense the school is the administrator's. Also, the consolidated school permits, or almost requires, a compound of federal employees who are thus distinctly separated from the homes of their pupils.

School employees enjoy living in the newer buildings and working with the more elaborate facilities. Yet the very modernity of the school deepens the gulf between school and home. Most educators think this a good thing, as it enlarges the horizon of the children beyond the Reservation and builds an appetite for modern (and expensive) consumer goods and the related style of urban living. While there is a blunt practicality to acquainting Indian children with the forms of modern living (for those who do not know the technique of using a flush toilet may find themselves embarrassed when they travel off the Reservation), nonetheless, insofar as this style of living is being presented to the pupils as socially proper and morally necessary, while their true likelihood of ever enjoying it is minuscule, then the educators are inducing, not motive, but shame and hostility.

## Invidious Distinctions

We are not asserting that familiarity with the diverse forms of contemporary, middle-class American living is harmful to Indians. What we have noted, particularly at Pine Ridge, is that most teachers seem unable to divorce their image of the "usual" urban or suburban life from a moral context. As Indian children are instructed, it is not that city people ride subways, get polio shots, and use handkerchiefs, but that these are the things good and admirable people do. People who do not do these (and hundreds of other things) are pictured as backward, ignorant and filthy. Many Indian children seem to accept these value judgments without becoming aware that they can be destructively applied to most of the residents of the Reservation. When, in adolescence and early adulthood, they begin to put two and two together, their usual reaction is acute embarrassment. As they see it, Indians who encounter Whites are always doing "awful things" like dressing oddly, eating with their fingers, or "making mistakes" in English. And, in consequence, White people must spend much of their time "making fun of" (ridiculing) or "looking down on" Indians. This is one of the major reasons why country Indians do not invite a White or Mixedblood caller into their houses, preferring to talk outside under the shade or in the car. Some reflections of this shame and hostility appear in parents' statements cited later in this chapter, in the section on Clothing in Chapter IV, and in interviews with high school students.

As much of this cruelly invidious comparison between country Indian and urban middle class living is justified by school and other Bureau employees on the grounds that it will motivate the Indian to "improve himself," it may be appropriate to digress briefly on this issue. A quite fitting parallel would be if some wealthy family, such as the Kennedy's, were to invite a Bureau teacher to spend a week with them at their yacht or winter mansion, not for the pleasure of their company, but rather to encourage him to "improve himself." Neither the teacher nor the Sioux nor the present authors lack motive for more sumptuous living; if none of the three is dwelling in a mansion, the reason is not lack of motive.

While Sioux desire better housing, they also desire many other things. If they are not excessively concerned about housing, the reason is not apathy or indifference, but two important, often neglected factors. First, the economically underdeveloped nature of the Reservation area and, second, the positive values that the Sioux place upon other aspects of living. In like manner if teachers do not dwell in mansions, the reason is not apathy but, first, their level of wages and, second, the positive values that they place upon their profession which led them to enter it in the first place. Admittedly, we are oversimplifying a complex question but, as we shall note later in this chapter, much educational confusion arises because administrators conceive of Sioux as lacking motive when in actuality the issue is rather that they value different things and are moved by different matters than the Whites about them.

## Figures: Budgets and Attendance

In a sense, the very expenditure of money on visible edifices constitutes an important element of B.I.A. public relations. The critic who might be inclined to question the relative lack of achievement of Indian pupils in formal education is disarmed by the tangible and costly evidence of governmental concern. Yet today on Pine Ridge, it seems that the larger and more modern the school, the worse the overall relationship between the school and the Indian community. This in turn affects the achievement of the youngsters. There are obvious advantages to consolidation and to decent school buildings and comfortable quarters for those who work in them. Nonetheless it must be said bluntly that expenditures on consolidation and construction may build bureaucratic empires without improving the quality of Indian education.

As the schools have been consolidated, their organization has become more bureaucratic. Of course, every school system is organized bureaucratically and, for that matter, the systems of the metropolitan centers suffer greatly from this rigidity because they are so huge and so straitened economically.[2] On the other hand, the Indian schools labor under subordination to federal civil service, the widely ramified Bureau of Indian Affairs, the Department of the Interior, and finally the U.S. Congress. School personnel are recruited, rewarded and punished, released or pensioned, according to the rules of the Civil Service. Construction and maintenance of buildings follow the policies, plans, and politics of Agency Offices, Area

---

[2] Compare Callahan, Raymond, *Education and the Cult of Efficiency*, Chicago: University of Chicago Press, 1962.

Offices, and Washington.[3]

When in the autumn of 1962 we witnessed an Orientation Program for the Employees of the Pine Ridge School System (teachers, guidance workers, matrons, cooks, bus drivers), we were disconcerted to observe that almost the entire week-long session was devoted to explaining the various tables of Bureau organization together with descriptions of procedures and protocol for action within that organization—forms in multiple copies with multiple signatures—and all this together with the injunction of patience, for the Bureau takes time to accomplish anything. The school personnel were exquisitely and painfully prepared for (or reminded of the realities of) life within the federal bureaucracy. Poor souls! One could not blame the majority of school employees for napping through lectures of several hours' length during which the speaker reviewed the number of square feet of each type of building under his care, the number of heating units in these buildings, the cost of utilities for each, and the like. While much time was devoted to this, none whatever was given to a specific discussion of the problems of teaching the Indian children. A half-day of the week long program was spent on a so-called "attitudes program," which had little to do with scholastic work, and will be reviewed in the next section under the heading of "The Ideology of the School Administrators."

[3] It is reported that the Dining Steward of the Oglala Community School objected strenuously to the plans for the new dining hall but that his words held no weight with the government office responsible for the design; the structure once built did prove to be so inefficient that it had to be changed as he said it would; meantime, he had transferred elsewhere. (The office responsible would have no difficulty in rebutting this kind of criticism with parallel tales of disasters wrought by local folk, e.g., contractors who poured the concrete foundation of a house in such fashion as to block the sewers.)

As one element in their bureaucratization, the federal schools have come to rely on attendance statistics to regulate their policies, their programs, and—most important—their budgets. Attendance is about the most easily measured quality of a school in operation, other than its sheer physical proportions, and its use as an index fits well with the currently popular attitude that the place for children is the school, regardless of the experiences they are having within its walls. Mere presence within the school has become a major virtue, and administrators pressure the teacher and he in turn pressures his pupils for high rate of attendance. Weekly or monthly attendance averages for each class are figured and displayed in the halls of the Day Schools. Pupils who have attended school every day are honored by certificates for perfect attendance awarded at school ceremonials. The parents of such a child will proudly display this certificate to any sympathetic visitor who inquires about the progress of his child at school. (Indeed, many regard these certificates as full and self-evident response to the question of whether or not their children are learning anything at school.) Within the school the work of morning classes may be disrupted while the school principal utilizes the public address system to announce the percentage of attendance of each class within the school that day and praises those classes with high figures of attendance. At the 1962 School Orientation Program the major exhortation made by any administrator to the Education Committee of the Tribal Council was "to twist the parents' arms and get them to make their children come to school."

The actions of the educators reflect not merely the exhortations of the Bureau officials but also the financial pressure that is put upon the school system. Average daily attendance figures are one of the principal bases used for budgetary assignments: Larger budgets mean more power for the administrator, more freedom to reward his favorite subordinates or his cronies elsewhere. Larger budgets also mean more purchasing and construction and this, too, can be an instrumentality of power for the administrator. This is so much the case that administrators have been known to speak of the absence of children from class as being dollars out of their pockets. In theory this should not be so, because the budgetary appropriation is supposed merely to reflect the need of the school as measured by the number of pupils enrolled and participating in its activities. In bureaucratic actuality, the larger the number of the pupils present, the larger the budget and the more powerful the administrator.

The pressure for high attendance figures is so great that school administrators have developed various devices to inflate their attendance records. Employees of some schools hinted at chicanery but were ignorant of or fearful of divulging details. Some of the devices seemed relatively minor, but some seemed to be of rather dubious legality. Project researchers noted that in the high school at Pine Ridge classes seemed to be far smaller than the official attendance figures would indicate. In this particular case, it seemed evident that pupils were being counted as "attending" providing they "checked in" at some time during the day, although they might be absent from most of their classes or even just be using the school as a dormitory. An average daily attendance figure for the whole high school can in this case be grossly misleading, if it does not show the proportion of children who are actually present in each class. When we began to check out this latter figure—the actual attendance at each class—we immediately ran into administrative resistance. Verifying attendance records is clearly a threatening

activity within the Bureau organization.

Unintended as such, but nonetheless a significant inducement to attend school, is food. In the elementary schools, children get snacks in the morning and a nourishing, hot lunch during the day. Given the poverty of the people the food is extremely appealing. A field assistant reports the words of a seventeen-year-old girl on her elementary education: "She said she got perfect attendance at the Day School: 'The only good meal I had was in school, so I would never miss a day.'" Teachers have remarked that children from the more impoverished reservation families gain weight during the school year and lose it during the summer vacation. Of course, our intention is not to denounce the distribution of food within the schools to needy children nor even to object to the gathering of attendance statistics, but rather to note the distorting effect which the emphasis on attendance has upon the educational situation. As we shall note in a subsequent chapter, the schools convey to Indian adults the illusion that if their children will attend faithfully then they will surely be educated.

Because attendance is so important to school administrators, some Indian pupils discover that they can violate the school regulations with impunity. Administrators do not want to suspend or expel a pupil, if only because this would mean the loss of a person from their school roster and therefore a loss of money from their budget. The result is that, especially in high school, a number of pupils live a rather carefree existence on the periphery of the campus, being assured of dormitory room and even board, attending classes as they like, feeling relatively free about obeying the school regulations, and knowing quite well from the behavior of the school officials that no serious punishment is likely to be in store for them as long as they comply with some outward forms of school attendance. Some of these may even graduate. Teachers who are oriented towards discipline or achievement within the classrooms find these pupils a source of profound irritation and some advocate all manner of coercion for dealing with them (including corporeal punishment). They feel frustrated because the school administration refuses to support them in a crack-down.

## Power and Property

The dynamics of reservation existence and the role of the Bureau on the reservation are perhaps most clearly illustrated in the problem of the care and handling of school buildings. On the one hand, the school building is designed for the Indian children; it is something to be used in their education. By extension, it can even be regarded as, in some sense, belonging to the Indian community. On the other hand—and much more realistically—the school building is property of the federal government, built by federal funds, and entrusted to federal employees who are held responsible for its care. A major concern and activity of Bureau employees thus becomes the guarding of school property. Charged with the protection of valuable school property, school administrators tend to regard Indian pupils and their parents as the main threat to this property, and thus to their own careers in government service.

The Indian attitude of destructiveness toward school property is widely interpreted as the product of a cultural heritage—a heritage of indifference to personal property, intensified by a poverty which makes people ignorant of how to treat modern construction. Accordingly, school administrators and most teachers devote an inordinate amount of school time to instruction of children in the handling of modern buildings and to exhorta-

tions on careful and respectful handling of property. In the early grades, much emphasis is placed on teaching children how to operate faucets, use soap and towels, and flush toilets. The marking or soiling of desks, walls, or floor is defined as an atrocity. (In one consolidated school there are classes in which the pupils, like Japanese, leave their shoes at the door and go all day in bare or stocking feet.) Children may begin their first reading lesson with the following ritualistic chant:

> Teacher: Who knows what you should do when you open books?
> Class: Don't lick your fingers.
> Teacher: What happens when you lick your fingers?
> Class: You get the pages dirty.

Despite, or perhaps because of, this excessively careful training, some children seem to take an inextinguishable delight in spraying or scattering water, urine, towels, and toilet paper around the washrooms. School administrators and teachers counter with peculiar practices. Women teachers accompany grown boys to the toilet; male administrators enter the high school girls' washroom while girls are using it. Except for a period at noon, toilets in the high school building are locked during school hours, for, as the administrator told the entering Freshmen: "Once in the morning, once at noon, and after school. Only babies go more often."[4] (Aug. 28) The first lecture given to the entering freshman class at O.C.H.S. was a one hour discourse, delivered with tremendous emotion, on the cost of the buildings and fixtures of the school campus, together with exhortations as to their proper care. The significance of such a dis-

---

[4] Members of our study could not always adjust to this Spartan regime and, on one occasion, one of them, after desperately charging to two different locked toilets, was forced to drive to the nearest Indian outhouse.

course can be better appreciated if one stops to consider what alternatively might have been said or mentioned—on the subject of greater maturity and freedom, the advantages of a high school education, work opportunities, social life, or the like. The spending of this amount of time on this one item of school property indicates the pressures which are placed upon school officials and pupils in the context of the federal school system.

In all likelihood Indian destructiveness of school property is much more than cultural habit or ignorant behavior arising from poverty. The dichotomy between things done to the Indian versus things which he does for himself is strikingly illustrated in the case of the modern schools. We have already indicated the preference of some Indians for the old-fashioned one-room school and mentioned that pressure for school consolidation and new buildings was generated by and within the Bureau organization, not the Indian population. When these new schools were built, they were presented to the Indian community as "theirs." In one case, this gave rise to events dramatically illustrating the gap between the federal school and the Indian community. The new consolidated school was dedicated with great ceremonial, including g u e s t speakers from Aberdeen, Washington, and New York. In line with current policy, the community was informed that this was not a "government school," not a "Bureau school," but the school of that particular Indian community. These words percolated about the populace for a while and soon local leaders approached the Principal, wishing to utilize the building for an evening's social activities. Worriedly, he consulted with his superordinates, who granted permission. ("Let's see what they're going to do," was the word.) The community flocked into the building, insisted on having the

entire structure opened to them, and used the facilities in what the anxious Principal felt was a careless and dirty fashion. Several community leaders (who do not like this well-intentioned but excessively sober Principal) repeatedly announced "This is *our* school!" Minor damage was done to the new walls and much debris was left about for the school personnel to clean.[5] The School Principal felt that the local community had demonstrated its basic irresponsibility. Clearly, he did not regard this as their school, but as his, and indeed it was he who had worked and schemed for years to bring the new consolidated structure into effect. The tale reveals the pathetic hope and enthusiasm of the local folk. Their destructiveness was not just ignorance or indifference, but a testing of reality: If the object was truly theirs, they could destroy it; if their alleged ownership of it was just another fraud of the Whites, they would be stopped. The statement that the school was "theirs" was but another instance of the familiar Reservation strategy of pretense, associated with statements as to what is being done "for the sake of the Indians." Sioux sometimes respond to this pretense by violence toward other objects which they have been assured are "theirs" but which somehow remain under the control of the federal government and at the disposal of Bureau employees.

Administrators seem to respond to Indian attitudes toward property by feeling that the most urgent thing that can be taught pupils is proper reverence for (federal) property. Hence,

---

[5] The conflict over use and abuse of consolidated school buildings is well established. Pedro T. Orata mentions the mess left by a community carnival in 1936 in the first of the consolidated schools (Kyle), *Fundamental Education in an Amerindian Community*, Lawrence, Kan.: Haskell Press, Bureau of Indian Affairs, 1953, pp. 26-7, 32-5.

teachers are not only saddled with the care of property placed in their custody, but also with the burden of knowing that injury to this property will be regarded as evidence that they are not discharging their function as teachers. The result is a self-confirming prediction: According to Bureau ideology Indians will not be ready to run their own affairs until they respect property. Insofar as Indians perceive that property is for them but not in their control or responsibility, they are inclined to be reckless with it. Meantime, because career advancement in the Bureau (as in most bureaucratic organizations) is associated with responsibility for property and supervision of others who have access to it, it is Bureau employees (rather than Sioux) who are being inculcated with a reverence for federal property that is almost fetishistic. As an illustration, we may mention the case of a relatively high-ranking Reservation official who spent much time tracing the whereabouts of a household appliance that was twenty years old and had evidently been purchased for special Reservation conditions now no longer present; it is doubtful if the appliance would have been worth repairing or if its net value would have been equal to that of a substantial part of the time the man devoted to hunting for it.

In summary, the bureaucratic organization of the school system serves to alienate the educational staff from the Sioux community. Judging by the reports of earlier students (Macgregor, Erikson, and others), the lapse of a generation or more has altered the form of this separation rather than affecting its nature. Occasionally, educational administrators profess to be interested in the background of their pupils, but when action is undertaken the needs of the bureaucracy tend to dominate and education comes to be redefined as instilling into the children convenient habits or attitudes, *e.g.,* attending regularly, respecting federal property, and respecting school personnel.[6]

This process is epitomized in a hortation delivered to the assembled school employees in August by a school administrator of high rank. After an introductory sermon in which he stressed the imperative need of making the Sioux parents conscious of the crucial importance of school attendance, he outlined what he termed the "Activation Program." It had been discovered, he said, that many Indian students fail in school because they are apathetic. When interviewed, some students complained that:

1. If they worked hard at school, they were ridiculed by other pupils;
2. They obtained no support or interest from home;
3. They could not see what good school was to them;
4. (Not heard by recorder)
5. The teaching staff was often indifferent to them.

In response to this statement of the problem [not wholly accurate but nonetheless formidable], an educational staff had been convened to consider the situation. At this conference the question was asked [note the redefinition of the problem], "How does one motivate Indian students and people toward a better life and higher standards when they themselves don't want it?" Having duly considered this question, the conferees drew up a list

---

[6] In this context, the criticism of Ruth Hill Useem seems even more utopian than when she wrote it in 1947: "Certain ideologies held by the dominant group [whites] such as racial equality, civil rights, sanctity of the home from interference, are not emphasized by the whites to the Rosebud [Sioux] either in the school system or council meetings because of the upsetting effect it would have on the superordinate-subordinate status system. . . . The items of behavior which are introduced are those which the superordinate thinks, consciously or unconsciously, will give greater advantage to itself." "Aftermath of Defeat," unpub. Ph.D. dissertation, University of Wisconsin, 1947, p. 100.

of guidelines, among which were "We had to make the students realize they had to change," and [although no goals had been specified] "Goals must be attacked in an orderly and systematic fashion." Finally, the staff decided to meet this challenge [again redefining the problem] by concentrating for one school year on teaching "common courtesy": children would be taught to say, "Good Morning," "Thank you," "Please," and "Excuse me." The administrator continued his peroration:

> This program fit the entire outline perfectly. We achieved this during the first year. Then we had an evaluation in the Spring, a long conference on why Indians had not achieved one hundred per cent courtesy during the year. We decided that seven months was too short a time to sell the idea of courtesy.

Undismayed by the fact that they had fallen somewhat short of their goal, the staff members selected an additional goal for their second year of the Activation Program—care and respect for property:

> We developed crucial attitudes, telling the children, "Get your heel off the wall," and "Don't make a mark on your desk!" (In consequence) you won't find a pencil mark on the wall of our new building or any scuffed floors or a name in the toilets. The building is in perfect condition. Not a mark on the desks! (Aug. 22)

[To what degree this program of teaching civility and respect for (school) property had affected the situation of the Indian students, as exhibited by their five initial complaints, the speaker did not say.]

## Other Issues

In most schools on the Reservation one afternoon hour a week is released for religious instruction by local ministers. The religious education sessions take advantage of the school building and the school bus system, and in their present arrangement it is doubt-ful whether they would win the approval of a federal court, if any parent had the knowledge and the inclination to challenge the practice. This religious instruction seems to be a relic of the earliest missionizing ("colonial") phase of Indian administration. If the question of which organizations and associations had the right to utilize school facilities and encroach on school time were a matter for public decision by representatives of the Sioux community, it is likely that some Indian "lawyer" would have raised the constitutional issue long ago. In that case, were the practice still desired, a more suitable and licit means of continuing it might have been arranged.

The consolidation of schools requires a system of transporting youngsters to and from their homes daily. Each Day School has a fleet of three or four buses for this purpose. The rolling terrain, the extremes of weather, the dust, and the stretches of unpaved road are hard on these vehicles, and as a consequence a major concern of the school principal is the maintenance of his bus system. Should one of his buses be out of service, the school day must be reorganized, and if two buses fail, he might as well close up school. His situation is aggravated by the great distance between the schools and an adequate servicing facility at a nearby town off the Reservation.

If the communication between the school administrators and the Indian community were better, it is highly likely that emergency systems of transportation could be improvised. Most local communities have enough functioning automobiles to bring the children to school if need be. Alternatively, there is the example of Rosebud Reservation, where the Tribal Council operates a bus system as a means of public transportation about the Reservation. Such a bus system could constitute an auxiliary or emergency system in case of failure of a school ve-

### TABLE 9
### FEDERAL SCHOOLS IN SHANNON COUNTY*
(Pine Ridge Reservation; Dec., 1962)

| Name | Town | Grades | Enrollment |
|------|------|--------|------------|
| No. 5—Loneman | Oglala | B-8 | 210 |
| No. 9—Red Dog | Manderson | K, B-8 | 228 |
| No. 16—Pahin Sinte | Porcupine | K, B-8 | 205 |
| Little Wound | Kyle | B-8 | 210 |
| TOTAL DAY SCHOOLS | | K, B-8 | 853 |
| Oglala Community School | Pine Ridge | K, B-8, U | 621 |
| TOTAL (Elementary Grades) | | K, B-8 | 1474 |
| Oglala Community (High) | Pine Ridge | 9-12 | 292 |
| TOTAL ALL GRADES | | K, B-12, U | 1766 |

Notes:  B—Beginners
       K—Kindergarten
      U—Ungraded room (all overage)
*Source: Office of Reservation Principal, Pine Ridge.

hicle. In any case, consultation between school administrators and representatives of the local community might improve the present situation, in which federal administrators insist on handling the problem themselves, while the Indian parents are happy to be free of all concern.

## THE VACUUM IDEOLOGY OF THE SCHOOL ADMINISTRATORS

By "Vacuum Ideology" we mean the disposition of administrators and school officials to support policies and programs (such as the establishment of nursery schools) with the assertion that the Indian home and the mind of the Indian child are meager, empty or lacking in pattern. On our first day at Pine Ridge, we were instructed by a high ranking Agency official:

The school got this child from a conservative home, brought up speaking the Indian language, and all he knows is Grandma. His home has no books, no magazines, radio, television, newspapers; it's empty! He comes into the school and we have to teach him everything. All right. We bring him to the point where he's beginning to know something in

high school, and he drops out. Our dropout figures are high. Because at this time he has to choose between Grandma and being an educated member of the community. . . . If we could reach the children at an earlier age, at kindergarten—or even nursery school, I believe we should have nursery schools here—then we might be able to accomplish more. (Aug. 1)

After we had lived for a time with Sioux families ourselves and had acquired some familiarity with the all too un-meager gamut of experience of their children, we sometimes could not resist a modest challenge to this philosophy. Once an educational administrator explained to us:

The Indian child has such a *meager* experience. When he encounters words like "elevator" or "escalator" in his reading, he has no idea what they mean.

But it's not just strange concepts like those. Take even the idea of *water*. When you or I think of it, well, I think of a shining, stainless steel faucet in a sink, running clean and pure, and of the plumbing that brings it, and chlorination and water purification, or of the half-million dollar project for the Pine Ridge water supply. But the Indian child doesn't think of water as something flowing into a bath tub.

## TABLE 10
### FEDERAL SCHOOLS ON PINE RIDGE RESERVATION: FISCAL YEAR 1962*

| Name | Town | County | Grades | Type of Student | Enrollment (1962) |
|------|------|--------|--------|-----------------|-------------------|
| American Horse | Allen | Bennett | B-8 | Day | 90 |
| Little Wound | Kyle | Shannon | B-8 | " | 230 |
| (No. 5)—Loneman | Oglala | Shannon | B-8 | " | 235 |
| (No. 9)—Red Dog | Manderson | Shannon | B-8 | " | 145 |
| (No. 16)—Pahin Sinte | Porcupine | Shannon | B-8 | " | 184 |
| (No. 24)—Wanblee | Wanblee | Washabaugh | B-8 | " | 171 |
| Oglala Community | Pine Ridge | Shannon | B-12 | Day | 329 |
|  |  |  |  | Boarding | 539 |

TOTAL ENROLLMENT 1923**

Note: B—Beginners (Pre-First) Grade.

*Source: Branch of Education, Bureau of Indian Affairs, Statistics Concerning Indian Education: Fiscal Year 1962.

**An additional dozen children went from Pine Ridge to attend the vocational boarding school at Flandreau, So. Dakota.

Names and "school numbers" in parenthesis date back to the period of one room schools; to some extent these remain in popular usage today, so that Loneman School at Oglala, So. Dak., is often referred to as "Number Five" by local folk.

As this person spoke, our minds were flooded with visions of the creek which ran a few hundred yards from the Sioux homestead where we had camped during the summer and we recalled its coolness and vegetation, the humans and animals that had come there to bathe, the flights of mosquitoes at dusk, not to mention the ancient cars and the yelping of their enthusiastic escort of dogs. So, one of us gambited, "I guess the Indian child would think of a creek." But the administrator insisted on the universally miserable quality of Sioux experience, "Or of a pump, broken down and hardly working."

Carried far enough, the Vacuum Ideology leads to characterizations of Sioux life which are deplorably fallacious. One person who had worked on the Reservation for many years asserted in a public meeting that "Indian children have no home experiences in art or music" and that Indian children are not told stories by their parents. (Even a music teacher in secondary school stated that Indians had no musical experience.) Another person, also of many years experience, remarked, "We must go back to the (Indian) home to find the lack of patterns that should have been learned."

In the face of this repetitive and rigid usuage of such terms as empty, meager, and lacking in pattern, we at length began to feel that these administrators were perceiving the Indian mind as the land-hungry settlers had perceived the continent:

> The White people speak of the country at this period as "a wilderness," as though it was an empty tract without human interest or history. To us Indians it was as clearly defined then as it is today; we knew the boundaries of tribal lands, those of our friends and those of our foes; we were familiar with every stream, the contour of every hill, and each peculiar feature of the landscape had its tradition. It was our home, the scene of our history, and we loved it as our country.[7]

---

[7] Francis LaFlesche, *The Middle Five*, Madison: University of Wisconsin Press, 1963, p. xx. LaFlesche, an Omaha Indian born about 1857, wrote this passage in 1900.

Supplying some intellectual rationalization for the Vacuum Ideology are the writings of Pedro T. Orata. A Filipino by birth, Dr. Orata served as Principal of the Little Wound (consolidated) Day School at Kyle during the school year 1936-37. He kept elaborate records of this one year's experience, producing a four volume report for the Bureau which he condensed into the book, *Fundamental Education in an Amerindian Community*. In Dr. Orata's writings the Vacuum Ideology has a simple purity: On the one hand, there is the secularized Protestant ethic with the virtues of diligence, prudence, thrift, cleanliness, etc., and on the other hand, there is—nothing. As he describes the Sioux, it is not that they have any set of values of their own but that, like the littlest babes, they have not been taught: So they loaf when they should work, they are messy when they should be tidy, and so on.

Even before the time of Orata's work, the Vacuum Ideology was undergoing attack from an anthropologist well familiar with the life of the Oglala:

> Education of a native people by representatives of an alien culture is essentially a re-education or a re-conditioning process, regardless of how it may be considered or what may be attempted. Formal education is but part of a process extending from birth to death. By the age of six or seven, when a Sioux child enters a school, he is already a conditioned being. He speaks a language alien to that used as a medium for teaching. He has studied the behavior of the adult and other children around him and has long been building his reactions accordingly for the minimum of frustration in his interaction with them. . . . In short, he is already a pupil of some years' standing in modern Teton-Dakota culture.[8]

In the light of this analysis of the process of cross-cultural education, written about Pine Ridge over a generation ago, it is especially noteworthy that when the administrators of the school system confer today about their problems, they should devote so much of their discussion not to an attempt to understand the nature of the Sioux child, but rather to a statement of his "deficiencies" of experience, as compared to their idealized image of a "usual American" child. Since the latter child and his family are ideal, rather than actual, they are credited with countless traits, unquestionably desirable because middle-class American. The longer the list of these traits the more defective the Sioux child is made to appear, until finally all present agree that, "The gap is terrifying!!"[9]

Note how in the following excerpt from an address at a conference of Pine Ridge educators, the speaker portrays an idealized, urban, middle-class family, which somehow has been labeled as "usual." Note also that, despite the high regard of the speaker for these familial activities, none truly has anything to do with the basic rudiments of education, namely learning to read, write or figure. Note, finally, that the Fullblood Sioux home is not actually as different as seems to be implied, for Sioux parents do buy toys for their children (insofar as they have the money), they do tell them stories and teach them songs, they take them on excursions, and they answer their questions—astonishing! The speaker is correct that urban middle-class children have more knowledge of jet planes, rocket ships, and hydrogen bombs, but in fairness she ought to allow that Sioux children have more experience with horses, cattle, and the

---

[8] H. Scudder Mekeel, "An Anthropologist's Observations on Indian Education," *Progressive Education*, XIII (1936), p. 156 The article seems largely identical with a chapter of his dissertation of 1932.

[9] "Reservation-Wide Pre-School Program" (Minutes of a Conference, February 23, 1961, Pine Ridge Indian Agency) Pierre, So. Dak.: Division of Indian Education, Department of Public Instruction, duplicated.

life of the prairie. In all, it is dubious whether any aspect of the background of this "usual" child would truly have any bearing on his scholastic abilities, except that he would be more congenial to the teacher because he shared more of the same culture.

I drew the topic that has to do with lack of constructive activities in the Sioux home previous to school age and, coupled with that, the lack of opportunity to sharpen decision-making skills. I believe that we'd have no trouble at all in agreeing that children of all races begin to learn at home. Doesn't the usual pattern in the home run something like this: We find the parents reading aloud to the children, telling them stories, and teaching the children to say a simple prayer at bedtime or at mealtime, teaching them songs, Mother Goose rhymes and little verses, looking at pretty picture books and coloring these picture books, and listening to endless questions, helping the children to satisfy their curiosity. And don't parents usually help with the make-believe play of their children and, as a rule, take them on walks, trips and excursions. There's no end of toys. As a usual practice we find that children's homes are flooded with toys, especially at birthday time and Christmas time. Nowdays there's a toy to represent every conceivable occupation, animal, person and thing. The dolls, you know, are packed with a Toni, and the cowboy outfits *have* to have two guns, or they're just not in style. And the cops and robbers outfits have to have a tear gas gun. We assume that these [Sioux] children have many home experiences. In fact, we assume that they all come to school with the same experiences. In reality we find too great a lag or gap between the actual background the [Sioux] child has and the assumed constructive home experiences, or the things that would build concepts. If this is out of balance as much as I think it is, then we must include a great many experiences, normally provided by the home, in the school program. [She lists these experiences as follows:]

Television
Jet Planes
Rocket Ships
Hydrogen Bombs
Helicopters
Polio + GG Shots
Supermarkets
Frozen Foods

Hundreds of Electrical Appliances
The Lag is Terrifying! ! [10]

However we wish to resolve this comparison between Sioux and "usual American" homes, the important consideration is that the approach of these educators is negativistic and contrary to basic educational theory, which says it is the task of the school to inquire about where the child stands now in his development and to pitch its educational efforts accordingly. Of what utility then is this Vacuum Ideology with its endless lists of traits that Sioux children lack and its lack of interest in the traits that these children *do* have. So far as we can see, the ideology is a rationalization for the educators' defeat, as given their pathetic image of the Sioux child, then surely it must be a miracle if the school manages to teach him anything. Moreover, the Ideology also has the convenient quality that it serves to justify *any* activity within the school as somehow being "educational." For if the Sioux child is presumed deficient in every realm of experience, then the task of the school can properly be defined as furnishing him with vicarious experiences to compensate in every aspect of life. So long as he is kept away from his home and in school, he is being educated—or so the Ideology would declare. And if he can be enrolled in school at age two or three, so much the better.

Given the Pine Ridge administrators' image of the ideal pupil in the off-reservation school, it is particularly ironic to note that urban administrators also have their problems and that they have coined their version of a Vacuum Ideology built about the concept of a *culturally deprived* child.[11]

----

[10]*Ibid.*, pp. 7, 13.

[11] For a critical review of this concept and of the limitations of present school programs for educating these urban children, see Frank Reissman, *The Culturally Deprived Child*, New York: Harper and Row, 1962.

With regard to that conception of the urban lower class and with regard to the problem of Indian education, the critical remarks of Eleanor Leacock seem most trenchant:

> All too often, the concept (of cultural deprivation) carries with it the uncomfortable implication that middle-class norms are *ipso facto* desirable, that "lower-class culture" [or Indian culture] is merely a subtraction from middle-class culture and has no positive attributes of its own on which to build learning, and that our goal should be to have all children reject any deviations from middle-class standards. Yet at the same time we question the meaning and value of these same middle-class norms, as evidenced by the writings of many novelists and social philosophers. . . . One can even play with the idea of cultural deprivation for middle-class children, since home and school join in building a protective barrier between them and so much of the modern world.

Dr. Leacock shrewdly observes that "cultural deprivation" helps to justify educators in a policy of "educational deprivation" so that in the case of lower class Negro children, the teachers do not expect that they can be taught "and the teacher's low expectations for these children are reflected by the children's lack of expectations for themselves."[12] The Vacuum Ideology serves a similar function on the Reservation.

The most stirring counter-ideology to the various Vacuum Ideologies of administrators of Indian and slum schools has been offered by Edgar Z. Friedenberg:

> To reach the dropouts and give them a reason for staying, the school would have to start by accepting their *raison d'etre*. It would have to take lower-class [or Indian] life seriously as a condition and a pattern of experience—not just as a contemptible and humiliating set of circumstances that every decent boy or girl is anxious to escape from. It would have to accept their language, and their dress, and their values as a point of de-

parture for disciplined exploration, to be understood, not as a trick for luring them into the middle class, but as a way of helping them to explore the meaning of their own lives. This is the way to encourage and nurture potentialities from *whatever* social class [or ethnic group]. . . . The fact that they may have reason to hate their life of fear and deprivation does not give us the right to force ours on them as the only acceptable alternative to it. This is something they must work out for themselves, and the school's job is to help them understand most fully the meaning and nature of what they have to work with.[13]

## THE TEACHERS IN THE BUREAUCRACY

### Composition

The teachers in the elementary grades are predominantly married women or widows, middle aged or older. Most of them are Whites raised in the communities of the Western Plains. A few of the women teachers are Indian, and they are as often single as married. The men in the elementary grades tend to be Indian or Negro, while the high school contains a high proportion of White males.

The social dynamics of this ethnic-age composition are relatively straightforward: The Reservation would not impress a young, White, female teacher as a good place to find a husband and few of its single men are college educated or beginning on promising careers. Even the better educated young Indians are saddled with numerous and impoverished kin and are unlikely to advance socially unless they move geographically. Besides, the social ecology of the school compounds is constricted and offers little opportunity for meeting new and possibly acceptable young men. An idealistic girl, fresh from college, and with a compassionate desire

---

[12] "Comment," *Human Organization* Monograph, No. 2 (1960), pp. 30-32.

[13] "An Ideology of School Withdrawal," *Commentary*, Vol. XXXV, No. 6 (June 1963), pp. 499-500.

to educate Indian children, would in any case tend to become impatient, frustrated, and embittered by the rigidity of the policies of the federal school and the skillful sabotage of her pupils.

Many of the teachers, especially the womenfolk, are attracted by the economic security of the federal school system. Civil Service regulations mean a tenure that is relatively assured, pay every month throughout the year, paid vacations and sick leave, and a good pension on retirement. Considering that the teacher is required to work eleven, rather than nine, months of the year, the wages are not high relative to Western school systems. On the other hand, on a comparative basis within the Reservation the pay and general social status are excellent; for a country Indian, the salary must appear astronomical.

For married couples Pine Ridge has definite attractions. If both partners are qualified, each may work for the Bureau and even teach in the same school, and the double income means a comfortable living. This, plus the federal rule against racial discrimination, makes Bureau employment especially attractive to those Negro couples in which both partners are college-educated. One may anticipate seeing more Negro couples on Indian Reservations as time goes by.

In addition to women whose husbands have school or other Bureau employment, there are those who are engaged in enterprises in nearby towns. The tourist industry, because of its seasonal summer nature, fits well with teaching. The man of the house can tend to the modest winter business of the motel or store and during the busy summer season have the added assistance of his spouse. In theory, a nine-month cycle of scholastic employment does not mesh with the Civil Service regulations which govern the federal schools, but with the current difficulty of recruiting experienced teachers on the Reservation, administrators are willing to stretch the rules. These nine-months teachers are necessarily absent from whatever summer duties or programs the Branch of Education may organize.

While teaching is not an occupation that recommends itself to the vocationally ambitious, some advancement is possible within the federal system, particularly for the men. Because the Branch of Education is the largest within the B.I.A., it is natural and frequent that Bureau administrators emerge from its ranks. The present Area Administrator was once a teacher in a one room school on Pine Ridge. Male teachers may hope to climb from the classroom, and so-called guidance workers from the dormitories, to the office of principal or other administrator. Also, mobility is possible within the federal civil service, and several positions congenial to both male and female teachers have been developed, such as those of community health worker and adult education specialist.

Of those few Indians who attend college, a great proportion major in education, and boys, especially, major in physical education. Those from the more conservative Indian backgrounds are likely to return to the Reservation and seek employment there. They encounter several handicaps. When it comes to hiring for Bureau positions civil service regulations do discriminate in favor of Indians. On the other hand, most school administrators seem to prefer that qualified country Indians work on a reservation where they have no kin. When an Indian member of our staff approached administrators on the question, he was told that a teacher's poor relatives would "pull him down." When White members approached them, they denied this policy and pointed to a young teacher of country extraction. Later another local school employee explained that, the administration would hire educated country Indians provided that they made it clear that they had severed their ties with their home community.

## Attitudes of Teachers Toward Indian Parents and Pupils

Many teachers look upon the Indian parents with attitudes very much like those of Whites living near the Reservation: "The trouble with Indians is that the government has been feeding them," or "When they get money they spend it like drunken sailors," or "They are the *laziest people!*"[14] One teacher told us, "They go back to the Blanket, you know"; though she, like a missionary teacher and certain Mixedbloods who contemptuously speak of country Indians as "bucks" and "squaws," was somewhat dated in her imagery. When teachers learned that we lived "in there" and visited with country Indians daily, a few clearly thought we were odd. Some were curious: "How do they stay alive when it gets cold? How do they stand it?" or, "I wonder what they do with the goods the government gives them, do they trade it off for liquor?" (Jan. 28) We found no White teacher who had country Indian friends and only one—an unusual, elderly woman of modest rank—who had taken the trouble to become acquainted with their ways, so that she might better instruct their children. On the other hand, there are a minority of teachers, especially in the high school, who would appreciate and enjoy meeting Indian parents, but find that in the present situation this is difficult to do.

Very few of the Day School teachers actively dislike their pupils; quite a few seem fond of them; very few respect them. At a meeting of supervisors and principals, all vigorously agreed with the statement that "the Indian child must be made to *feel* that he is important." But very few teachers, either then or later, in word or

deed, have ever suggested that in their opinion he truly *is* important. The most common attitude is condescension, sometimes kindly, often well-meant, but always critical:

> One of the things I try to instill is not to lie or steal, because by nature they are that way.
>
> They all seem to want to copy, copy, copy. Give them a thought problem and they won't do it; they'll all just copy from each other even if it's all wrong. . . . If you show them where to get information, you open the book and point to the paragraph, they'll just copy the whole paragraph. . . . They just don't seem to care or try.

The first six statements at a teacher's (B-3) session (Aug. 22) of the Orientation Program were—

> Some of their attitudes really have to be changed, for example, they have to learn to respect the employees, the teachers, the bus drivers, and the cooks.
>
> It isn't that they should fear authority but that they should respect the authority that is doing things for their own good.
> Yes, they need to learn to conform.
>
> We should get across to our little ones that they should approach any teacher with their little wants.
>
> It takes constant reminding so that they learn to share.
>
> Some children use improper [obscene] language without knowing that it is improper. They have learned it from their fathers. They need a lot of reteaching.

If properly cued, many teachers will recite portions of the supervisors' Vacuum Ideology: "We try to give them experiences, because their background is so meager; for example, they don't know what an escalator is." On the other hand, most of the teachers, and especially those who work in the Day Schools, apply the ideology more reasonably than do their supervisors. While they grant that the Indian home lacks the conveniences of the usual American home (though they have never been in an Indian dwelling), their daily experiences with the chil-

---

[14] Two statements by teachers, one by dormitory official.

dren makes them aware that somewhere outside school the child has
learned and is learning many things
that do not make the teacher's life
easier. Thus, while the supervisor re-
iterates that the Indian's life is empty,
many teachers tend to see the child as
acquiring habits that "must be broken."

Teachers differ from their supervisors even more sharply in their open
recognition of the most obvious and
agonizing problem in Sioux education:
the "withdrawal" or "lack of response"
of pupils in the late elementary grades
and the high school. Though supervisors did not even mention this phenomenon, most teachers told us it was
their gravest problem with students,
and a few asked if we could give them
any suggestions on teaching methods.
A teacher of many years' experience
lamented:

> When I give a lecture I'm lucky to
> have the attention of more than a few;
> the rest look out the window. Even the
> few don't give their attention for long.
> On class recitation, some students just
> won't speak up. One girl—I asked her a
> question I know she could answer. She
> just looks up at me a minute and then

---

15 Howard S. Becker notes that it is in
the nature of institutions "to try to become
self-contained systems of power and to protect themselves against interference from
the outside." In the case of colonial and underdeveloped countries, the educational institutions have an easy time in this respect
because "parents are relatively unable to
assess the school's work and deal with educational authorities." This also holds true of
schools in urban slums and it allows the
teachers "just to get along and not have
too much trouble; educational standards
come second. It is only where the institutional defenses are breached, as they are in
[urban] middle-class areas, that this can be
avoided and educational standards maintained. One of the elements preventing the
lower-class from receiving the full benefits
of education in a class society is its lack
of organization and effectiveness in pushing
teachers to do better work." "Schools and
Systems of Stratification," reprinted in *Education, Economy, and Society,* A. H. Halsey, Jean Floud, and C. Arnold Anderson,
editors, New York; Free Press, 1961, pp.
101-2.

looks back to her book without saying
anything. I've tried everything. I've scolded her, I've encouraged her, I've spoken
with her after class. Nothing works.
(Dec. 10)

Another teacher who has served on
Pine Ridge for over five years—

> When I began to teach here, the chil-
> dren didn't even answer when I took
> roll. I got very upset. They would sit
> right there and wouldn't even say "Pres-
> ent." I had no idea what that was all
> about. I think the Orientation Program
> here needs a great deal of improvement.
> I don't know much about this, but I
> think the teacher should be given a much
> clearer idea of the kind of children, the
> kind of group, that they are going to be
> meeting . . . what they are going to
> face. Then, they may not be so taken
> aback by the reaction or, I should say,
> no-reaction of the students.

And another teacher of similar experience—

> I tell the new teachers that they just
> have to learn to be philosophical about
> it. The pupils withdraw in the later
> grades and there is just no way you can
> reach them no matter what you try. I
> know.

In addition to the ecological separation of the school campus from the
residential areas of the community, a
number of other factors help to isolate the teacher from the children's
parents. The school day is long, and it
is made longer by the Bureau's inflexible requirement that the teacher put
in an eight-to-five day centering at his
desk. In addition, many teachers are
pressured into working several evenings a week or occasionally on weekends. The furthest most Day School
teachers will roam during the day is
immediately outside the school building to supervise the children at play.
Teachers are not inclined to devote
weekends and evenings to school business unless it is work directly connected with their classes (*e.g.* grading papers) or unless it is commanded by
their superiors (*e.g.* monitoring evening movies at the boarding school).
Journeying about in a strange and ap-

parently trackless community to visit impoverished parents of unknown temperament is hardly likely to appeal to the ordinary teacher as an after-hours' recreation. Conversely, most Indian parents avoid the school and its teachers, visiting only for a crisis and often not even then. It is likely that they feel uncomfortable in this strange and modern building which is devoted to arts beyond their ken. Many Indian women are acutely aware of the differences between the teachers' modish garb and their own old-fashioned and well-worn clothing, and, moreover, find the administrators' exaggerated emphasis on cleanliness insulting.

> I was kinda scared to go to school. At "Number Ten" the teachers really dress up. They use makeup and lipstick and everything. I don't know how to dress to go to that school (April).

> No sooner do you step into Howling Bear (Day School) than they clean it up right after you. They come after you with a mop! (Sept. 27)

Many Bureau employees feel that the present Indian "problem" can be "solved" only by disrupting or minimizing the tie between the children and their elders and so they are not inclined to encourage participation or visiting by the latter. Schools vary in this regard, depending a great deal on the principal, but Project staff rarely saw an Indian parent at a Day School while classes were in session. Most teachers regard the social distance between themselves and the Indian parents as a blessing or benefit of Bureau employment, and they are quick to recall the nuisance White parents can be with their complaints about grades, assignments, and honors.[15]

Educators with children of their own may face a problem in the adjustment of their offspring to Indian children. This is the kind of thing that varies so that it is difficult to say anything generally valid. If the teacher is unpopular with the pupils and the community, her children may have more than usual trouble. Likewise, the situation at the school in Pine Ridge town is sometimes troublesome because a large proportion of the young Indian boarders come from broken homes and are neglected by their families; such children can be mean and spiteful to outsiders. On the other hand, most children of educational personnel have little difficulty in excelling in school work and in assuming leading positions in school activities.

## Better Schoolrooms

Despite the general attitude of the Bureau and School administrators there are a few teachers who develop fine classrooms and teach their pupils a great deal. These teachers are difficult to describe because they are remarkably different in background and personality and some are "real characters" in the sense that this word was used fifty years ago. In general, they differ from the less successful instructors in that they respect their pupils. By this we mean that they treat them as if something worthy of respect is already there.[16] If a child errs they imply that this is not because he is innately stupid but because he is not using the intelligence or talents he possesses. They also differ from other teachers in that most of the statements they make about their pupils are positive: "Indian kids are smart," or "They can be awfully good students if you understand them." These teachers are strict disciplinarians and do not tolerate non-

---

[16] In an exhortation for improving the teaching of children from the urban slums, Goodwin Watson urges: "The starting point is respect. Nothing else that we have to give will help very much if it is offered with a resentful, contemptuous, or patronizing attitude. We don't understand these neighborhoods, these homes, these children, because we haven't respected them enough to think them worthy of study and attention." "Foreword" to Frank Riessman, *The Culturally Deprived Child*, New York: Harper and Row, 1962, p. xi.

sense. Some speak to their students in impersonal or sometimes even in gruff tones. But all are very fair and all are extremely skillful in avoiding a situation which would embarrass a shy student before the class. They tend to place a heavy emphasis on scholastic work and they often behave as if such matters as pupils' neatness in dress and eating habits, or how pupils spend their money, do not fall within their province:

> I don't feel that we should always be fighting the force of culture in the home. They (Indian children) like to eat their hotdogs rolled in bread and they like to dip their bread in the stew. It's not bad manners for them. I don't think it matters, and we shouldn't interfere. One teacher is always going around at meal time and saying: "Don't dip in the stew—don't make sandwiches." But they like it and we shouldn't interfere (Jan. 28).

Most of the teachers with good classrooms spend relatively little class time on the Attitudes Program or on the exercises designed to give the pupils vicarious experiences. Bluntly, in their work with pupils they tend to ignore top-level directives.

### Recruitment and Orientation

Recruiting new teachers for the federal schools on Pine Ridge has become something of a problem, and it is our impression that the turnover of new teachers during the first weeks of their work is extremely high. One source of new staff has been the retired teachers from nearby public school systems. They have the asset of abundant experience in teaching, but the handicap of having gained that experience among White children rather than country Indians. For those who are elderly and inflexible, the task of adjusting to children who speak English so poorly and have such different ways may simply be too severe.

As we have noted, the annual orientation program for Pine Ridge educators provided no help or guidance for dealing with any pedagogical problems. When we asked a responsible official why teachers on an Indian Reservation were not given any introduction to the special problems they might encounter in teaching Indian children, we were given contradictory excuses and the information: "We used to have staff meetings on this kind of thing out in the Day Schools once a month. Now we have millions of meetings but none on the teacher's level and it doesn't trickle down." (Dec. 17) After we had completed our observation of the situation in the classrooms, we wondered if it might not be wise to hold some meetings at which there was less trickling down and more seeping up.

Whatever orientation the new teacher now receives comes from her (or his) superiors, the local school principal and the Education Specialist in the Office of the Reservation Principal. As the turnover of teachers accelerates, these persons find themselves running very fast to remain in one place. If turnover could be reduced, not only would the education of the children be improved, but also there might be enough saving of administrative time and expense to more than justify a better, though costlier, program of orientation. The situation might be one where *team teaching* would be worth a trial, as this would facilitate the apprenticeship training most likely to equip novices with the skills and insights effective in working with Sioux children. Watching experienced teachers work with pupils and then attempting similar tasks under their supervision wuld be the kind of internship that should sharply reduce initial turnover among teaching staff. Also, team teaching might permit suitable scheduling of classes so that individual teachers could be absent for occasional half-days for meetings, instructional periods, or for visiting and observing teachers working with classes at similar levels in other schools. Observing other teachers in operation and chatting informally with them is worth any amount of formal instruction and might even prove helpful and stimulating to teachers who are becoming jaded. Some formal instruction and discussion, especially centering about Sioux ethno-history and current Reservation affairs might be useful as background. As a final measure, new teachers might well be introduced to the local folk at one of their ceremonials or gatherings.

---

*Excerpts from a Field Diary:*
*A P.T.A. Meeting—January, 1963*

About twenty people are present, mostly school employees (teachers, bus drivers, cooks) and their families. The chairmen from last year and this year are present; both are ranchers, slightly Indian in their legal genetics, scarcely Indian in their culture. Two other officers are sociological Fullbloods, but one of them is absent tonight; the one present is wife of a school employee. In all, representation from the Fullblood majority of the community (except school employees) consists of one male, who may be angling for a school job.

The business of the evening revolves about a change in date of meeting. According to the ByLaws the regular meeting is the second Tuesday of each month, but the Principal and some of the teachers have been attending an evening class at a neighboring teachers' college every Tuesday. As a result, no meeting has been held since October when new officers were elected. Accordingly, the Chairman entertains a motion to change the date of meeting to Wednesday and this is passed unanimously. At this point, last year's chairman rises to point out that such a change in the meeting date is equivalent to a change in the ByLaws: hence, it requires notice to be made at a prior meeting; plus two-thirds approv-

al by a formal quorum; and finally notice to and approval by the state chapter of P.T.A. He concludes on a plaintive note,

This is what hung us up last year. You have to have a quorum to transact business, and we could never get a quorum present, and so we could never change the ByLaws so as to take care of the quorum. No legal quorum ever attended our meetings, so we couldn't do anything, and we couldn't change the ByLaws.

Discussion continues around this frustrating situation, and it is finally decided to lay the problem before the visiting speaker, an officer of the state P.T.A. who has just arrived. At first, the problem is posed abstractly, and she declares that the ByLaws should be like the Bible of the Chairman; amending them is a serious thing which you wouldn't want to have performed by a rump session with only five people present. She conjures up an image of five clever people perverting the Howling Bear P.T.A. by judiciously amending its ByLaws. Meetings must be held on the scheduled date, she declares. (No one dares to explain that meetings have not been held or that, when held, no business can be transacted.) Finally, someone does explain that with the present meeting date the Principal does not attend, and the visiting expert relents from her judicial severity:

Oh, the Principal can't come. Well, he should come. Then, well, if it's the Principal, then maybe you should make the meeting for Wednesday, but notify everyone you are changing the ByLaws because the Principal can't attend, but then you can take a vote on it at that meeting.

Consideration of this difficult and frustrating topic has taken over an hour and a half, and everyone present is weary. (At the next P.T.A. meeting, on a Wednesday some two months later, the Principal was moved to say, "I think we should have more members at P.T.A.")

Comment: This P.T.A. is in effect a closed corporation of the school employees. Attendance from the Sioux community is very slight, and those few who do attend almost never participate. At these meetings the only communication between (Fullblood) Indian and White is between the teachers and the blue-collar school employees (bus drivers, cooks).

# Chapter VI

# WITHIN THESE SCHOOLS

## THE LOWER ELEMENTARY GRADES[1]

### Initial Interest

An observer's first impressions of the lower elementary grades (Beginners, First, Second, Third) at an Indian Day School are likely to be positive. If the teacher is fairly competent and the class small, the children appear attentive, obedient, and eager to learn. An Indian observer reported of the Third Grade:

(They) jump up and answer right away. They talk real loud and read real good. Out of eleven only three missed one word! (Jan. 7)

Or of the First Grade:

It looks like they really mean business. If a kid gets stuck (reading) they all help her—they really help out each other. If somebody makes a mistake they (courteously) don't pay no attention. They don't laugh at each other. I think these beginners are more serious with their lessons (than the older kids) (Jan. 10).

Some children seem to take delight in scholastic activities and drill. Thus, we have seen children in the First Grade voluntarily working away at a reading assignment while their fruit juice is poured and served. Or again in Beginners[2] class:

Miss Rose brings forward a large display board with leaves that turn like a calendar. "Let's all look this way." It is a picture of a boy with the word *Dick* under it. Miss Rose asks a boy to come forward and point to the word *Dick*. (This is not hard because *Dick* is the only

word on the leaf.) A Fullblood (country Indian) kid gets up, smiles, and swaggers to the front of the room. Grinning, he points to *Dick*. Miss R. turns the page and shows us a picture of a boy, a girl, a dog and several short sentences, some of which contain *Dick*. Miss R. asks three boys to come forward and point to *Dick*. Three little boys come up and look carefully at the picture. Then they turn to each other and hold a brief consultation in Lakota. Suddenly one boy turns around and shoots his finger at *Dick,* just as if he were playing the handgame. The boys return to their seats, looking pleased. Miss R. asks: "Who else can show us where Dick is?" Four hands go up. Most of the kids are watching all this keenly. But the girls, though they watch carefully, are shy about leaving their seats. Of three called on only one goes up—slowly—with the task of pointing to Spot (name of the dog). Another then follows her and, after considerable coaxing by Miss R., the third goes up also. Meanwhile, most of the other kids eagerly take it all in (Sept. 5).

During the first weeks of school these beginners are phenomenally quiet. They sit like little birds, ever alert for a guiding cue or (if they feel naughty) for an inattentive moment of which they can take advantage. Adult visitors, such as ourselves, noisy and aggressive school mates, and many other potential distractions are ignored:

---

[1] Observations on the lower elementary grades were made by four members of our Project. Most of the quotations in this section came from the reports of Dr. R. Wax or an Indian observer. We have not attempted to translate the latter's vivid and expressive Pine Ridge dialect into middle-class or academic English. All names of persons mentioned in the text are pseudonyms (e.g., "Miss Rose").

[2] "Beginners" is a special, preliminary grade level of these federal schools. The rationale is that these children, being deficient in English and other skills, require preparation for the work of the First Grade. "Beginners" is differentiated from "kindergarten," because, so it is said, "Congress won't support a kindergarten." Presumably, some Congressmen at some time thought of kindergarten as simply a place of supervised play and therefore as a luxury inappropriate to a federal school. The fact is, of course, that the work accomplished in the Beginners grade of the federal schools is quite akin to the work of any kindergarten with the important qualification that many Fullblood children enter school with little or no fluency in English.

These little kids are enormously "teacher oriented." Whenever they are not working by themselves, they usually just look at the teacher in an unwavering, attentive stare. I have never seen anything quite like it (Aug. 28).

Indeed, when a lower-elementary class room becomes noisy, the racket sometimes does not so much emanate from bored or defiant trouble makers as from over-eager learners demanding attention, approbation, or instructions from their teachers. Clearly, most of these children wish to please their teachers and most of them, as they themselves assert, seem to "like school."

The classroom situation is the more impressive because of the disadvantages with which the children begin their school careers. Many know no English at all. They are, as we have noted, accustomed to being petted and helped by elders and they have no familiarity at all with "discipline" as it is defined by their teachers. Many are so shy and some are so frightened that for the first few days of school they may not say a word even to each other. Nevertheless, within a week or two of the opening of school, they become interested and willing pupils.

## English as a Second Language

At the same time that the observer is impressed with the positive attitude of the youngsters and the devotion and conscientiousness of the teachers, he is distressed by a highly significant anomaly. The teachers believe that they are helping the children to become competent and fluent users of the English language and they devote a majority of the class time to the achievement of this goal. The pupils similarly believe that they are "learning English." In point of fact the children are *not* learning the English language in a fashion that will aid them in becoming even competent Fifth and Sixth Graders. Instead, they are, year after year,

being instructed in reading "loudly" and in writing a language that they do not understand and in which they rarely (so far as the activities of the school are concerned) develop any ease or fluency.

Before elaborating the above statements, let us look at what is going on in the classrooms:

There is a lot of pencil rattling, squirming, pushing, and general carrying-on. Miss Rose tells the children to be quiet but they pay no heed. Then she says very loudly: "When Miss Rose says put the pencil down, she means put the pencil down," but half the kids playing with their pencils don't seem to understand what she is saying.

There follows an exercise which (I think) is intended to familiarize the children with the elements of English grammar. They have an exercise book with pictures open before them and they are supposed to put their pencil on Sally and take her to get her dress (Sally and the dress being pictured in the book). Nobody catches on (including me). But Miss R. persists with loud rhetorical questions: "Why did we have to take Sally to get her dress? Why did we have to take John to get his shirt?" A few kids look baffled or concerned, but most stare at their books or look around, unaware that they are being asked a question, "Because," says Miss Rose, "the dress can't move; because the shirt can't move." On being urged, everybody catches on that they should say this in unison. They do so with expressions of pride and relief, though nobody seems to understand what it is all about. "OK," says Miss R., "you can close your books." Some children close their books; the others, seeing this, close theirs (Sept. 5).

Miss R. starts part of the class to work in a book in which the children are supposed, for example, to color three apples if the arabic numeral three is present. When she checks their work, most have not followed her cryptic instructions, "Draw your three over there." But now I, at least, catch on: she meant them to draw a line from the arabic three to the three colored items. Miss R. went back to the other group and everybody peeked at the page of the kid Miss R. had praised, noted the line she had drawn, and proceeded to copy it (Oct. 19).

The teachers themselves comment on the fact that their pupils achieve little understanding of English:

On August 28, I had been favorably impressed by the clarity and competence with which the Second Graders read aloud, though (remembering Milton's daughters) I could not help wondering whether "reading aloud" is not a skill distinct from reading for one's own edification or pleasure. I was, moreover, struck by the irony of the fact that Miss M. kept urging the children to read loudly before the class, but scolded them when they read aloud to themselves. (Incidentally, everyone kept r e a d i n g aloud to themselves.) . . . Then I went to observe the Third Grade. I remarked to Miss Bardey (a new teacher) that I had been surprised at how well the Second Graders read. "Yes," said Miss Bardey, "but they (other teachers) say that though the children read well, they don't understand any of the words they read."

After arithmetic sessions a number of teachers have remarked that the Indian pupils could do quite difficult problems providing the numbers were placed before them, "But give them a word problem and they fall flat every time." Even the math teacher in the high school emphasized this.

As the months passed, we noted that even in the higher grades the children rarely spoke to each other in English, either in the classroom or on the playground. When answering a teacher, they limit themselves to the briefest possible replies. If any voice was to be heard in the classroom speaking English, it was that of the teacher, exhorting the children to take care of school property, giving instructions, reading aloud, or asking rhetorical questions. Indian observers also commented on this phenomenon:

I noticed that these little kids don't speak English in class. The only time they talk in English is when they talk to the teacher. When they talk to each other, like when they visit when they (should be) studying, they talk in Sioux (March 21).

The linguistic needs of most of the country Indian children are so peculiar as to be almost unique. If they are to do even moderately well in the higher elementary grades (not to speak of high school or college) they must rapidly develop a fluency and ease in the use of the English language that is at least roughly comparable to that of a native English speaker of the same age. But while the Indian children spend a great deal of time on what they and their teachers think is the study of English, they develop no fluency and very little understanding. Knocking about the Reservation, they do develop some fluency in the Pine Ridge dialect of English, but their fundamental vocabulary is small and their acquaintance with scholastic English is nil. In consequence, even the brightest Indian child looks stupid when, for example, he is asked to cope with an Eighth Grade curriculum taught in a language in which he has, perhaps, the comprehensive skills of a three or four year old child.

There are two obvious reasons for the unusual linguistic difficulties of the country Indian child: the first is situational; the second has its source in the way English is taught in the schools.

On the situational level the major disadvantage is that the country Indian child does not communicate or converse in English either in the home, in play or peer groups, or with other children in school or in the class room. His linguistic communication with his teacher is minimal, being limited to monosyllabic responses or such well-learned expressions as "Good Morning," "Thank you," or "May I go to the toilet?" In or out of the classroom, he speaks in Lakota to his friends and intimates whenever he wishes to express something important, subtle, or complicated. On the other hand, in school, he learns to "read" English aloud with a fair pronunciation (but little comprehension) and

82

he may learn to write a legible hand and to spell fairly well (though, since he does not speak the standard colloquial dialect, his written English tends to be obscure and stilted).

The techniques or methods of teaching English in the Day Schools seem unconsciously designed to re-enforce the situation described above. A disproportionate amount of time is spent drilling children to speak up "loudly" while reading, asking them questions in English (which they do not answer), on "phonic" reading drill (which neither the children nor the teachers seem to understand), on reading aloud to children (who do not seem to listen), while no time at all is spent on facing and (hopefully) dealing with the fact that most if not all of this activity is futile until and unless the pupils converse fluently and colloquially with the teacher and, especially, with each other. Meantime, these pedagogic activities are carried on with so much energy and devotion that they convince teachers, educational supervisors, visiting dignitaries, and sometimes, even the Indian school children themselves, that the "language problem" is being dealt with adequately.

Unfortunately the Pine Ridge "language program" makes almost no use of the linguistic techniques pioneered so successfully by the armed forces, i.e., repeatedly listening to and immediately duplicating commonly used phrases. In fact, on the several occasions we heard a child ask a teacher how to pronounce an English word, the teacher refused, saying: "Look it up in the dictionary."[3] Unfortunately, a dictionary is not the place to learn how to pronounce the sounds of an alien language.

When children do speak English in class, they tend to employ the familiar Pine Ridge dialect. Teachers are trained to criticize this as "bad English," and so, no sooner does the Indian child open his mouth to speak English, than he is branded publicly as speaking incorrectly. Such criticism reinforces reticence to speak up. The educational task here is particularly difficult for teachers ignorant of the fundamental principles of linguistics and aural-oral teaching of languages.

### Patterns of Learning and the Indian Family Group

When the Indian child enters school he is accustomed to see himself as part of a local kin group distinct from other such groups. He may love, hate, obey or fight with his immediate kin but, nonetheless, they are his folks and he is obligated to and responsible for them. Toward "outsiders" he has no such relationship or responsibilities though they may live only two or three miles away, ride to school on the same bus, and sit in the same class.[4] Of course, his parents expect him to listen, learn, and mind the teacher, and most parents expect that the teacher will keep order and not permit the children to abuse each other.

When the young child leaves his "little community" and enters the school, he has a problem in defining his own place and that of other children. Outside of school, if a young kinsman should get into trouble with "strangers" the child knows that he is supposed to stand by him. But within the school, if the same kinsman stands squirming before the class because he does not know an answer, the teacher says he is not supposed to help him.

We observed that in the early ele-

[3] Two teachers, one an Indian and the other a White woman interested in what she called "Indian ways" had, apparently, hit upon the Army technique by accident and employed it consistently with marked success.

[4] There are devices by which older folk mingle politely with outsiders, but we doubt that the little children are aware of these.

mentary grades the children sometimes follow the pattern of mutual help and sometimes that of ruthless individualism. For example, an Indian observer was pleased with what she considered the commendable behavior of First Graders:

> Those kids—they really help each other. If a kid is reading and she stops (because she doesn't know a word) the others tell her. If a kid gets stuck, they all help her. They really help each other out. They don't laugh if somebody makes a mistake (Jan. 10).

She reported quite different behavior in the Second Grade:

> They really were having a hard time with their reading—even the White kids. They go a little way and then they stop again. Then the teacher gets up and helps them. They hide their books from each other and they won't tell any other kid if they're having a hard time. They don't help each other. So the teacher has to run back and forth helping just one person at a time (Jan. 10).

So far as we could tell, the children in both of these classes worked diligently and seemed to be learning at about the same speed. (Though the Principal told us that the pupils of the First Grade teacher did outstandingly well on their achievement tests.) The most significant difference was in the wear and tear on the teacher.

## Fighting, General Disorder and the Overcrowded Classroom

Pre-school Indian children have little experience in playing or fighting with strange age-mates. This may account for the fact that during their first weeks at school, Beginners do very little of what White parents would call "fighting with" or "fighting back." Instead, a few boisterous ones nudge and punch the others. Those struck stand amazed, as if this had never happened to them before:

> One little boy, who, at first, had seemed shy, was now running around and tapping or tagging other children. Those

struck did not seem to resent this, but merely turned to look at him with an expression of surprise. . . . One light hued little boy grabbed a Fullblood boy by his shirt, shook him and said (I think) "Blackshirt! Blackshirt!" The Fullblood kid just looked at him. . . . Later, the light kid began to tease a hefty Mixedblood girl. But she turned around and swatted him (August 27).

As the weeks pass, fighting begins to take on different patterns. Sometimes, as in the first example below, it turns into rough play. At other times, as in the second example, it becomes what Indians call "picking on":

> Just in front of me sits the light hued boy who on the first day of school was rather nasty to "Blackshirt," the Indian kid. On each side of him sits a Fullblood kid. These three keep poking and nudging each other like puppies, in complete good nature, each socking the other with equal but not lethal forces, all giggling softly and paying little heed to the teacher (Sept. 5).

> Next to each other were seated two girls: one large, stolid and sad looking; the other, small, alert and covered with impetigo sores. While Miss Rose had her back turned, the little one reached over and gave the big girl's braid a terrific yank. It was not what I would call a teasing pull—but a tug into which she put all her strength. The big girl did not even wince. A few seconds later, the little girl tried to pull the big one's color book away from her, but desisted when she noticed that Miss Rose was turning around. . . . In the three examples of "picking on" I saw in this class today the kids are already adept at noticing whether the teacher can see them. . . . When we went out for recess I asked Miss Rose whether she thought Indian children tended to pick on or abuse each other. "That hardly ever happens," she assured me, "though a few parents complain about it all the time" (Oct. 19).

After the children have attended school five or six months, most have learned to fight back. As children fighting each other make much more disturbance than a bully and his mute victims, this contributes considerably to the noise and disorder of large class-

84

es. The following observations were
made on what a teacher would call a
"bad day." Possibly a White observer
might have found some of this fighting
"natural" or even "playful." The Indian
woman, however, finds it uniformly
distressing. All parties would have
agreed that this class was too large:

> These little kids are really mean to
> each other. . . . They fight over books
> and papers. They fight over just any-
> thing! There was a new boy there—
> everybody that passed him just turned
> around and hit him. . . . I was really
> mad at one little boy. They (children)
> lined up and he kicked them to put them
> back in line. He doesn't even smile! . . .
> Boy it's crowded in that place. . . . They
> talk in Sioux when they quarrel or fight.
> Oh, they talk nasty. He was talking so
> dirty! They know that the teacher doesn't
> even understand them. . . . This room
> is really small for that many kids. . . .
> I went out at 12:30 to watch the kids
> play. My! These children are really rough.
> They fight over the rubber balls. Some
> call each other dirty names in Sioux. . . .
> (Later) I said to my sister: "When I
> send my boy to school I'm going to
> teach him how to fight. . . . If he doesn't
> fight, boy, they will really pick on him
> and take his papers and books away from
> him!" (March 21)

In the early elementary grades, fighting and teasing do not interfere seriously with scholastic accomplishments, so long as the class remains
small. Most of the teachers of these
early grades are competent disciplinarians. When class attendance is twenty
or below (which is rare), the atmosphere of the class is pleasant; most of
the children seem to be happy and
progressing; the teacher has time to
help those who are slow, and in some
classes the children help each other a
great deal. When attendance rises
much over twenty (twenty-five to
thirty-five are usual classroom loads),
class procedure becomes chaotic, and
the teacher is obliged to spend most of
her time keeping order. Very little is
learned, and as an Indian observer put
it: "the teacher has to keep hollering at
them all the time."

## The "Backward" Child

Some of our Indian observers were
more inclined than the White observers to note and comment upon the behavior and plight of the individual
"odd-ball" child—the child who is left
behind.

> One little Fullblood boy was having a
> hard time. He wanted to copy off two
> girls but they would kinda hide their
> papers. When Miss McCoy would say:
> "All of you who are finished raise your
> hands," he would raise his hands, too.
> But I looked at his paper and he hadn't
> done anything. . . . He must have been
> doing this kind of thing for a long time,
> because every kid around him was really
> hiding their papers from him. He was
> the only one that didn't seem to know
> what was going on (Jan. 4).

> When Mrs. Forrester has penmanship
> she makes the kids sit real straight. They
> are supposed to move their whole arms
> like this (with movement from shoul-
> der). One little boy doesn't understand
> her at all. He's a Fullblood and he doesn't
> know English. He was writing just with
> his hands (small finger movements). The
> teacher says (to him): "Move your
> whole arm." But everytime she does that
> he writes like this (finger movements).
> But she says: "Use your whole arm!"
> Finally she got so mad—she had a pen-
> cil—she just hit him on the head—like
> that. Everybody kind of giggled. I was sure
> glad I wasn't in his shoes. I'd sure hate
> to get hit on the head like that (Jan.
> 22).

An Indian staff member interviewed
several of these children and their
mothers. Two "backward" Third Graders stated that if they had their choice
they would stay home and not go to
school. One added: "I don't understand
some of the things we're learning, like
arithmetic. If I ask the teacher, she
tells me, but if I still don't understand
and I ask her again, she gets mad. So I
copy or I ask one of the boys next to
me because I don't want to ask the
teacher." (Jan. 23)

The mothers of these children said
that they had done good work the
year before with a different teacher.

Both felt that the best thing to do was put the children back to the Second Grade so they would be with the teacher they liked. One mother stated:

> At first (this year) he came back and told me the teacher was too rough with him. I told him he was just making up stories. And now he never tells me anything, but he doesn't do his school work.

The other stated:

> He acts real funny ever since he started in Mrs. ............ room. Everytime I holler at him, he'll jump up and he looks kind of lost, like a stray puppy. I don't know what's wrong with him. . . . He sure hates to go to school in the morning. When it's Saturday, he says, "Gee, I'm glad I don't have to go to school." But the other one (a younger brother) he's sure anxious to go to school.

We suspect that both of these children are not so much suffering from a "mean" teacher, as from the fact that they have left a class which is usually kept in excellent order and entered one they must share with noisy and extremely unruly Fourth Grade. In fact when asked what they most disliked about school, both boys said: "The big Fourth Grade boys are real rough to us."

While quite a number of the children in the first four grades are not doing satisfactory work by their teachers' standards, neither the children nor their parents seem to be especially distressed if they fail and must repeat a grade. In the lower grades little children as wretched as those described above are rare. And they, it should be noted, are unhappy not because they do poorly in school but because they are afraid of their teacher and of the big bullies who sit in the same room. When a child of this age can obtain help neither from his parents nor his teacher, he literally has no other resources. Little wonder that he begins to look "kind of like a stray puppy."

## The Parents

Most parents are pleased, if a little surprised, by the enthusiasm with which their younger offspring go to school. They rarely, however, visit the school themselves, except to take a child on his first day. When our Indian observer began to attend classes, one teacher (of seven years' experience) told her: "This is the first time an Indian mother has visited my class."

A few of the younger mothers try to teach their children the A-B-C's and the numerals (perhaps because it is said that children who know the A-B-C's and can count may go into the First rather than the Beginners Grade). On the first day of school, some of the children in the Beginners class began voluntarily to demonstrate their scholastic knowledge. The teacher's attitude toward the parental interest in instruction is noteworthy:

> Several children were writing on the blackboard. One girl had printed her name and the other was chalking up numbers from 1 to 9, but doing this from right to left, e.g., 987654321. Miss Rose called my attention to this and said some mothers went to a lot of trouble to teach their children to print. "Then it may take me months to break them of the habit." I asked why it was necessary to break this habit and she explained that one must learn to "write" first. She related an anecdote of a little girl who had stubbornly refused to give up printing and had insisted: "I was borned of my mother and she should know how to write my name." Miss R. thought this was kind of cute, but added: "It took me till Christmas time to break her of it." "Then there's that girl writing her numbers backward. I'll have to break her of that too. . . . *When the mothers ask me what they can do to help their children, I tell them: 'Don't do anything.'*" (August 27).

## Scholastic Achievement and Age-Grade Level

Table 11 presents the distribution of ages for the various grade levels of the Federal schools in Shannon County of

Pine Ridge Reservation.[5] Basically, the pattern is one of an initial overagedness which becomes increasingly marked in the higher grade levels. Thus, in the First Grade, where normally children are six years of age, a full half of the Indian children were older and over one-quarter were aged eight, nine, or even ten years of age. By the Sixth Grade, three-quarters of the youngsters were overaged, and the teacher was dealing, not with just twelve and thirteen year olds, but with a substantial group of fifteen, sixteen, and even seventeen and eighteen year olds. (An Eighth Grade classroom containing such young adults has quite a different flavor than one composed largely of early adolescents.)

The fact that overagedness increases with grade level is testimony that many Indian pupils do not appear to be learning the subject matters of their grade level in school and so fail of promotion. During the course of this study we attempted to gather the scholastic records of a sample of country Indian children then aged thirteen to twenty-one. We were able to obtain only partial records for many of those on the sample. Even so, the pattern is highly significant: Almost half of these children had been held back one or more grades during the interval between Beginners and Fourth Grade. In addition, we encountered records indicating that a substantial group of these young people had been "socially promoted"[6] for one or several of the elementary grades; usually these promotions were justified in the record on the grounds that the child was becoming excessively overaged for his grade. Consequently, one may argue that the actual overagedness of Sioux children is not as extreme as it might be.

The relative lack of achievement of Indian children generally (throughout the nation) has been documented by an analysis of their scores on nationally standardized tests of educational achievement.[7] These show that Indian pupils generally score better than average at the Fourth Grade level and then progressively decline in achievement. A recent, Federally sponsored study explained its findings as follows:

Since a great majority of the pupils in the present study took the test in October, or the second month of the school year, we will consider their actual grade placement to be 4.1 for Fourth Graders, 5.1 for Fifth Graders, and so on. The mean, or average, score for the composite group of Fourth Graders fell at the 4.3 grade level and that for Fifth Graders at 5.0. This may be considered as not different from "normal" achievement within the meaning of the published norms. However Sixth Grade pupils were at grade 5.5 or 0.6 of a grade level lower than the published norms. Seventh Grade pupils were at grade 6.6, Eighth Graders at 7.2, a retardation of 0.9 of a grade level, and Ninth Grade pupils at grade 7.9 or 1.1 grade levels below "normal" achievement.[8]

---

[5] A study of Indian children in the public schools of South Dakota, 1957-8, shows the proportion overage for their grade as averaging 22.3% for all twelve grades, being about twenty percent in the Second and Third Grades and fluctuating as high as thirty percent in selected grades, such as Eighth, Ninth, and Tenth. (On the whole, the public school situation is superior in this regard to that within Pine Ridge.) "The Age and Grade Placement of Indian Children in South Dakota Public Schools," by John Artichoker, Jr., Pierre: Division of Indian Education, Department of Public Instruction, June 1958, mimeographed.

[6] Various parents and tribal officials question or oppose this practice. Indeed, several adults have told us how they, as Day School pupils, unsuccessfully tried to resist social promotion so that they might repeat a grade and "really learn arithmetic."

[7] In "A Study of the I.T.E.D. Achievement Scores of High School Freshman Indian Students in the South Dakota Public Schools" (unpublished M.A. thesis, State University of South Dakota, 1960), Kenneth L. Deissler has shown that Indian freshmen achieve below the state norms in all nine areas of the Iowa Tests of Educational Achievement.

### TABLE 11

### Class Enrollment By Age

### Composite, Day Schools, Shannon County
### (Kyle, Loneman, Porcupine, Manderson)*
*Date of Report: December 14, 1962*

| Grade & Appropriate Age Level | | 4 | 5 | 6 | 7 | 8 | 9 | 10 | 11 | 12 | 13 | 14 | 15 | 16 | 17 | 18 | 19 | 20 | 21 | Total | Number Over age | Percent Over age |
|---|---|---|---|---|---|---|---|---|---|---|---|---|---|---|---|---|---|---|---|---|---|---|
| Kindergarten | (5) | 1 | 27 | | | | 2 | | | | | | | | | | | | | 31 | 3 | .09 |
| Beginners | (3-6) | | 28 | 73 | 14 | 2 | | | | | | | | | | | | | | 117 | 16 | .13 |
| First | (6) | | 1 | 44 | 20 | 21 | 6 | 3 | | | | | | | | | | | | 95 | 50 | .52 |
| Second | (7) | | | | 29 | 32 | 21 | 8 | 1 | | | | | | | | | | | 91 | 62 | .68 |
| Third | (8) | | | | 1 | 23 | 36 | 20 | 5 | 8 | | | | | | | | | | 93 | 69 | .74 |
| Fourth | (9) | | | | | 1 | 27 | 28 | 22 | 6 | | | | | | | | | | 84 | 56 | .66 |
| Fifth | (10) | | | | | | 2 | 35 | 22 | 19 | 11 | 3 | 2 | | | | | | | 94 | 57 | .60 |
| Sixth | (11) | | | | | | | 23 | 23 | 25 | 31 | 14 | 5 | | 1 | | | | | 99 | 76 | .76 |
| Seventh | (12) | | | | | | | | | 20 | 18 | 18 | 12 | 8 | 1 | 1 | | | | 78 | 58 | .74 |
| Eighth | (13) | | | | | | | | | | 18 | 16 | 14 | 14 | 7 | 2 | | | | 71 | 53 | .74 |
| Totals | | | | | | | | | | | | | | | | | | | | 853 | 500 | .58 |

*The Day Schools outside Shannon County (at Allen and Wanblee) are not included in this tabulation. Also excluded is the Oglala Community School located at Pine Ridge town, which serves both boarders and day scholars.
Source: Office of Reservation Principal, Pine Ridge Agency.

Scores on the California Achievement Tests administered on the Reservation in 1960 and 1961 show a similar pattern of declining achievement.

The results of this program of testing have stimulated a great deal of discussion and speculation among educators. Clearly, most country Indians enroll in school with a tremendous linguistic handicap and nonetheless they are doing exceptionally well by the time they reach the Fourth Grade. Yet, from then onward, when they might be expected to accelerate even more rapidly, presuming they have now mastered the English language, they instead progressively decelerate. The materials we have already presented in this report cast some light on this problem, for it is clear that the children, far from learning English fluently, have been getting by with a rather meager fluency. Moreover, their fluency does not usually improve with age or grade level. We also feel that persons relying on these tests may have been deceiving themselves about the rate of accomplishment in the lower grades: Our own observations of the lower elementary grades indicates that while the atmosphere is happy and busy (and far superior to that of the more advanced grades), nonetheless, there is good reason to doubt whether the children are being adequately prepared for work in the middle and upper grades; this ethnographic observation finds confirmation in our study of grade failure and promotions mentioned above. Perhaps if children in the Fourth Grade are doing so well on national achievement tests it is because they have been exposed to early primary grade work for more than the normal number of years?

---

[8] *The Indian Child Goes to School*: A Study of Interracial Differences by L. Madison Coombs, Ralph E. Kron, E. Gordon Collister, and Kenneth E. Anderson, United States Department of the Interior, Bureau of Indian Affairs, Lawrence, Kans.: Haskell Institute, 1958, p. 35.

In any case, as we turn our eyes toward the intermediate levels of the primary grades, we shall observe abundant reasons for the relative lack of accomplishment on national achievement tests.

*Alienation from School*

When we planned this study, we envisaged the problems of Indian education as being rooted in a struggle between educators, on the one hand, and the Indian community, on the other. As our research progressed, we perceived that these two are, not so much dramatic antagonists contending for the souls of the Indian children, as mutual avoidance societies—neither daring to behold the other. The Indian parent initially brings her child to the awesome school campus, but she rarely ventures to return and penetrate the door to the schoolroom. The teacher, especially if female, fears to leave the campus and the paved roads in order to penetrate into the humble and sometimes squalid Indian home.

In the early elementary grades, children tolerate this dissociation fairly well. Their parents tell them to mind the teacher and to learn and, since their teachers are not ogres, this is what they tend to do. The fact that the teacher may have a rather low opinion of them as Indians is not visible, because characteristically adults regard young children as irresponsible and requiring supervision. So long as their teacher cares for them and maintains enough order in the class to protect them from excessive assault by their peers, they enjoy school. In social psychologese, they have not yet learned to take the role of the other (especially when this other is a non-Indian adult), or as Indian parents characterize these young children, "they don't care."

But Indian children of ten or eleven find themselves in a very different situation. They have learned "to care" with such intensity that a joking or malicious word from a peer or elder can throw them into agonies of mute and blushing embarrassment. They have learned that their peers will laugh, sometimes politely and sometimes maliciously at the slightest error of any child who is engaged in a public performance and that their laughter will always be critical if he has attempted what they define as a "show-off" performance. They have learned that they must stand by or help a member of their gang (or their kin) before outsiders or enemies and that, under no circumstances, may they betray (tattle) a peer to an authority.

With this growing consciousness of social realities, the children find themselves spending most of their waking hours in an environment from which elder kin—a major source of authority —are mentally and physically excluded. Meantime, they have been confronting a teacher whose basic conception of his pupils is extremely negative: On the one hand, he regards them as incomplete beings of "meager experience," and on the other hand, he sees them as dirty and depraved because of "too much of the wrong kind of experience." To counter this, he has been presenting them with moral and practical counsel that is fatuous, given the nature of Reservation life and their own abundant experience of human relationships. Basically, he does not respect them, and as the children begin to realize this, they lose their respect for him and thus the moral basis of his authority is eroded.

If the teacher had the active and intelligent support of the childrens' parents, this might be overcome, but in the present condition of mutual avoidance all the school can obtain is the passive wish of the parent that the child finish school. Again, if the teacher had more potent instrumentalities of discipline at his disposal (such as the corporeal punishment some ad-

vocate), he could maintain the mechanical control characteristic of slavery. However, administrators are loathe to enforce even a mild discipline for fear that this will affect attendance records or cause a scandal in the community.[9]

As Howard S. Becker remarks of schools generally in the world's underdeveloped areas:

> One result of the lack of cultural support of the educational enterprise . . . is that education cannot be really cumulative, cannot progress year by year to new and higher subjects and skills. The teacher can never count on his pupils having already mastered some set of facts or skills just because they have had so-and-so many years of schools, and each year tends to become a repetition of the last, devoted to attempting to make sure that everyone has at least mastered the basic skills of reading and writing. At each higher grade level the gap between what should be learned and what actually is learned becomes greater; teaching degenerates into a desperate attempt to instill some minimum amount of learning. Teachers are tempted in such a discouraging situation to take the easy way out, either giving up completely or devoting their efforts only to those few students who will accept them wholeheartedly and are comparatively easy to teach. The teachers' stereotypes about the subordinate group's lack of ability tend to be confirmed by their experience and leads to less effort being expended where more is in fact required, thus increasing the school's failure.[10]

In the most highly developed situations—of avoidance between teachers and parents and of a lack of respect between teacher and pupils— the schoolroom becomes a veritable no-man's land, where the only check on the Indian pupils is the regard of their peers and the fact that the school

---

[9] Ironically, many Indian parents are critical of this mildness. Their attitude is that children who break a rule of which they are aware should be punished.

[10] "Schools and Systems of Stratification," in *Education, Economy, and Society*. A. H. Halsey, Jean Floud, and C. Arnold Anderson, editors, New York: Free Press, 1961, p. 97.

does provide some basic satisfactions of food, shelter, and a place for communal (peer) amusement. Most parents are ignorant of what goes on within the school, and the embittered teachers take the breakdown of discipline as further evidence of the uncivilized state of their charges.

Since teachers do not know what goes on in each other's classrooms, they are ignorant, not merely of the atrocities perpetrated by undisciplined pupils and outraged teachers, but also of the outstanding performances of the few colleagues who are wise and able. Where a teacher treats the children with firmness and respect and presents his subject matter with devotion, he is rewarded by a peer group that obeys him, quiets the roughnecks, and even encourages the bashful into speaking. An Indian teacher who was outstandingly successful with children of this age group explained his technique to us in the following guarded words:

> Indian kids are good kids; they'll work if you give them work. But they are very sensitive. They know what people say about them. They know. You can't fool them. (Sept. 13)

Given the nature of school systems, this kind of teacher is not likely to be rewarded outside of his classroom. To the extent that his abilities are noted, the administrator will saddle him with the oldest and toughest pupils, and it will not likely be a matter of comment or reward that he brought some sixteen year old's from a Second to a Fifth Grade level of scholastic achievement.

## THE MIDDLE ELEMENTARY CLASSROOM

All in all children of lower elementary grades seem relatively attentive, busy and happy. While a critical observer may often doubt the worth of what they are learning, nevertheless, their classes have an air of order, bustle and general well being. The intermediate grades (Fourth, Fifth, Sixth) generally present a sharp contrast, especially in large schools and large classes (twenty-five and over). Children of the typical rooms appear shy, withdrawn, stupid and sullen. In the "poorer" rooms their shyness is transformed into terror and their sullenness into insolence and cruelty. In this section we will be focusing on the worst rooms not to exaggerate, but because in them the mechanisms that disturb the educational process are more clearly visible.

I enter at 10:30, after recess. The pupils are beginning an arithmetic lesson taken from a book with large and highly colored illustrations representing a circus ring, with clown, horses and acrobats.

Mrs. Walker asks, "How many have ever been to a circus?" There is absolutely no visible or audible response. It would be inaccurate to say that there is silence, because there is enough squirming, whispering, page ruffling, and desk creaking to make the room quite animated.

Mrs. Walker waits a moment and then asks, "How many have been on a trampoline?" Again, there is no visible or audible response. It is as if Mrs. Walker were not there.

Mrs. Walker waits again and then says, "What do you suppose the horses do?" Again, there is no visible or audible response.

Mrs. Walker now explains at some length that in a circus the horses go round and round the ring. As she talks the noise level rises, so that I have difficulty in catching what she says. No one, not even the Mixedblood pupils, pays attention. They whisper, nudge each other, giggle, riffle the pages of the book, open desks and look inside, or sit and stare vacantly as if in a dream.

Mrs. Walker: "How many have ever seen them doing tricks on a horse?" A White boy raises his hand and says, "At the rodeo."

There were more questions but the only one to which any Indian children responded was, "How many have ever seen a clown?" Three raised their hands but said nothing.

As Mrs. Walker continues to ask questions, it becomes clear (to me, at least), that she does not much care whether her queries are answered or not, and she does not herself seem to listen for or to any answers. She now rapidly babbles one question after another, like a radio to which no one present is expected to respond (Aug. 28).

This teacher had taught these same two grades the year before, so she and the children were well acquainted with each other. Some time later, these grades were separated and the "lower Fourth" placed in the same room with the diligent Third Grade and a strict and demanding teacher. Four months later the pupils' behavior had not changed:

Mrs. Forrester really tries, but they wouldn't listen to her. She was trying (to instruct them) in lots of ways, but they are just giggling. . . . If she corrects a girl, she (the girl) won't talk for a long time. She just sta-a-a-nds there. . . . It's just as if she was teaching Beginners. They won't even *listen* to her! She has to talk two or three times, but they won't even listen or answer. They just kind of drove me crazy! I felt like getting up and beating them on the head! They are just like a bunch of dumb Indians! (Jan. 21).

It is highly significant that the breakdown in communication occurs between teacher and pupil and not among the children themselves.

There is a little boy in Mrs. Gruber's class (Sixth Grade) who talks real loud and makes noise to (other) kids. But when she (teacher) asks him to read (aloud) he holds the book right in front of his face so nobody can hear him. She (teacher) says: Mrs. (observer) can't hear you. Talk louder." But he just mumbles and nobody can't hear him. Then when he sat down he was talking real loud again to the kids (Feb. 5).

In Mrs. Walker's class (Fifth Grade), the boys talk in Indian (Lakota) all the time (Feb. 4).

The cooperation and efficiency with which these children sabotage any suggestion made by the teacher is remarkable. Sometimes, as in the following example, the sabotage appears to be undertaken for its own sake. At other times, it enables the children to devote themselves to their own affairs:

Mrs. Walker now calls on a pupil to read a problem aloud and answer it. Immediately two children and then a third get up and go to the back of the room to sharpen pencils. I cannot hear whether the pupil called on answers or not. Singly or in twos, more children go to the pencil sharpener. As they pass me, two of the boys grin at me knowingly. For ten minutes there is bedlam—a rising and falling grind—grind—grind—and sound of moving children. During the less intense grinding periods Mrs. Walker's voice can be heard but not intelligibly. By listening very carefully I, at length, make out that she is calling for somebody to go to the board and write out a problem. Nobody pays any attention to her and as soon as it looks as if the noise might stop, another cluster of kids walks to the pencil sharpener. Still, she keeps trying to make herself heard, and when relative quiet descends it is because the pupils grow tired of their game (Aug. 28).

On occasion a big boy will make a picaresque display of insolence:

At long last Mrs. Walker reads the first problem. "Peter had 85¢ when he went to the circus. He spent 75¢. How much did he have left?" There is still so much noise that I am sure many pupils do not hear the problem. But some begin to figure on paper and some still fool around. One rather big boy volunteers an answer, which I cannot hear, and Mrs. Walker tells him to go to the board and write it down. He rises, strolls regally past the windows, looks out, pauses, looks back at the class and then proceeds to the board. He gives the impression of taking his damn sweet time. At the board he writes numbers less than an inch in height. I cannot read them though I am less than ten feet away (Aug. 28).

More common behavior is a display of bashfulness or fear (which is sometimes genuine) or of stupidity (which is often assumed).[11] Or, perhaps it

---

[11] These children often are very much afraid that their peers will laugh at them if they speak. But their teacher will be angry if they do not speak. By assuming a cringing or idiotic expression they avoid the wrath of their teacher and the scorn of their peers.

would be better to say that the children often behave as if they can not or dare not speak and meanwhile they may giggle or look abjectly terrified. At other times, they behave as if they cannot hear.

> (When the) Fourth Grade . . . took up reading . . . you can't even hear what they are saying. They held their books right in front of their faces. Mrs. Forrester said (to them): "Put the book down." But they'll be ba-a-a-rely talking! (The) next one gets up and does the same thing. . . . I don't know what's wrong with them. (Listening to them read) I felt like I was deaf. . . . When the Fourth Grade kids do arithmetic they just *act* dumb. All they do is copy it off from each other. One gets it wrong and then the whole aisle gets it wrong. The teacher gets mad (Jan.).

> When the teacher turns to the problems on the board, the children stand in front of their work (in an attempt to hide it). Some of them, like the first boy, have written in minuscule hands. Some will not answer her. . . . Once she (teacher) calls on Buddy (a child of our Indian neighbor) and asks him "What is five times two?" Since I had heard Buddy reciting his tables the day before and doing even the "sixes" correctly, I perk up my ears. But Buddy merely looks stupid and shakes his head. I am able to watch as Mrs. Walker corrects papers on the two times five problem and it seems as if only three out of eighteen kids in the Fourth Grade have the right answer (Aug. 28).

Whereas in the lower elementary grades an observer often feels that the children are eagerly learning (be it material of little value), in the middle elementary grades he searches in vain for evidence that they are learning anything at all—except, as some of the critical parents put it, "to fool around":

> Boy, they really had a hard time. And some of them are real big girls! Mrs. Forrester gives them real easy numbers, but they still couldn't get it. Some were standing there counting with their fingers. . . . But it was with the New Basic Readers that she (teacher) really gave up on them. She told me to correct one book and out of the whole book he

(pupil) only got two right answers! All of (the others) were wrong!

> From here on I cannot pretend to follow and record what goes on because most of the time there is so much noise that I cannot clearly hear Mrs. Walker or the "responding" children. What seems to happen (through the noise) is that she reads a problem and asks for an answer. This goes on for twenty minutes with rising and falling waves of sound so that I, though I listen with might and main, never once find out what a correct answer is (Aug. 28).

> The Fourth Grade(rs), nobody will work if she (teacher) leaves them (to instruct Third Grade). One big kid just wrote letters (illicit notes). Out of nineteen kids only three of them were studying. The boys roll up papers and then they throw it at the girls. One little girl worked, but the others were just doing something else, talking and writing notes, and just so *noisy!* They'll be so noisy and talking and like a bunch of magpies, but when the teacher comes over they won't talk at all. They'll just sit (she illustrates, crouching over with eyes on floor). It was just awful with them. . . . Behind and under their desk they (Fourth Graders) will have funny books (comic books) and they'll be reading. She (teacher) didn't see them. They'll even trade the funny books in class instead of studying. They'll hide them under their jackets. She (teacher) told me "I tell them to take off their jackets when it's warm. But they wouldn't take it off." (That's because that's where they hide the funny books.)

> (In the Sixth Grade) one boy sits way in back and he had his arithmetic book out—and right on top he had a comic book. He had it some way that Mrs. Gruber couldn't see it. She didn't even see it when she went right by (Feb. 5).[12]

On one occasion a teacher who had just taken over a class like these, made a particularly poignant comment to an Indian observer.

---

[12] Compare the high noise level and disciplinary problems reported of the Negro slum school by Martin Deutsch, *Minority Group and Class Status as Related to Social and Personality Factors in Scholastic Achievement,* "Human Organization Monograph" No. 2, 1960, chap. vii.

White kids really want to learn. Poor things, they're dumb some times, but they'll try. Indian kids—they're smart, but they wouldn't try. They wouldn't talk to you and they get mad and act mean to you.

The aggression which among the smaller children is often diffuse (in the sense that they run about pushing and nudging any other child within reach) here turns into merciless bullying and teasing of the meek, the helpless, and the handicapped:

A little cross-eyed girl, she was working. She doesn't bother them (other children) but they keep bothering her and hitting her. She just stared real mad at them. . . . Then Mrs. Forrester went out, and I was sitting at her (teacher's) desk. That little cross-eyed girl—the boys and girls just pushed her around right in front of me. They just hit her right in the back, really hard, and they just slapped her. She (cross-eyed girl) was so mad! I said, "Leave her alone." Gee, they were mean to her—they kicked her around. One little boy said (to her) in Indian, "Cross-eyed." . . . By the time the teacher came back everybody was reading and writing. The teacher told me that the other day she (cross-eyed girl) wouldn't go into the classroom. She was just standing there crying. The teacher said (to me), "I don't know why she doesn't want to come into the classroom" (Jan. 21).

Those Black Spider boys were pushing a small boy around—then they grabbed another little boy (held him up?) and let him go so that he fell. He was just helpless! I got after them. I said, "Leave him alone. You're going to kill him" (Jan. 22).

A big boy will make a sign (fist striking palm) to a boy in front. The boy in front will hit a little kid in front of him. The little kid will turn around to see what hit him and the big boy will make a sign at him to show that he made the other kid hit him. They don't make noise at this because they do it by signs (Feb. 4).

Some of the children are clearly distressed by the disorder in which they are obliged to spend their school days:

In some of the classrooms you can see how some of the kids are unhappy.

They just sit there kind of sad. (I think) this is because the other kids are so noisy they can't study. . . .

In the Fourth Grade only three boys were trying (to learn), two White boys and one Indian. (The teacher told me that) the Indian boy is so far ahead of his grade he just wastes his time. . . . These kids try to sit away from the rest of the class so they won't bother them (Jan. 21).

For what it reveals about the dynamics of the middle elementary classrooms, the following observation is extremely significant:

(When the teacher asked questions) one little boy did raise his hand, but he raised it right in front of him, with his elbow close to his belly button and his hand in line with his nose. The other students could not see his hand but the teacher could. He seems not to want the other students to see him raise his hand (Nov. 26).

The Indian bus drivers and cooks are probably more aware of (and certainly more embarrassed by) the gross disorderly behavior of the school children than are the teachers. Some of them recommend the institution of severe corporeal punishment. Our country Indian observer also felt that most of the middle grades lacked discipline, but tended to criticize the current policy of inconsistency and the use of noisy threats which were never carried out:

Sometimes Mrs. Walker hollers real mean and the next time she pets them. They don't listen; they don't care (Jan. 17).

Mrs. Walker and Mrs. Forrester and those others, they are always threatening the kids. You can hear them a mile off. But if they tell them that they are going to keep them in for recess, they ought to do it. Now Mrs. McCoy doesn't holler. She is quiet and she makes them stand in a corner if they are bad. She told me she learned that from Mrs. Blackbird (an Indian teacher) (Jan. 21).

As our observations proceeded, we often wondered what effect the sight of these classrooms was having on our Indian colleagues. On one occasion, after she had described a particularly disorderly room, we asked an Indian mother: "What would you do if one of your kids told you that the other kids were picking on her and keeping her from learning?" She immediately replied just as almost all Indian mothers do: "If any of the big boys is picking on the little ones, I would tell them to tell the teacher. That's what she's there for." But then she added with less confidence: "That's what anyone would say, I guess." Then, softly, to herself, "But it seems as if the kids are afraid to talk to the teacher about their troubles." Now, many months later, we hear that she plans next year to send her children to the little local public school.

*The Peer Society of Indian School-children*

When we first observed the bizarre activities of the worst classrooms of the intermediate grades, we were blinded by our own sophistication. When children refused to speak in class or would respond only in quiet voices, we thought we were observing a shyness that was culturally traditional among Indian peoples and somehow rooted in the personality of the Indian child. Having lived close to Indian families for several months, we had observed how hesitant children were about approaching strangers and how difficult it was initially to engage them in conversation. In speeches and in literature most Bureau administrators also treat this shyness as a historical characteristic of the Sioux. Yet, as we continued to visit classes, we were struck by a most peculiar shift with age: the older the children, the shyer and the less vocal. Fullbloods in First Grade would speak up boldly, whereas in the Eighth Grade they might remain mute to all interrogation. Surely after eight or more years in school, any child should be familiar with it

and have lost whatever fears of the alien surroundings he initially had? What was troubling the older children—were they afraid, and if so of what?

When we asked Indian children, "Why is it that some kids won't answer the teacher?" and, "Why do some kids just go mumble-mumble when called on to read aloud?" and, "Why do some kids write such tiny numbers when at the blackboard?" a number were willing to respond. Shyly, and with giggles, they said, "They are afraid the other kids will laugh at them," or, "They are afraid if they make a mistake they will be teased." Our fullest description came from a Fullblood woman who, although she had not herself been employed by the Bureau, had been in a position to observe the children and the schools for a number of years. She explained,

> When some of the kids try to read or study, some of the others really make fun of them. They even make fun of the writing. If they make one little mistake in writing, the other kids make fun of them. . . . If a kid is very quiet and likes to study, then they tease him about (romancing) some girl that he doesn't like. When the teacher calls on him, he hates to talk because they will make remarks about him.

Little children, she emphasized, were different, because even if teased by adults or older children,

> they don't care; they're still small; they don't know anything. They don't mind about the other kids making fun. . . . But the older ones, they tease each other, and they get more and more bashful.

We had known that the Sioux, like many other Indian tribes, had traditionally utilized teasing as an important instrument for socializing and controlling the child.[13] We had also

---

[13] Cf. Gordon Macgregor, *Warriors Without Weapons*, Chicago: University of Chicago Press, 1946, pp. 135-38.

known that the Sioux had relied on older children for training a child, where Europeans had relied on adults. (Though differences between the Indians and Whites in these matters are real and significant, they can easily be exaggerated. Teasing by peers is an important part of the upbringing of most "White" children, just as admonition by parents is important for Indian children.) What we had somehow not anticipated was that the shyness and bashfulness of Indian children in school would be the reflex of the activity of the peers.

We were also, at times, shocked by the cruelty of the Indian children in their "picking on" some victim, and we realized that parents were truly justified in complaining that the major reason a child might not wish to attend school would be that he was being made the butt of some group of children. For example, a youth in our home neighborhood was a notorious truant; on inquiry, we were surprised to learn that he claimed to like school and to like the learning that took place there. His problem became intelligible when we discovered that, being over-age for his grade, he had been made the butt of a group of younger boys whom he felt he could not combat. They had succeeded in making the school so unpleasant for him that he was loath to attend. We do not claim that this boy was a model of scholastic virtue or ability, and we confess we do not know how well he would have done or how reliably he would have attended in a group of age peers; rather, we direct attention to the difficult situation of children who come under sustained attack by other pupils in their schoolroom.

Performance of a child within the schoolroom is affected in two different ways by the attitudes of his peers. On the one hand, Indians tend to ridicule the person who performs clumsily: An individual should not attempt an action unless he knows how

to do it; and if he does not know, then he should watch until he has understood. In European and American culture generally, the opposite attitude is usually the case; we "give a man credit for trying" and we feel that the way to learn is to attempt to do. Federal schools conform to this principle, and Indian children are thus faced repeatedly with the difficult task of having to perform before an audience of critical peers when they are unsure of their abilities and have reason to expect negative comment from their teacher. Since Pine Ridge dialect English is the continual object of "correction" of most teachers, a Fullblood child can scarcely open his mouth in class without exhibiting himself as the target of possible criticism:

> Another reason they get bashful is that the teacher don't explain. They make a mistake and the teacher gets after (scolds) them, but she doesn't explain. They get ashamed. Then they make another mistake and the teacher doesn't like it. Then they get more ashamed.

This comment, uttered by the same woman who had explained the nature of teasing within the school, refers to the fact that, when Indian children err, their elders "explain," which as we understood it means that they painstakingly and relatively privately illustrate or point out the correct procedure or proper behavior. However, as she had noted, teachers in school do not understand this. Their irate scolding becomes an assault on the child's status before his peers. (At the same time, the teacher diminishes his own stature, inasmuch as respected elders among Indians control their tempers and instruct in quiet patience.)

If a child may suffer then by performing inadequately before his audience of peers, he also has a problem if he is able to perform correctly or excellently, as this may be interpreted as collaboration with "the enemy," i.e. the teacher. In schools, in factories, in armies—wherever an organizational structure imposes one group over another—the subordinates develop a private set of understandings concerning the tasks they are supposed to perform and the deference they are supposed to display. A vocabulary of nasty expressions and gestures emerges for teasing individuals who are suspected of going too far in accepting the authority of the superior. (For example, Indian children often engage in "mock applause" in judgment on the collaboration of a fellow with the teacher.) Yet, while this counterorganization of subordinates acts to limit the exercise of authority, it is not necessarily hostile to the assigned tasks as such but may be even more rationally or efficiently oriented to their performance than is the superior. Military history is replete with tales of insubordinate men who win battles by violating the orders of their superiors. And scholarly biographies likewise contain many instances of crucial learning coming via peers rather than masters.[14] Considering the ubiquity of this phenomenon, one might say that the test of a school is, not what its masters teach, but rather the atmosphere it creates such that children do learn the significant subject matters from each other instead of devoting their energies principally to the inhibition of scholarly learning. We have already referred to one crucial condition for the creation of this educational atmosphere, namely a relationship of mutual respect between teachers and pupils; a second condition appears to be the establishment of a stable society among the pupils such that assault and harassment is kept within limits.

The nature of the peer group and of the teasing that occurs within it, does seem to have been greatly altered by the consolidation of schools. Where Indians attend a small, local community school, they belong to families that are kith and kin. The children tend to know each other and to follow the already established patterns linking their families. A pecking order based on age, physique, and skills gets established, and, after an appropriate period of hazing and testing, a new child is fitted into that order. We had the opportunity to observe the behavior of a local group of about a dozen school children daily over a period of some months. Our office contained some things of great attractiveness to them, especially a typewriter, which they were allowed to use. After our observations of teasing and chaos at school, we were astonished to see how quietly they handled this prize that only one could enjoy at a time. A well-defined system of status existed such that when a superordinate child appeared at the side of the one typing, the latter at once gave way and left the machine to the other. A half-dozen of these shifts might take place within an hour, as children came or went, or were interested in typing or attracted to some other activity; yet, all this occurred without a blow or often even a word.

Bullies do exist within a local community, but their impact is often lessened by the care of the older children for younger relatives and by the knowledge which the teacher (or other adult) develops of the children and their families.

With consolidation of schools these patterns are disturbed. Children now interact with others whose families are relative strangers, and with the establishment of separate classrooms for the various grade levels the older children are effectively separated from

---

[14] Thus the Omaha Indian, Francis LaFlesche, describes how in a mission school of the nineteenth century he was taught English by his chum, who wanted him promoted into the same class as himself. Later, he and this chum instructed two other newcomers, so that they might also join this same class. *The Middle Five*, Madison: University of Wisconsin Press, 1963, pp. 13, 22.

younger ones whom they might shelter. (Ironically, bullying of younger children by older ones sometimes continues, with the older child escaping from his classroom in order to assault a younger child at recess.) The society of children changes from being one representing diverse ages but similar locality to one representing similar ages but diverse locality.

## The Overburdened Peer Society

By its very system of organization, every school provokes the growth of a semi-independent society both among the children of each classroom and among the school children as a whole. Within these societies there flourishes a set of norms and values which may be tangential or even opposed to those of the educators. Notoriously, within the school of the metropolitan slums, adolescents (and even juveniles) tend to prize sexual attractiveness among the girls and physical strength and skill and the willingness to utilize it among the boys. School administrators in this environment judge the competence of teachers by whether or not they can exercise enough control to protect the school property and inhibit the children from open assault and sexuality.[15] In the upper middle class suburbs, the activities of the peer society are not so directly challenging to the educational system. While cars, dates, and

athletic success are far more valued than scholastic competence, still teachers find it easier to maintain order within the schoolroom and children do manage to acquire more of the subject matter taught there. The big difference between the situation of slum and suburb is, not the literacy of parents, but the meshing of values of parents and and teachers. By providing an understanding support of their children in school, parents reduce the necessity of the child to rely so heavily on his peers in his struggles with educational authority. The child who feels abused by the arbitrary authority of the despotic teacher has a higher court of appeal. Also, by the very fact that they have such significant control over privileges and powers, the parents themselves become the target of the adolescent rebellion and demand for greater independence.

In the Indian schools, the children are usually lacking a supportive understanding from their parents and likewise lacking in respect for the teacher. There is then no adult present with the authority and respect which would be required for the establishing of order in the classroom. Because the pupils do value coming to school—both because their elders value education and because school is a relatively pleasant place to be during the day, offering food, shelter, and companionship—they have the motivation to avoid any radical actions that will result in their being expelled. However, if order is to be maintained, then the pupils must themselves create it. To do this, they have to assess each other's qualities and abilities, measuring themselves against each other in the ways children do. They have also to form and enforce a code of behavior. If the mechanisms which they utilize for these purposes are sometimes crude and barbaric, this is not because Indians are barbarians, but because they are children, and children living within a barbaric situation.

---

[15] Cf. the studies of the Chicago public school system, executed under supervision of Everett C. Hughes, as theses and dissertations in the Department of Sociology, University of Chicago: Howard S. Becker, "Role and Career Problems of the Chicago Public School Teacher," (Ph.D., 1951); Miriam Wagenschein, "Reality Shock," (M.A., 1950); John Winget, "Ecological and Socio-Cultural Factors in Teacher Inter-School Mobility," (Ph.D., 1951); Harold MacDowell, "The Principal's Role in a Metropolitan School System" (Ph.D., 1954).

# THE UPPER ELEMENTARY GRADES

## The Silent Classroom

Before proceeding to a description of these classrooms, we remind the reader that about a third of these pupils in the Seventh and Eighth Grades are fifteen years of age or older and seven percent are seventeen and eighteen years old. By White or Indian standards, they are young men and women and, given the nature of Reservation society, most have had a great deal of experience with the elemental facts of life. They have also developed a great deal of self-discipline (which many teachers would regard as stubbornness) and a common stock of values and understandings with their peers.

If the major characteristics of the typical classroom of the intermediate grades are noise and disorder, then those of the corresponding classroom of the upper grades are silence and order. Hours may pass without a publicly audible word being uttered by a student. The extraordinary discipline of these upper grades is the creation of the Indian pupils, who enforce it upon themselves and upon their teachers.[16] It serves as a shield behind which any unprepared, unwilling, or otherwise indisposed pupil may retreat; it transforms most teachers into ridiculous and futile figures; it provides (for the first time in years) a quiet and

orderly classroom in which pupils who wish to daydream, exchange notes, read library books or even study, may do so, disturbed only by the voice of the instructor which they have anyway long ago learned to tune out. Teachers tend to respond in any of three ways: They may resign themselves to the silence and work individually with those pupils who indicate that they are willing to study privately; they may boldly and blindly devote their energies to maintaining the stream of talk and (rhetorical) questions; or, if ruthlessly indifferent to cultural norms against corporeal violence to students, they may shout at, shake, and otherwise assault the silent pupils, until they terrorize them into mechanical responses or into truancy.

The casual visitor to a classroom of these grades may not be aware that the silence is imposed by the students, as most teachers have become adept at concealing their state of Coventry. Thus, teachers will avoid any situation calling for a public verbal response from their pupils and instead give long assignments of seat-work; or, when they have several grades in their rooms, they may work publicly with the younger and more responsive pupils. Leaving such a schoolroom, the casual visitor may feel he has witnessed a well-disciplined class—and he is right!

The teacher who conscientiously refuses to resign herself to the stillness finds herself engaged in an exhaustive struggle. She is continually attempting to gain the public attention of her class by verbal sallies, while they in turn direct at her an unbroken shield of indifference and boredom. The inadequacy of her public posturing is constantly threatened with exposure, as if she were a comedian struggling to elicit a laugh from a difficult audience. One teacher brilliantly supplied all parts to her performance, mystifying the White observer and provoking the Indian observer into the

---

[16] Even in the public schools of the middle class suburbs children sometimes act to restore quiet, when the authorities themselves refrain from action. Jules Henry reports of a "democratically" run Sixth Grade: "As the school year entered the last month, evidence began to appear that impulse release and noise had reached a point beyond the endurance of the *children,* for the children, particularly the girls, began spontaneously to *shush* the class." "Spontaneity, Initiative, and Creativity in Suburban Classrooms," reprinted in *Education and Culture,* edited by George D. Spindler, New York: Holt, Rinehart and Winston, 1963, p. 224.

most careful scrutinizing of facial muscles:

(First day of academic year; Seventh and Eighth Grades combined in one room; there followed a session on rules:)
Teacher: "What do we do while we are in line?"
(Silence)
Teacher: "Do we push; do we try to trip somebody?"
(Silence to my ears, but visibly to her some of the pupils must have indicated the sought for negative.)
Teacher: "No, we don't push. . . . If you spill something (on cafeteria floor) what do you do? Do you just leave it there? . . . "
(Again, silence to my ears, but teacher carries on:)
"No, you are responsible for cleaning up what you spill. So we write: 'Carry trays carefully.'"
She now asked for a volunteer to write the rules on the board and stood there at the front of the room with chalk in hand, pleading for one. Half the boys at the rear of the room raised the tops of their desks, some making a pretense of looking for materials, others just plain hiding behind them, while other boys tried to make themselves invisible. . . .
By a process of pseudo-interrogation which may have yielded some class response I could not detect, the following rules were written on the board:

1. Don't run.
2. Sharpen pencils before school time.
3. Go to the bathroom as we go out.
4. Walk to the right.
5. Come in when the bell rings.
6. Play safely.
   Etc. . . .

(I felt that the absence of the kind of response White kids would have given, must have been a great irritation to the teacher (Aug. 27)
(Same class, Feb. 8, Indian observer)
They were having Reading Skills when I went in—they were reading something called "Atomic Submarines." When she asks them questions about it, I don't see none of them answer. But she says they answer . . . maybe she's a lip reader. Out of the whole room no one made a sound except one boy. He barely whispers to her. He sits in the back of the room. But she says: "That's right. That's right." But I can't hear what they're saying. . . . Maybe he whispers. . . . When I couldn't see who was answering, I moved to the other side of the room to watch. But even then I couldn't see anybody's lips move. I even watched here (pointing to

juncture of jaw bone and skull) because that way you can see if somebody is talking—but nobody moved there." . . . It was just awful. . . . It reminded me of when I went to visit Pierre and there were some blind and deaf there. They were quiet but they made signs, and at least you could see them make signs. But in this class they didn't even make signs. . . . It was like she had a room full of dead people and she was trying to talk to them.[17]

So far as we were able to observe, these young people rarely tease each other in the classroom. Evidently they feel that such an act would detract from the dignity of their combined resistance to the teacher. But as soon as they leave the classroom and teacher, their behavior is transformed.

At about 11:00 she gave them a three minute recess. I went and watched them and, boy!—they were really teasing each other. Noisy—like other kids. Three girls had one of the boys down and they were beating him up and he was hollering. They really act different out of the classroom. But when they went back in the room they didn't make no sound.

*Passive Resistance*

As the pressure of the teacher becomes greater, the resistance of the pupils becomes more grotesque, so that like plantation slaves, they appear stupid or infantile. This, in turn, provokes the teacher into treating these adolescents with a condescension that only little children could tolerate (note the rules written on the board in the example above). Even the tone of voice is that which most adults reserve for babies or idiots, and the pupils exhibit a counter-display of physical helplessness or utter incompetence:

Tests are passed out. Teacher says in whiny voice, "Carmelita, what do we *not* do when we take a test?" (Carmelita says nothing.) "What is the first thing we

---

[17] While this teacher told us that "lack of response" was her most serious classroom problem, she added that she had found the students of another Northern Plains group even *less* responsive.

do?" (Carmelita says nothing.) "Don't draw with your ruler. You'll run into the lines (Nov. 15)."

About 10:30 she (teacher) says: "Get ready for spelling. Come get your papers." But nobody moved. So finally she got the papers and passed them out to them. I wished I was going to school there, because the teacher does everything for them. . . .

(Later) with penmanship she told them just how to fold their papers. Then she said, "Have you folded your papers?" But no one done anything, so she went down the line folding the papers. She treats them like little babies and they act real helpless, like little babies. . . .

A boy busted his pencil and she took it and sharpened it. He could have sharpened it himself. When she gave it back to him, he never even said "Thank you," or nothing (Feb. 8).

When a teacher is excessively stern, the pupils respond with a mechanical execution of the materials:

This teacher is a well-built man. Folks in the community have accused him of violence to the pupils. This may be exaggeration, but he is one of the few upper grade teachers who would be physically competent to battle with the older pupils. His manner is brisk, preemptory, brooking no nonsense, and the youngsters respond dutifully, if quietly and monosyllabically.

All the kids (except one girl who is likely White) have followed the arithmetic model unthinkingly, so that the usual error was failing to reduce the fractional answer to lowest terms. For example 8½ divided by two was always worked as 17/2 times ½ leading to 17/4, and no one looked at the problem as one which could by inspection have been answered as 4¼. Pupils were continually arriving at such awkward answers as 9/60, so that the teacher was finally provoked into scolding, "Have you kids forgotten how to cancel already?!" (May 6)

If the observer has any illusions that the indifference and incompetence of the pupils is not a mask that conceals both shrewdness and a capacity for interest, they are dispelled by events like the following (basketball and the prowess of local athletic teams being the passion of the contemporary Sioux):

About 11:20 the teacher had a phone call. She came back in smiling, real happy, and she thought the kids ought to be happy. She says, "I have good news for you. The boys won the basketball game!" But nobody cared. They just looked at her. And she said: "Well, my goodness, doesn't anybody care at all?" But they was just sitting there. I think I was the only one that smiled. . . .

## Underground Scholarship

Even in the extremely unfavorable conditions of these higher elementary grades, some formal education takes place. In our interviews with these adolescents, we were at first taken aback when pupils who would not or could not converse in English would insist (in Lakota) that next to basketball the thing they liked best about school was reading books.

In the rear of the class is a table with chairs, situated near some bookshelves. Since the class has not yet started and all the pupils not yet present, this constitutes the only clearly vacant area, so I seat myself here. A young man appears, Fullblood in appearance and quiet, standing uneasily near the table. The teacher walks up and says, "Reuben is our librarian." The boy seats himself, facing the rear of the room, and for the next hour and a half reads "Classic Comics" (pamphlets in comicbook format that are based on classical works of literature). The teacher is engaging in public work with the lower grade, and the children not involved are reading, daydreaming, or, rarely, writing at what might well be school work (May 7).

Those children who develop a genuine interest in academic studies have a difficult role to play, since they dare not engage in any public interaction with the teacher, whether seeking assistance or testing their knowledge by answering her questions. They listen to the teacher without appearing to do so, working at their lessons as best they can, occasionally aided by the teacher when she roves from the desk of one pupil to another. A few even spirit books home, for further reading or "illicit" homework. This privatized learning seems especially favored by girls. Comparatively speaking, these pupils do manage to learn a fair amount, for teachers frequently comment that some of their most "withdrawn" or "bashful" students make the highest scores on examinations.

A device favored by the young men is the classroom gang organized about a bright boy. (Unless the teacher intervenes, classes naturally segregate themselves by sex with the boys sitting toward the rear.) Whenever the teacher asks a question, the bright boy answers in a tone of voice audible to the gang but not clearly audible to the teacher. Recently, this method of learning, while excluding the teacher, has been aided in some Day Schools by a policy of dividing the class into groups, each of which sits around its own table:

Mrs. W. began on her health lesson which she meticulously charted on the board and which, I think, none of us at this table saw because of the window glare. She questioned the students with little success. Roy and his friend were busily paging through their health books and held their own conversation on health, sometimes arguing over the lesson. Harry (bright boy) who was doing my questionnaire, had an ear open and would give the answer in a loud whisper directed at the boys across the table, but also loud enough so Mrs. W. could hear and did hear, yet weak enough so she could not be positive who said it. This interchange of lesson continued without any knowledge by the teacher. . . . When I left she said to me with an uneasy giggle, "We arranged the desks so the students would talk more. They do, but not to me." (Feb.)

Before his parents and other elders of the community, this particular bright boy poses as one of the few boys courageous enough to "speak up" in class. His family see him as a brilliant student, the pride of his teacher, and his mother boasts to neighbors that her son learns so fast that he spends most of his time in school "helping other boys."[18] In many upper elementary classrooms, if the Indian pupils learn anything of a scholastic nature, it is through such devices as these. An observer expressed this in more concrete terms:

Little if anything has been done by the teacher for the students. What learning that is done is done by the students themselves. They very easily could have let the first part of the morning go by without doing a thing, however, some of them worked quite religiously (Nov. 15).

---

[18] Two young men who are now university graduates and professionals acted as Day School "bright boys" twenty years ago. Speaking of them, a school fellow said:

Boys like Ezra and Martin, they were not ashamed. They would go up (to teacher) and ask questions. The kids would laugh at them but they didn't care. Then the rest of us kids, after Ezra and Martin did the problems, the rest of us would copy the answers.

Nevertheless, one gathers that in those days peer group organization against the teacher was not so strong as today. A pupil might ask a question of a teacher without becoming a social outcast and, as a number of informants have told us after recounting school escapades, "Somebody always tattled." Today, from about the Fifth or Sixth Grade on, almost nobody tattles.

# Chapter VII

# SUMMARY AND RECOMMENDATIONS

## SUMMARY ANALYSIS: ISOLATION AND EDUCATION

Isolation—lack of communication, social distance—is the cardinal factor in the problem of Indian education on the Pine Ridge Reservation. Because the isolation affects so many contexts—the community as a whole, the school within the community, the pupil within the classroom, and the teacher within the educational system—its effect is greatly intensified.

The Sioux community is isolated from the mainstream of national life and isolated especially from the current where literacy and education are important and common. Sioux do journey from the Reservation area, but in most cases their experiences outside are as unskilled labor and this does not serve to enlarge their educational horizon. Most know that education is important in gaining jobs that pay well, but they have not yet learned what an education consists of or what the individual must do to obtain it. Here, the second context of isolation, that between the educators within the federal schools and the parents of the Sioux children enrolled in them is important. Rarely do parents visit the schools and their classrooms. In turn, teachers rarely leave the school campus and the paved roads to observe any aspect of Sioux life. As a result, parents do not understand what their children should be doing or learning in school and, even when they wish to help their children obtain an education, they do not know what they might do to assist them. Conversely, most teachers know little about Sioux life, and what little they know tends to repel them; thus they find it hard to reach out to their pupils. When classes are small (below twenty) and the teacher and children come to know each other, then a helpful educational relationship may nonetheless develop between them. As classes reach thirty or more in numbers, most teachers find themselves unable to communicate with their pupils and spend most of their time in the vain attempt either to establish discipline or elicit any (scholastic) response from them; this difficult classroom situation leads to a high turnover in teacher personnel, which in turn further aggravates the situation.

Indian children perceive very early what most Whites think of their parents and themselves. Once past the primary grades, they approach each teacher with caution, testing her response to them; if it is negative, they quickly retreat. Some educators and administrators feel that Sioux children should be happy and eager to alienate themselves from a community that seems to those outside to be inferior or repulsive. However, Sioux children do not share the teachers' judgment; they find warmth and security among their family and kin, their world and their life. Attachment to their homes does not inhibit Sioux children from attending and enjoying the federal schools: They like the food, the shelter, the companionship of their peers, and the opportunity for learning and intellectual stimulation. Yet, insofar as the Sioux children and their teachers come to reject each other, their peer society solidifies about activities and values that effectively limit or sabotage the educational process.

The school isolates the Sioux children from their elders who can control them. The school personnel and the Indian community isolate themselves from each other. When, in addition, the teacher and her pupils reject each other, then the pupils are isolated from adult supervision, and the strength and influence of their peer society suffer no checks. Children everywhere tend naturally to organize themselves as peer societies; among some peoples this tendency is limited by other principles of organization, such as kinship and social status. However, among the Indians of the Plains this grouping by generations has been of major significance. Because the modern school system groups and governs children according to grade (and age), it maintains and emphasizes this native Sioux tendency.

When adults—Indians or Whites—cannot reach within the peer society to influence its members, children will organize themselves informally—crudely and even savagely. For the Sioux child, the nature of this peer society and his place within it becomes the greatest factor in his performance within the school: whether or not he is happy and willing to attend, what he learns, and whether or not he dares to recite in class. The child who becomes the butt of his peers—beaten, picked on, robbed—may often be so miserable that he refuses to attend school, despite the encouragement of his elders. Some scapegoating within the peer society is usual, but within the Bureau school it seems to become more severe and cruel as the children become sensitive to the critical judgments of the educators regarding "Indian" behavior. Perverted versions of the values preached in the classrooms enter into the peer society as the basis for invidious comparisons and teasings. Of especial significance here are clothes, their style and impeccable cleanliness—this among a people of minuscule monetary income and lacking running water and electricity in their homes!

Where children come from a conservative, "country Indian," community maintaining Lakota as a domestic language, they tend to continue its use among themselves in school as a strategic device, excluding the teacher and school administrators from their activities. English is regarded, not as an alternate means of communication which brings them into contact with the national society, but as the language of the teacher and other Whites. Accordingly the children have little inclination to utilize English in any context except the classroom or to develop any fluency with it. Disregarding the efforts of teachers, the English they do learn is the dialect characteristic of Pine Ridge, which is substandard in its status within the national dialects of the U. S. and not suitable as an instrument for more advanced education. Accordingly the isolation of the children from the school system and the national society is strengthened and deepened by their lack of fluency in the national language.

A final significant variety of isolation is that experienced by the teachers themselves. As in most schools, teachers seldom visit each other's classes or really assist each other in their management. Meantime, as in most schools, the educational administrators are more concerned with the protection of government property and the maintaining of high attendance and enrollment figures than they are with the formal learning in the classrooms. As a consequence, each teacher is left more or less on her own to struggle with the difficult task of teaching these culturally alien children, most of whom cannot speak English fluently and most of whom are cautious about revealing how much or how little they actually know. Since most of the teachers are of rural Western background and many of them are elderly, they are themselves quite isolated from the metropolitan society of the modern United States. Even if their classroom relations with their Sioux pupils were greatly improved, it is doubtful whether they could do much in the way of preparing them for dealing with modern urban life, except by assisting them to fluency in a standard, colloquial dialect of American English. Unfortunately, few teachers have any training or skill in the teaching of English as a foreign language.

Because the school system is isolated from the Sioux community, the pressures associated with its linkage to the federal bureaucracy are intensified. Administrators find that their careers are more tied to the protection of federal school property and to the securing of high rates of enrollment and attendance than they are to the scholastic achievement or vocational success of their pupils. Especially on the high school level, the concern with "keeping the kids in school" leads to a comedy in which the pupils are neither in school nor out of it, classwork suffers, and conscientious pupils and teachers are frustrated. Likewise, on the elementary school level, the same concern leads to boarding school care for neglected children, an arrangement which may not be the most suitable for the emotionally disturbed.

Among the Pine Ridge educators an ideology has arisen which serves both to justify their current teaching practices and also to insulate themselves further from any contact with the Indian community. According to this ideology, the Sioux pupils are woefully lacking in knowledge, morals and manners because of an inadequate home life. Thus the blunt facts of cultural difference and social isolation between the Indian and the national society are converted into matters of cultural "lack." In fact, contrary to this ideology, the Sioux do not suffer from an absence of culture, except in the sense that they do suffer from social isolation and lack of responsibility and political power. Sioux children are reared at home within the spirit of contemporary Sioux culture, and this is as visible as their speaking of Lakota. The educational and social problems of Pine Ridge do not stem either from a cultural lack or from the simple fact of cultural difference. A

people may be as different from those of the White residents of our Western Plains as are the citizens of Japan or the Soviet Union and still perform creditably in science, scholarship and art. Moreover, the history of the immigrants to this nation demonstrates how people of the most varied ethnic backgrounds adapted themselves to the American economic and educational system, sometimes with outstanding success and virtuosity.

It is true that because the Sioux children are culturally different from the middle class children of urban centers, the educational curriculum and techniques that work well with one will not automatically work well with the other. If educational specialists were thoroughly familiar with Sioux culture and willing to improvise experimental programs with the children and their parents, they might be able to devise educational materials and techniques that would result in high rates of scholastic achievement. This would be the justification for continuation of a federal school system for the Sioux (or other Indians). At the present time, however, the failure of teachers and pupils to perform well using the nationally standardized materials leads to a situation in which teachers and pupils lose respect for each other. The educators believe the Sioux children are so lacking in culture that they cannot master scholastic materials, and the children regard the teachers and their subject matters as "White" and hence legitimate targets of their hostility and indifference. Under these circumstances an enormous amount of time in school is wasted, so far as formal learning is concerned.

By way of contrast, we might mention the Holy Rosary Mission School operated by the Jesuit order on Pine Ridge. Financially, it operates on a meager budget compared to the federal schools. Yet because it respects its pupils and requires more of them it achieves more. Moreover, the Jesuit fathers are far more knowledgeable about the daily life of the community than are the Bureau teachers.

Many readers will wish to know how general are our findings, how applicable to reservations for other Indian tribes of other regions. We can only speak here by inference and hearsay, as we found the task of understanding the community dynamics of Pine Ridge so demanding that we did not have the time to study other reservations and other school situations involving Indian children. It would be our guess that the fundamental problems of isolation and social distance would distinguish most reservation communities and significantly trouble the relationships involved in schooling. However, the particular form that the school problem assumes on Pine Ridge—the struggle between teacher and peer society of schoolchildren—would be limited to the Plains Indian peoples and would not be so marked among peoples who preserve strong clan organizations. Thus we were not surprised when a teacher informed us that among the Northern Cheyenne the children were even less responsive than among the Sioux. On the other hand, we would not expect southwestern peoples (e.g. Navaho and Pueblo) to develop the same kinds of problems within their schools, although other kinds of problems might be equally troublesome.

Concerning public schools, we hear mixed stories. Some situations are reputedly scandalous with Indian children being the targets of discrimination and discouraged from attending school. Other situations of mixed federal and local support have been highly recommended to us, but we have not personally observed them. If possible, selective studies in various areas, focused on the social processes of the school and the community would be desirable. Where statistical studies of educational achievement are used, it will be especially important to deal with random samples or cohorts of the population of Indians and not simply with the proportion who happen to be attending school.

## RECOMMENDATIONS

The isolation and social distance which we have seen as crucial to Reservation problems have been associated with the traditional governmental policy of determining programs and policies independently of the Indians themselves. What is needed in the educational sphere is precisely a thorough application of that principle which has characterized the inception of the present administration in Indian affairs—an involvement of the Indians themselves in the formulating of policy. At the same time, we must caution that Sioux are themselves so varied in their circumstances and so individualistic in their desires and needs, that it is hardly likely that any single program will meet the needs of all. The best that can be done is to construct some range of programs, so that in the best tradition of American life each individual can choose the kind of path that seems most suited to his needs as he understands them.

At the most general, we would suggest that the Sioux be involved in the schooling of their children. At present, the educational administrators of the Bureau prefer to hold the Indians at arms' length, away from the schools, and the parents are content to let others worry about the education of their children. Administrators assure the parents that their children will be educated (and vocationally qualified) if they attend school regularly, and most parents believe this. As we have demonstrated in this Report, the consequence of this policy is chaos within the schools.

Neither resolutions from Area and Washington Offices nor P.T.A. type organizations can bridge the gulf between Indian community and federal school. Only an organizational change, such as transferring some authority and responsibility to community representatives, offers the probability of being effective. The most drastic procedure might be the simplest and most effective—namely, transferring control of the elementary school system to a board elected or otherwise selected by the Indians themselves. Funds would continue to be advanced by the federal government under Johnson-O'Malley or parallel legislation and would be subjected to the same types of budgetary and auditing controls as are routinely applied when agencies or institutions receive financial support from the federal government in return for performance of specific services.

The process of transition may be awkward unless there is careful preparation and unless the Sioux population has some period of time to discuss the change. If the Sioux generally disapprove of the change, then it should not be attempted; more temperate proposals (to be discussed later) involving joint boards of Bureau officials, Tribal representatives, and outside parties may then be appropriate. Whatever organizational changes are proposed, consultation with the Sioux and careful preparation should make the period of transition less troublesome. However, since altercations about curriculum, moral values, graft and nepotism, are aspects of the political dynamics of school systems generally throughout the U. S., observers should not be startled when they occur within a tribal school system on the Pine Ridge Reservation. The advantage of democratic organization anywhere is not its superior efficiency to a benevolent autocracy but rather its salutary and educational effect on the populace that participates; in the long run, it is the total Sioux community (rather than merely their children) who will become educated through assuming responsibility for

the operation of their school system. Accordingly, we have specified that control of the school system be turned over to the Indians rather than to a public school board. While we ourselves have not thoroughly examined the public school systems serving Indians, it is our impression than in too many situations the Indians themselves still do not participate in the educational process and have not become involved with the selection of the school board and the setting of policy. Even on Rosebud Reservation, which has an energetic tribal political machine, the Sioux have not so far attempted to elect anyone to the school board. Accordingly, we advocate transferring control over the elementary schools directly to a board elected or otherwise selected by the Sioux themselves. In the long run, we would hope to see amalgamation of the Indian and public school systems, but we feel that this kind of integration might best be left to the local populace itself to negotiate, when the various parties are ready for it.

The matter of secondary education is more complex because of the desirability of providing abundant opportunities for off-reservation schooling, from junior high school onward. For most Sioux and most Indians generally, economic and social betterment means involvement with modern urban society; it means familiarity with the great metropolitan centers where most of the factories, educational centers, governmental offices, business enterprises of the nation are located. Adjustment to urban life is not something than can be learned in a school in an isolated Reservation area, especially when most of the educators are themselves country folk preaching small-town attitudes and values. The natural and time-honored age for migration and acquaintance with the city is adolescence. Present programs for introducing Indians to the city ("Relocation") are designed for older persons, usually married and with family responsibilities; the strain of adjustment to urban life for a family with young children is extreme. Accordingly, we suggest that programs be established whereby Indians, *if they and their parents so desire,* could receive their formal education, from junior high school onward, in the regular schools of metropolitan communities. On Pine Ridge, most high school students are boarders, supported by the federal government. The fundamental modification here being suggested is the establishment of dormitories or boarding homes in urban localities, from which Indians would leave daily for instruction at some local (urban) school, together with other pupils residing in the area. Operation of this program should to some extent be under the control of adult representatives of the Indian community.

We do not assert that urban schools are ideal or even good, and we recognize that many schools in urban slum neighborhoods offer no better scholastic or social training than the present Reservation schools. But even at their worst, they give a pupil the chance to learn to speak English fluently and to learn about city life.

We also recognize that some cities which already have what they judge to be an "Indian problem" (e.g. Rapid City) would not be hospitable to the introduction of adolescent Indians into their school system. On the other hand, we would guess that other urban school systems would welcome the federal monies that would compensate them for educating Indian youngsters. We also recognize the knotty legal and moral tangles ensuing from the fact that the federal government would be paying the cost of board and room for some Indians (those living on Reservation) and perhaps not for those whose families had migrated to the city. Yet we feel there is a fundamental need for urban, off-Reservation schooling for adolescent Indians, and

that the present disposition to educate Indians in isolated rural regions is a socio-cultural anomaly that defeats any program for encouraging Indian adjustment to modern society. Since the beginnings of civilization, a fair number of young people from outlying or rural regions have migrated to the cities for various combinations of education and employment. Denying this opportunity to the young Sioux seems to be doing no one any good. Of course, the educational effects of living and attending school in a city can be negated by following the pattern of the present Reservation boarding schools, *e.g.,* confinement of pupils to "campus" after class hours, tolerance of poor scholastic work, rules inappropriate to age level of students, penalties which are rarely enforced, supervisors (White or Indian) who see their major function as training the pupils in their conception of middle-class morality.[1]

Whatever the school arrangement for the Sioux (whether on or off the Reservation), the mingling together of their children with children of other ethnicity and other language could be markedly stimulating. The Sioux perform best under the challenge of outside competition (witness their triumphs in intermural basketball) and attending school with different children might encourage the powerful Sioux peer groups to coalesce about success in that struggle, rather than devoting their major energies to frustrating the educators. Matched against children from well-educated families, the Sioux might find the contest so difficult as to be humiliating, but with other children who also suffer from an educational handicap, they might be on a par. Perhaps the best and simplest dormitory arrangement would bring together children of several different

---

[1] Some otherwise able high school teachers automatically call a boy-crazy girl a "poor student."

Indian language stocks. Here the commonness of being "Indian" would be helpful, while the language differences would encourage the usage of English as a *lingua franca*. Instead of the Reservation situation where E n g l i s h is the "White" language used only in dealing with teachers, E n g l i s h would become the natural language for communication among the students themselves.[2] Significantly, many Indians on Pine Ridge recognize that the schools do not motivate their children toward competence or excellence and there might be much popular support for any reorganization that would increase the demanding nature of the schools—short of the point where the children felt so incompetent that they felt they had to quit.

Because of the clear advantages of this mingling together of different types of pupils and of bringing Indian adolescents to u r b a n environments for their secondary studies, we are inclined to favor the maintenance of a significant role for the Bureau of Indian Affairs in the educational area. At the same t i m e, we feel that the present o r g a n - izational structure placing all power with the Bureau and none with the Indian community has many drawbacks both for the operation of the schools, the education and development of the Indian communities, and (not least) the education and self-respect of Bureau employees. As one type of suggested organizational change, we propose that the educational policies for secondary level schooling within each Area of the Bureau be placed in the control of a Board, some of whose members would be Bureau administra-

tors, *ex officio,* and some of whose members would be elected by the Indian communities in the area, and some, perhaps, educational consultants.

The foregoing represent our major policy suggestions. In addition, we offer a number of minor suggestions with reference to the current situation on Pine Ridge. First and foremost would be to improve the system of teaching English. Most Sioux children live in environments where little English is spoken and where that which is spoken is a substandard dialect ("Pine Ridge English"). The work of structural linguists in developing techniques for the efficient teaching of languages, including English, is now well known. At Pine Ridge, English is still being taught by traditional methods that emphasize reading and the formal grammar of written English. To the extent that spoken English is presented, it is non-idiomatic. As a result, most pupils in the Eighth Grade are not able to speak English fluently. Pine Ridge teachers need training in aural-oral techniques of teaching English.

Second, the school should solicit volunteers[3] from the local community to assist both the teachers in controlling and operating their classes and the bus drivers in maintaining order on the buses. Auxiliary personnel are especially necessary when classes climb in size over twenty. They would also be especially useful in handling and aiding youngsters who are in difficult emotional situations, whether because of troubles at home or conflict and teasing from their peers. As professionally trained teaching help becomes scarcer and more expensive, there will be increasing advantage to having local folk available to assist the school staff. Professionally trained guidance workers or psychologists are too scarce

[2] Sioux today commonly speak English in the presence of Crow, Navaho, and other tribal visitors or in-laws. Ironically, the best English we heard Sioux speak was at Fairs or other entertainments when they were addressing themselves not to White people but to Indians who could not understand Lakota.

[3] Ladies Aid societies might be induced to assist on a rotating basis among their membership.

and too costly; besides, even those who have been with the Bureau for some years tend to be ignorant of Indian domestic life. Finally, it should be mentioned that insofar as teasing and related phenomena of the peer society utilize Lakota and other devices understood within the Sioux community (but not evident to teachers), there is additional advantage to the presence of Sioux adults.

Third, the school day should be examined from the perspective both of teachers and pupils. Teachers who are expected to perform the difficult task of handling large classes of Indian youngsters should not be saddled with excessive hours of required responsibilities, and certainly so much of their responsibilities should not center at their desks. If p r i n c i p a l s are going to be allowed or encouraged to impose extra-curricular projects (such as monitoring evening movies, leading Boy Scout troops, or hauling children on a weekend excursion), then these should be considered part of their formal hours of responsibility. Teachers need free time to read, keep abreast of their field, plan lessons, and simply relax by themselves. Moreover, the present system of assigning those particular civic responsibilities keeps teachers so occupied that they do not have the time to relate informally and naturally to persons within the Indian community. Conversely, the present (nine to four) day of classwork might well be shortened for the benefit of the children, especially the young. The present assumption that confinement within the school building is equivalent to education simply means a lot of wasted time in the classroom: Neither children nor teachers are capable of that sustained study. Shorter class periods with more concentrated and effective work would benefit pupils and teachers alike. What might be a far more desirable situation would be to have a free hour every day within the school where children might select among clubs, library work, personal projects, or athletic activities. If, in these clubs children conversed with *each other* in English, so much the better. Younger children might simply be released for informal play, with an adult present.

Fourth, teachers should be given the opportunity to learn from each other via a program of systematic visiting of classrooms of the same grade level in other schools. By watching other teachers and talking informally with them, much of benefit could be transmitted in the way of techniques of working with Indian youngsters. The present system leaves "indoctrination and orientation" to overworked superiors who themselves are no longer actively engaged in teaching. Teaching Sioux children is not easy. It requires care and understanding, and there is much that a good teacher can illustrate in her actual operation of a class. Verbal orientation and teachers' meetings are relatively unsatisfactory and have a tendency to become ideological, *e.g.,* "they (pupils) should be taught to respect the staff."

Fifth, measures should be taken to increase the opportunity for Indians to tune in on events in the Bureau and the national society generally. Sioux response to Bookmobile service might be surprisingly high; alternatively, each school might have a modest library available for loan to adults—preferably staffed by volunteers from the local community. A radio program for a brief period each week with news and announcements in Lakota and English could be arranged with stations near the Reservation, either as a public service or sustained by advertisements from merchants and manufacturers who sell to the Sioux.

Sixth, there should be a parent's evening at the school one night a month, using the school bus system to transport parents both ways. Programs of educational films together with discussions by teachers of the nature of their classwork and the tasks required of the youngsters should be presented. A real effort should be made to induce Indian parents to attend. If necessary, a "feed" complete with boiling meat could be provided, for it is only in the relatively relaxed and informal atmosphere of a social affair that congenial parents and teachers may meet on a level of parity, develop relationships of mutual respect and, perhaps, initiate friendships. (The present P. T. A.'s might well be dismantled, since they tend to be vacuous organizations that do not involve the community with the schools.)

Seventh, to the extent that there exists a policy against hiring local personnel as teachers, this should be reversed. Local Fullbloods should be hired, just as anyone else, on the basis of whether or not they can demonstrate competence to conduct classes and encourage learning. If difficulties with kin in the community affect their performance within the school, then they should be subject to the same sanctions and alternatives as other teachers. This kind of personnel problem is an additional reason for transferring control of the elementary schools to the Indian community itself.

Eighth, the present system for caring for young children by a boarding school facility schould be examined critically. The Oglala Community School operates a dormitory for children age six and older who do not have a stable family; in effect, this constitutes an orphanage for emotionally disturbed children. Supervision of the care of orphaned and neglected children requires specially trained personnel and it might well be detached from the school system itself. Depending on the arrangements that can be worked out, placement in foster homes might well be superior to the present orphanage system, at least for the younger children.

Ninth, the present curriculum should be re-structured so as to provide vocational programs for those adolescent pupils whose interests and abilities turn in that direction. The closing of the program in vocational agriculture should not mean that the Sioux child can only select an academic program. Vocational opportunities for skilled laborers are numerous throughout the U. S., and many Sioux youngsters display marked gifts in these directions. Here, especially, the opportunity for migration to trade schools in urban settings might be appropriate, providing the young people were sent together in clusters of a half-dozen or more. Vocational training needs to be stressed because some Indian leaders have been so concerned about the problems of the Indian student in college that they have neglected the large numbers of youngsters who drop out of elementary or high school with insufficient training for gainful employment. At present, the large proportion of Sioux children do not graduate from high school, and when they drop out they find themselves ineligible for further schooling of any variety and unable to obtain employment. Haskell accepts only graduates of high school, and other federal programs of vocational training are open only to adults. If the program of the Oglala Community High School were to be stiffened and made academically adequate, this would benefit those youngsters who are oriented toward college, but it might further discourage those whose interests and talents lie in the direction of the skilled trades. Many urban high schools and trade schools are designed for youngsters whose interests and talents are not directed toward an academic curriculum, and similar programs ought to be made available to Sioux youngsters.

Tenth, school and dormitory regulations and discipline for adolescent pupils should be re-examined by a committee including representatives of the entire Indian community. Present disciplinary programs are formulated by educational and guidance personnel, most of whom have little awareness of Reservation life and fail to distinguish properly among educational, moral, and administrative goals. These programs of discipline cannot really be enforced, because of counter-pressures from the Indian community protecting the violators. Strikingly enough, many Sioux adults express themselves in favor of stern regulations and discipline for the school; yet, at the same time, a fair number feel that the present personnel are often unfair or cruel in their actions. A public review of such chronic dormitory problems as theft, drunkenness, truancy, inadequate clothing, and neglected children is sorely needed. While no system of rules and discipline can ever be wholly satisfactory, it seems likely that, with the cooperation of the Sioux community, policies can be formulated that will improve the atmosphere of schoolroom, dormitory, and school campus.

Eleventh, in line with suggested new policies for vocational training and discipline, it should be desirable to improve the situation of the over-aged pupil. Today, the adolescent within a classroom of juveniles is the source of profound disturbance: either they taunt him or he bullies them and the regulations of the teacher seem wholly inappropriate to his age and situation. Social promotions solve this problem at the cost of creating others. Ungraded classrooms may be a solution.

Twelfth, educational materials in the area of Indian and Sioux ethnohistory and current affairs should be introduced as units in the school program of U. S. history and social studies. High school programs might feature guest speakers on such topics from the universities at Vermillion and Brookings.

Thirteenth, the Tribal Council should establish a guidance and counseling office designed primarily to assist Indian youngsters in educational and vocational choices. The most important duty of this office would be to collect materials on scholarships, vocational programs, colleges, trade schools and the like and to make this information known and available to all Sioux youngsters. Because youngsters do not know about these programs and benefits, many of them fail to prepare themselves properly to take advantage of them or do not apply early enough and soon enough to the right agencies. The person or persons working in this office should be urged to journey to all parts of the reservation and to speak both to parents and children in homes and at public gatherings about the opportunities available to Sioux youngsters and about the steps that need to be taken to secure them. Also, youngsters should be encouraged to form small groups for taking advantage of off-reservation schooling and jobs, rather than going out individually.

Fourteenth, the tribal councils of the Western plains should organize themselves collectively to assist off-reservation Indians in obtaining schooling for their children. We have been informed that because of their migratory status and their poverty and because of discrimination against Indians, children of some Indian families may be deprived for months and years of the schooling to which they are legally entitled. In some situations, children are discouraged from attending school either by the educators or by other children. Tribal officials investigating these matters might secure valuable assistance both from the BIA and from the various national organizations devoted to Indian interests (the National Congress of American Indians, the Indian Rights Association, and the Association on American Indian Affairs).

Fifteenth, area and Reservation administrators might review the literature on team teaching and experiment with its feasibility. Possibly it might facilitate the orienting of new teachers and reduce turnover during the first few months of work with Indian pupils. Team teaching might also reduce the isolation experienced by most teachers and stimulate those who have become jaded. Ideally, teams might be ethnically and geographically mixed in membership, including both Sioux or other Indians and persons familiar with urban and off-Reservation areas.

## RESEARCH RESULTS AND THE ORIGINAL THEORIES

For convenience in discussion, let us state again the original theories by which we oriented our research efforts:

*Theory 1. Cultural Disharmony.* To children reared in conservative Indian fashion, the atmosphere of a normal, American school is painful, incomprehensible, and even immoral; whereas, to teachers of (normal) lower-middle-class American background, the behavior of these students is often undisciplined, lacking in scholastic initiative, and even immoral.

*Theory 2. Lack of Motive/Unappealing Curricula.* The notions of the Indian people themselves as to careers that are possible and desirable are sometimes much at variance with those of the educators. Where this variance exists, dropout of adolescent students is exceedingly likely.

*Theory 3. Preservation of Identity.* To conservative Indians, their identity as Indians is the last and most valuable treasure remaining to them. Insofar as education is presented to them, or perceived by them, as a technique for transmuting their children and their people into "Whites," then it becomes freighted with all manner of emotional complications and is likely to be rejected.

Let us begin with the second theory. Here our findings partly contradicted and partly confirmed our expectations. Sioux parents and their children generally see education as the key to vocational success. Conscientious parents, therefore, assist and encourage their children to attend school so far

as they can. However, there has been little employment available on or near the Reservation where most Sioux would prefer to dwell, and so most folk have modest occupational goals. Girls generally say they wish to be (practical) nurses, and boys more diffusely speak of being ranchers or rodeo-riders. If the girls do stick it out through high school (and eschew marriage and pregnancy), they can go on to nursing school in a neighboring city, and employment is thereafter available to them. Or girls may study secretarial skills and seek work with the B.I.A. However, for the boys the situation is less promising: many drift into occasional work as farmhands or ranchhands. Otherwise, they can migrate to nearby cities, but without definite skills and occupational savvy, their job careers are uncertain. Sticking it out through high school scarcely seems to lead anywhere, although many boys (even dropouts) will themselves declare that, without schooling, they can only look forward to being "bums." An elite few of the pupils do graduate from high school and go on to college; of these many have a difficult time even at the modest teachers colleges operated by the State of South Dakota. However, those who have some college education tend to be respected on the Reservation, and if they do not secure positions with the Bureau, they can occasionally obtain employment with the Tribal Council.

Some of the older Sioux think of ranching as the natural vocation of boys. They talk with nostalgia of the farms and livestock formerly maintained by the federal schools (especially the school at Genoa), and recall the days when a lad could earn a calf or colt by faithful tending of a herd. These adults think that the elimination of the vocational agriculture program in the schools has been a mistake. This was about the most serious criticism of the school curriculum that we heard from anyone. Here it is relevant that some college educated young men, not trained in agriculture, nonetheless look forward to establishing a herd on their land. We could not ourselves decide whether their goal here was to provide occupations for their kindred or simply that of investment—in the sense that land and cattle represent wealth to the Sioux (as silver and sheep do the Navaho).

The federal educators are not so vocationally oriented as their charges. Rather, they see education as a good in itself and as good for the Sioux in the sense of training him in a set of "unIndian" virtues. While the now-discarded vocational agriculture program was conceived as equipping the Sioux for ranching and subsistence farming, the present courses are more academic and in accord with the general national philosophy that almost every child needs a reasonably tough, reasonably academic schooling in the first twelve grades. Accordingly, trade school work is conceived of as post high school, although the irony is that the pupils for whom this might be most suitable have by then dropped out. Some Bureau officials point out that if vocational programs were standard high school fare, the problem would be that the graduates could not obtain jobs because of their youthfulness and their lack of social maturity. As to chronological age, they are perhaps not correct, because so many of those whom trade courses might otherwise induce to stay in school are already fourteen and over in the Eighth Grade; if such persons were to remain in school for an additional four years of largely vocational training, they would be eighteen and over on graduation, which is not too young for the labor market. On the other hand, youthful Sioux, especially those fresh to the city and isolated from kith and kin, are likely to have a difficult time adjusting to the rhythm of regular factory employment (al-though they might do much better with the intermittent pattern associated with the skilled construction trades). Bureau administrators prefer to educate—and business personnel offices to hire—the older, married man with children to support, and they have experience on their side; however, the consequence of this preferment is to create a profound social and educational problem concerning the Sioux adolescent who finds the academic curriculum and atmosphere of high school intolerable.

In summary, then, one dimension of the problem of Sioux education is posed by the lack of coherence between the school curriculum and the vocational possibilities open to the children, especially the boys. As this is, basically, a problem that plagues school systems all over the country, it is not particularly attributable either to the Indians or to the Bureau. It is however a problem somewhat exacerbated by the isolated location of the Indian Reservations.

With regard to the third theory, we found that while the federal educators do think of the schools as designed to make the pupils "less Indian," the Sioux adults do not seem to be concerned about this, but take the more pragmatic attitude toward education as qualifying them for better paying employment. They tend to think of their Indianness as an intrinsic part of their being, not to be altered by scholastic experience. Those persons who consistently disobey community norms are either "crazy" (i.e. youthfully wild and undisciplined, but nonetheless "Fullbloodedly" Indian) or they are "Mixedblood," the latter condition being spoken of as if it were a matter of heredity.

However, insofar as the educators orient themselves toward rendering their pupils "less Indian," they tend to foster a situation that, aggravated by the "Cultural Disharmony" of the first theory, tends to gravely handicap the operation of the school system. Here, the first theory requires reinterpretation. We found, generally, that Sioux children do like school. When they dislike school (and are moved to play hooky or quit), the immediate cause is more often their Indian classmates than their teacher. Some teachers are considered "mean" and accused by parents of cruelty to their youngsters; however, in general, teachers either are liked or do not constitute the primary source of student woes.

Teachers do encounter difficulties in conducting their classes, because some pupils do not wish to recite publicly or do not wish to be placed in a competitive situation with their classmates, but the difficulty here is not one of direct conflict of White and Indian values, so much as a struggle between school and Indian peer society.

As has been noted by other students of school systems, the school tends to foster the growth of a peer group or peer society among children of the same classroom, grade, and school. This peer society tends to organize about a set of values and behaviors quite distinct from those formally espoused by administrators as suitable for the pupils. What we find in the federal schools is an elaboration and intensification of this process. The cultural and linguistic gulf between teacher and pupils, augmented by the great social distance between federal employees and Indian parents and augmented further by the bewildering impact of a curriculum supposed to render the children socially more acceptable (to a small-town or lower-middle-class milieu), creates a situation in which the teacher finds herself with virtually no influence over the peer society. Since her pupils are not hostile to her or the school or to lessons in and of themselves, she can often accomplish something with the individual pupils, insofar as she can free them from interaction with their peers. However, the instrumentalities in her hand are relatively feeble, and many teachers in the intermediate grades find their primary task is that of gaining enough attention and response from their classes so that any kind of formal educational activity can proceed.

## FINAL COMMENT: THE SCHOOLS IN THE U.S.

Especially in the slums inhabited by ethnic minorities, the tensions of urban schools are markedly similar to those which we have been describing in the reservation context. The picture of an exotic community, such as Pine Ridge, sometimes furnishes the contrast by which we can perceive more clearly the functionings and malfunctionings of parallel institutions in more conventional settings. This illumination is the more valuable in the case of our schools, as these tend to be surrounded by a continual fog of rhetoric, hope, and abuse, so that their actual problems are hidden by attack and critique of particular educational and social ideologies.

Urban educators are isolated from the cultural and social milieux of their pupils, as are reservation counterparts. Knowing little of their pupils' life, and terrified or appalled by what they do discover, they justify their avoidance with a "vacuum ideology" of cultural deficiency and deprivation which ignores and derogates the values and knowledge that the pupils have acquired in their homes and neighborhoods. Meanwhile, the educators preach morals and manners that are vacuous or fatuous given the realities of the domestic lives of the children.

The gulf between educators and pupils is deepened by differences in language or dialect of English. The children are subjected to courses designed to teach them a dialect of English that is considered "correct" by pedagogues, but since few of the latter have any skill in linguistics or have the assistance of the electronic equipment so helpful to efficient instruction in spoken language, the coursework is usually more productive of classroom tension than of learning. Moreover, children from an ethnic slum see little utility (and much possible loss in prestige) in acquisition of the dialect associated with the overlords of the educational establishment; yet without oral fluency in a "bookish dialect" they will find themselves increasingly handicapped as they move upward through the grades. Learning to read a language is not difficult, providing that the alphabetic representation is reasonably phonemic and that the written messages correspond reasonably (in morphology, syntax, and subject matter) to the spoken utterances; but when these correspondences are slight, as when oral and written dialects differ markedly, then learning to read becomes a chore requiring the ablest intelligence and keenest motives. Phrasing the problem as one of "why children can't read," befogs the profundity of the linguistic and cultural separation between the pupils and the learning materials proffered by the schools.

The adults who are parentally responsible for the slum children are usually as hesitant as their reservation counterparts about involving themselves with issues of schooling. Being themselves poorly educated, they find the new lessons beyond their ken. Should they dare to enter the school building, they confront educators who are armored in more stylish dress and who wield a polysyllabic vocabulary of educational technicalities. With more elemental needs pressuring them, the slum parents are usually satisfied to leave schooling to those who claim competence and to hope that their children will thereby or somehow become vocationally qualified.

Given the abdication of their elders, and confronting teachers across a gulf of difference in age and culture, the slum pupils organize themselves into a cohesive society. The school campus provides an essential locus for their meeting and activities, but the values of the school personnel are seldom their values. Some few educators do manage to work through the peer society to transmit some formal learning; however, most educators fight a continual battle just to maintain classroom discipline, and the turnover of new teachers is high.

Thus, in a basic sense, the problems of the Pine Ridge schools are not problems of "Indian education" so much as problems of "general education" in a society which requires the schools to be ethnic melting-pots and ladders of social mobility.

# APPENDIX: RESEARCH PROCEDURE

## STAFF

The principal staff of the Project and the co-authors of this Report were:

Murray L. Wax (Ph.D., Sociology, University of Chicago), Project Director, Associate Professor, Division of Teacher Education and Department of Sociology and Anthropology, Emory University.
Rosalie H. Wax (Ph.D., Anthropology, University of Chicago), Research Associate.
Robert V. Dumont (B.A., Montana State University), Research Assistant. Mr. Dumont is a Sioux-Assiniboine from Fort Peck, Montana, and has been named a John Hay Whitney Scholar for 1963-64.

As these principal members of the staff were strangers to Pine Ridge, a number of persons native to the reservation were recruited as field assistants. Of these, the most important were Mrs. Roselyn HolyRock (née JumpingBull) and Mr. Gerald One-Feather. Mrs. HolyRock was interpreter, companion, and friend of Mrs. Wax and accompanied her in most of her visits to Sioux homes. Later, Mrs. HolyRock worked as an independent observer and interviewer. Mr. One-Feather served as a field assistant for the first six months of the Project. He and his family introduced the principal staff of the Project to many aspects of Sioux life which they might otherwise not have come to observe and experience.

Several other residents of Pine Ridge were employed temporarily by the Project and contributed to the collection or recording of data: Henry BlackElk, Jr., Marlene Foote, Calvin JumpingBull, David BlackCat Long, Vivian Arviso OneFeather, Eugene Redearhorse, Moses TwoBulls, and Patricia Catches Whalen. Besides these persons named, many others, Indian and White, contributed generously of their time, counsel, and opinions.

The following persons acted as consultants to the Project:

Robert K. Thomas, Director, Carnegie Cross-Cultural Education Project (University of Chicago);
Robert Rietz, Executive Director, American Indian Center, Chicago;
Tillie Walker, Field Director, United Scholarship Service for American Indian Students, Denver;
Everett C. Hughes, Professor of Sociology, Brandeis University;
Sol Tax, Professor of Anthropology, University of Chicago;
Staff of the Division of Teacher Education, Emory University, especially Edward T. Ladd, Chairman, who proofread our manuscripts with a keen and critical eye.

In addition, encouragement and suggestions were received from Jay Brandon, Edgar Z. Friedenberg, Eleanor Leacock, Gordon Macgregor, Phyllis Pearson, and Omer C. Stewart. Field notes and working manuscripts were exchanged with two other scholars currently studying the Sioux, Robert A. White, S.J. and Robert E. Daniels, and with two scholars studying mental health problems of the boarding school at Flandreau, Donald D. Hartle and Janet A. Hartle. Dr. Philleo Nash, Commissioner of Indian Affairs, provided great assistance to the conduct of this Project by instructing the staff of the Bureau to provide us with whatever information we required for the Project. Most of the secretarial labors for the Project were performed on the Emory campus by Mrs. Karen Bishop.

## RESPONSIBILITY

This report is the responsibility of the senior staff members, Murray and Rosalie Wax. Robert V. Dumont contributed in so many ways to the collection of data and its interpretation and analysis that he must be considered a co-author; however he bears no responsibility for the specific recommendations. While these principal staff members benefited greatly from the comments and criticisms of others, no other persons—Indian or White—can be regarded as responsible for the text or the recommendations.

Throughout this report all proper names of teachers, pupils, parents, and even schools have been altered in an effort to preserve the anonymity of those with whom we talked or whose actions we observed. If there is coincidence between a name in the text and that of some person on Pine Ridge, it is sheer accident, and all the reader can be certain is that the person in this text is not the person who does in actuality bear that name. The only names preserved in the text are those of key administrators, insofar as they are mentioned by our respondents, as when a mother spoke of wishing to talk to Mr. Penttila (the Reservation Principal) or Mr. Towle (then Agency Superintendent).

## FIELD WORK

This research was designed as a social-anthropological study of a community with especial emphasis upon its system of education. The basic research technique was observation as a quasi-participant or full-participant, supplemented by formal interviews.

The Project Office was established in a rural location midway between the town of Pine Ridge and the hamlet of Oglala, within an ancient building that had formerly been No. 4 Schoolhouse. The Waxes lived there during most of their residence on the Reservation; after their departure, Robert Dumont replaced them there. This location was convenient both for the observation of "official" events at Pine Ridge (and the Oglala Community School located there) and of local community events among the country Indians of the Reservation prairie. It also proved to be an excellent point for meeting and chatting with school children, as it was a major stopping point (end-of-the-line) for one of the school buses.

As usual in this type of research, the principal members of the staff maintained field diaries in which were recorded events that seemed significant,

as soon as possible after their occurrence. Wherever possible, detailed notes were made during the course of the events themselves. At various times, questionnaire schedules or other research instruments were utilized. However, since our fundamental task was to understand the social dynamics of a complex interethnic situation, and since we often did not know what questions were significant, we frequently relied on relatively unstructured conversation. Wherever we went on or near the Reservation we met folk who wanted to know who we were. When we defined our interest as being the schools and the Sioux children, many chose to comment, some briefly and some at length. Others chose to visit us and express their considered opinions. In this way, we accumulated records of some forty-seven lengthy unstructured interviews with Sioux adults and about twice that number of briefer conversations and communications, all bearing on the topics of school and education.

In due time, we were able to formulate a questionnaire schedule for use with parents, and the female members of the Project staff visited Sioux homes and interviewed mothers (or other adults in their absence). As we found that some questions did not elicit useful answers or did elicit answers that were the same from all respondents, we modified the schedule; two different versions are appended herewith. Forty-eight interviews using this type of schedule were obtained. This brought our total of recorded, formal interviews and conversations to ninety-five, plus about a hundred recorded, shorter episodes.

From the start of the school term, Project staff toured the Reservation, attending school functions (orientation programs, P.T.A. meetings, pupil assemblies), observing school classes, and conversing with educators. Observations were conducted in every federal school, every mission school, and sev-

## TABLE 12
### Educational Administrators Interviewed

| Location | Officer |
|---|---|
| Day Schools | Three Principals |
| Boarding School | Academic Heads (2);<br>Department Head, Guidance;<br>Assistant Head, Boys;<br>Assistant Head, Girls;<br>Supervisory Instructional Aids (2). |
| Office of the Reservation<br>Principal (i.e. Superintendent) | Education Specialist;<br>Adult Education Specialist (2). |
| Aberdeen Area Office | Director of Schools,<br>Assistant Director of Schools,<br>(and non-educational officials,<br>including Area Social Workers). |
| Washington Office | Education Specialist |
| Holy Rosary Mission | Principal |
| Shannon County (Public)<br>School System | Superintendent |

eral of the public schools on the Pine Ridge Reservation, as well as at a number of schools in neighboring areas. A total of seventy-two class sessions in sixteen schools were observed and are the subject of detailed notes in Project records. (Accordingly, this Report does not purport to describe any particular school and does not single out any particular school for mention, except where it is unavoidable as in the case of the single reservation boarding and high school.)

In addition to numerous informal conversations with teachers (recorded in Project files), twenty-two were interviewed personally and at some length. With ten of these teachers, the interview schedule appended was utilized; with the remainder, the interview was unstructured. In like manner, unstructured interviews were conducted with the following administrators:

To gain a picture of the problems of Sioux young people with their schooling, we began a study of the Oglala Community High School, located in Pine Ridge town. This study was to be the central focus of most

of the work of Robert V. Dumont, although other members of the Project also worked in cooperation with him. Interviews were conducted with all of the upper-classmen. In addition, the scholastic operations of the school were observed, as part of the general research activity of attending classes and interviewing teachers.

High school pupils from families living in Pine Ridge town and classed as Mixedbloods proved relatively easy to talk with. However, pupils from country Indian families speaking Lakota as their preferred tongue, were shy and uncommunicative, regardless of the language in which they were approached. Our attempts to converse with these young "Fullbloods" made us sympathize with the teachers and officials who work with these youngsters. Also, we realized that persons who were so shy and reticent in English would have grave difficulties when they sought employment or attempted to deal with the general institutions of the national society.

Our discovery of how to elicit attitudes toward school from these young

TABLE 13
ATTITUDINAL INFORMATION FROM SIOUX YOUNG PEOPLE

| | Personal Interview | Sentence Completion Schedule | | Total Persons |
|---|---|---|---|---|
| | | Brief | Long | |
| Loneman district (65) | 49 | 16 | 6 | 49 |
| Pine Ridge town (42) | 1 | ---- | 20 | 21 |
| Others not in samples | 103 | ---- | 7 | 103 |
| TOTAL | 153 | 16 | 33 | 173 |

Fullbloods was accidental: One of our Indian assistants who appeared to be making at least some progress in accumulating "interviews" had in fact been leaving a copy of the schedule with each youngster, and the latter had then filled it out at his leisure. We then began adding sentence completion items to our interview schedule, and as these proved useful we composed a longer and self-contained sentence completion schedule. Meantime, as we became better known in the community we found more acceptance in personal interviews with young people, and we devised a separate schedule to be used with girls (aged twenty-one or less) who had dropped out of school and married.

In order to insure a proper diversity of adolescent respondents, we proceeded by selecting a random sample. From the Agency office of the B.I.A., we secured census lists for the area corresponding to the Loneman School (including Slim Buttes, Number Six, Oglala, and Calico Hall North) and selected one out of four of the persons aged thirteen to twenty-one (born between the dates, Sept. 1, 1941 and Aug. 31, 1949). This yielded a sample of sixty-seven young people, of whom two proved to be deceased, reducing the sample to sixty-five. Forty-nine of these persons were traced and interviewed; eleven seemed to be off the Reservation—in the Armed Services, at school in Pierre or Haskell, or re-located; and five could not be located or traced.

Since it seemed that it might be valuable to supplement this sample of "country Indian" youth by a more systematic representation of the "urban" side of the Reservation, we drew a random sample of forty-two persons in the same age range from the population listed as residing in or near the town of Pine Ridge. Because time was running short, we did not attempt personal interviews with this group but rather requested completion of the sentence completion schedule. Completed schedules were secured from twenty of these, and a personal interview had already been obtained with another.

Table 13 presents the data assembled from research with Sioux young people (aged thirteen to twenty-one).

Of the youngsters interviewed, twelve of the sample from the Loneman district and seventeen of the other children had dropped out of school, so that our files contain either interviews or sentence completion schedules with twenty-nine drop-outs.

Late in the Project, we began to turn our attention toward children in the elementary grades, especially because Sioux parents and federal teachers asked our assistance in dealing with children who were problems in one way or another. While we did not feel we knew enough to be helpful as counselors, we did feel that we might learn much from talking to these children and trying to understand their troubles. Mrs. HolyRock, especially, proved highly skillful in this effort. A questionnaire schedule for young children was developed, using as a model a schedule developed by the Bank Street College of Education. Through the efforts of Mrs. HolyRock and Robert V. Dumont, interviews and observational data on sixteen grade school pupils were assembled.

## ANALYSIS AND INTERPRETATION

Many of the people of Pine Ridge —both Sioux adults and federal educators—made it plain to the Project staff that they regarded our study as important and urgent. They felt the local educational situation was plagued with difficulties and they seemed to feel confident that this study could provide answers. Accordingly, the members of the Project staff labored hard and long to produce a useful report as speedily as possible. In the process, much useful data and partially analyzed materials had to be set aside. Outstandingly, the discussion by Mr. Dumont of the federal high school has had to be omitted, simply because the problem of the elementary schools was more basic. Moreover, any full discussion of Pine Ridge education should consider the problem of adult education, and this the staff was able only to notice.

## INTERVIEW SCHEDULE FOR SIOUX PARENTS
### *Early Version*

1. Do Indian children ever learn things at school that make them be disrespectful or mean to their parents— or makes their parents feel sad?
2. Have your children ever learned anything at school that makes you and your family feel pleased?
3. Is there anything parents can do if their children learn things at school that their parents do not wish them to learn?
4. Have you ever helped your child with lessons?
5. Do you think Indians who go to school get better jobs than Indians who don't go to school?
6. What kind of a job do you want your kids to have when they grow up and finish school?
7. In what way is going to school going to help them get such a job?
8. Has your child ever said he didn't want to go to school?
9. Who do you know who is an educated man and a good Sioux?
10. Is there any Sioux you know who's worse off because he went to school?


## INTERVIEW SCHEDULE FOR SIOUX PARENTS
### *Final Version*

1. Do Indians ever learn things at school that make them be disrespectful or mean to their parents—or makes their parents feel sad?
2. Have your children ever learned anything at school that makes you and your family feel pleased?
3. When it comes to teaching your children English and Arithmetic, do you think the teachers do a good job or a bad job?
4. Does the school do a good job or a bad job in teaching children competition?
5. Sometimes children get ashamed in school and don't like to go. Have you heard of anything like that?
6. Have you ever helped your child with lessons?
7. Do you think Indians who go to school get better jobs than Indians who don't go to school?
8. What kind of a job do you want your kids to have when they grow up and finish school?
9. In what way is going to school going to help them get such a job?
10. Has your child ever said he didn't want to go to school?

## INTERVIEW SCHEDULE FOR BUREAU TEACHERS

I'd like to know how you feel about teaching here—the good points and the bad points.

1. What are the nicest things about teaching here?
2. What are the worst things about teaching here?
3. What are the special difficulties about teaching Indian children here?
4. Are there any respects in which it is easier to work with these children than with others?
5. What do you feel these children need most in the way of education?
6. What are the things that make it hardest for you to do a good job teaching these children?
7. What changes would you make or what programs would you initiate to improve the situation here?
8. As you see it, what are the biggest problems of the Indian people on this Reservation?
9. Since you have been working on this Reservation, have you had any special training in the teaching and handling of Indian youngsters? Please describe it. Do you feel this was enough training and of the right kind for you, or should it have been something else?

Now, I'd like to know something about your own background.

A. Where did you get your training as a teacher? (schools, years of training, degrees)
B. What schools and grades have you taught in? (schools, grades, years, kinds of pupils)

## BRIEF SENTENCE COMPLETION SCHEDULE FOR

## YOUNG PERSONS

1. Write about your first days at school. Were they easy or hard? Did you ever want your teacher to speak Indian?
2. How is your English now? Do you ever have trouble understanding your teacher's English now? By the time you were in Fourth Grade did you understand English pretty good?

3. Would you rather speak Indian or English? Have you ever been afraid to speak English in front of White people?
4. Have you ever wanted to quit school? What made you stay in school?
5. What is the hardest thing for you to do in school? What are some of the things that make this hard for you? Could you do this better if it was in Indian?
6. Have you ever played hooky (skipped school)? What were some of the things that made you play hooky? Would you rather play basketball or go to school?

THANK YOU

NOTE: *This sentence completion schedule is printed with the responses of a young teenage girl.*

# EMORY UNIVERSITY

## OGLALA SIOUX EDUCATIONAL SURVEY

Please fill in the spaces indicated. You may write anything you wish.

1. Please list the schools you have attended and the grades for years that you went to school.

| SCHOOL | GRADE LEVEL OR YEAR |
| --- | --- |
| _____ | _____ |
| _____ | _____ |
| _____ | _____ |
| _____ | _____ |

2. What school are you attending this year? _____
   If you are not in school what are you now doing? _____
   _____
   What grade are you in _____?
   If you quit school, what was the last grade you finished? _____
3. What is your birth date? _____
4. When you were a small child, which language was spoken mostly in your home?
   Indian ___√___ or English _____? (Check one)
5. Are you a boarder _____ or are you a day scholar ___√___?

## FINISH THE SENTENCES BELOW ANYWAY THAT YOU FEEL IS RIGHT FOR YOU.

A. In the classroom, I am usually "sometimes sleepy"

B. If school teachers could talk Indian "it would be better to understand what they say."

C. When I talk to White men "I usually get nervous."

D. To earn money "I babysit."

E. Most teachers "always help me when I don't know something."

F. The worst thing about school _____

G. When I need help I can usually turn to "my parents or the teacher or anyone who is around to help me."

H. The nicest thing about school "is the teacher never scolds us."

I. What I hate most around here "is in our classroom it is kinda cold and isn't in order like."

J. The other kids in my grade "looks like most all of them are a little smarter than I am."

K. When I feel like playing hooky "I pretend I am sick but not always."

L. I feel proud when "the teacher asks a question and my answer is right."

M. A good teacher is one "who trys to help in everything we do and explains what she is saying."

N. When I am thirty years old "I would like to get a job."

O. Reading books "will help me to speak correctly and"

P. The kind of school I would like best "is a boarding school."

Write your name here _____ Beatrice Black Badger _____

When were you born? _____

Is there anyone in your home who cares whether you do well in school or not? Who is this person? What does he or she tell you about school? "Yes. This person is my oldest brother. He tells me to study hard and try to get things in my head."

THANK YOU

# INTERVIEW SCHEDULE FOR MARRIED DROP OUTS

## (Age 21 or less)

Ask how long married—children if any—phrase questions accordingly.

1. Where do you think you'll send your children to school—
   Loneman—O.C.S.—Rosary—Public.
   Why so?

2. When you yourself went to school did you have anything happen to you that was unpleasant or may have discouraged you—that you wouldn't like to happen to your children?

3. When you yourself went to school did you have anything happen to you that you liked—that encouraged you— that you would like to have happen to your kids?

4. Do you think your children will get better jobs if they finish high school?

5. Have you ever wished you could go back to school?
   What kind of job prepare for?
   What kind of schooling needed?

6. When you dropped out of school, did anybody object or put up a fuss?

7. What happened?

8. Did you ever quit school and then go back?
   If yes, what happened?

9. When you finally quit school—what led you to quit?

## INTERVIEW SCHEDULE FOR CHILDREN

### (Age 12 or less)

1. Suppose tomorrow someone told you it was up to you as to whether or not you went to school. What would you do: would you go to school anymore or would you stay home? Why would you do this?

2. Do you think you would miss anything if you didn't go to school?

3. What kinds of things do the children in your class do that you would like to do if you could?

4. What kinds of things do children in your class do that annoys you the most?

5. What work (subject) in school do you like the best?

6. How are you at arithmetic? Are you good, medium good, or not so good? What happens when you can't do an arithmetic problem?

7. How are you at reading? Are you good, medium good, or not so good? What happens when you can't read something?

8. What about most children in your class? Are they good at arithmetic? Are most of them better than you or not so good?

9. And reading, are most of the children better than you or not so good?

10. What kinds of things do children do that makes your teacher particularly happy? What does she do then?

11. What kinds of things do children do that your teacher doesn't like? What does she do then?

12. What would you like to do in school that you don't do now?

13. Does the school teach you anything about taking care of yourself? What does it teach you?

14. Does the school teach you anything about how to act to other children and other people? What does it teach you?

15. What do you think you would like to be when you grow up?

16. Do you think going to school will help you to become that?

# Great Tradition, Little Tradition, and Formal Education *

## Murray and Rosalie Wax

From a comparative and historical perspective, the vast body of research literature on schools and education appears both pseudoempirical and pseudo-theoretical. Researchers have been administering hundreds of tests to thousands of pupils and intellectual critics have devoted countless pages to the criticism of textbooks and other curricular materials. Yet, the bulk of their efforts contrasts markedly with its quality and its impact, because their vision has been constricted by an interlocking chain of assumptions: that schools are primarily and exclusively agencies of formal education (rather than being social institutions); that pupils are isolated individuals (rather than social beings who participate in the life of peer societies, ethnic groups, and the like); that formal education is synonymous with education; and that the principal task of the teacher is to educate. Thus, instead of inquiring what sort of social processes are occurring in — and in relation to — the schools, researchers and critics have defined their problem as being one of discovering how to make the schools teach their individual pupils more, better, and faster. Only a few of the many researchers and critics have had the patience, fortified by the faith in ethnographic empiricism, to observe the social processes actually occurring in relation to the schools: among the pupils, among the teachers, within the classrooms, between the pupils and their parental elders, and so on.

Teachers and pupils being docile and available, it has been far easier and far more pretentiously scientific (while less threatening to the local power structure) to administer reams of tests that are then scored mechanically. As a result, the research literature lacks a solid body of data on the ethnography of schools.

Seemingly, the theoretical literature on education would be far superior. The intellectual critics number some of the most formidably trained scholars in the country, as well as some of the most irate journalists and pontifical classicists. Unfortunately, most seem to lack that sense of history and feeing for comparison that the Classical Curriculum (or its modern "Liberal Arts" variant) is presumed to produce. As but a small instance, consider that most of the classically trained critics laud the Hellenic system of education, and, from that vantage point, denounce as trivial and unworthy of our schools such courses as driver

---

* "Great Tradition, Little Tradition, and Formal Education" by Murray and Rosalie Wax first appeared published in *Anthropological Perspectives on Education,* edited by Murray L. Wax, Stanley Diamond, and Fred O. Gearing (Basic Books, 1971), pp. 3-18.

127

training. Yet, it is surely arguable that being able to drive an automobile courteously, deftly, and responsibly, restraining aggressive impulses, and focusing attention upon the task, is a sign of good citizenship and moral excellence. Really good training in driving an automobile would merit as much approbation as the Hellenic cult of body culture. If the invidious slur on driver training courses is typical of the logic of the critics (and we take it to be so) then they are sadly deficient in the perspective and knowledge required for an evaluation of modern schools.

Asking the right questions is the path to acquiring wisdom, but to ask good questions, rather than trivial ones, the investigator has to break out of conventional frameworks. In the early part of this essay we proceed autobiographically, outlining how this happened to us so that we came to perceive freshly some of what is going on in relation to the schools. Later in the essay, we build on these experiences and elaborate a more theoretical argument which, in turn, leads us to a series of research questions for the study of the culture of schools.

## The School and the Little Community

We begin in traditional anthropological fashion by describing some of what we learned about the educational problems of the Oglala Sioux on Pine Ridge Reservation. The patient reader will find that this is not simply an ethnographic excursion but leads to a consideration of the nature of education in a modern industrial society.

Our interest in Indian education developed during the several years in which we directed the Workshops for American Indian college students held during the summer on the campus of the University of Colorado. These workshops had been designed to provide young Indians with a broad perspective about Indian affairs, so that they could later serve their communities as advisors and leaders. As we worked with these young people, we were appalled. Supposedly the cream of the Indian population, they were so provincial in their knowledge of the United States and so ignorant of Indian history and current affairs as to make us doubt their rank as college students. Yet, at the same time, most of them could be excited, and to an intense glow, by lectures on Indian history, or on Indian religious cults or social organization, in which we treated these phenomena as worthy of serious intellectual attention. Judging by their response, none of these students had ever participated in a discussion that treated Indian religious cults as vital and meaningful subjects (rather than as superstitious, primitive, or archaic). Accordingly, we developed a critical curiosity about the nature of the educational system in which these students had been schooled, and we deliberately decided to study an Indian population (the Pine Ridge Sioux) that had for some years been subjected to federal programs for education and assimilation.

At the time we designed the study, we envisioned the school as a battleground: on the one hand, the educators—flanked by the Bureau of Indian Affairs, the mission churches, and kindred agencies—would be fighting to pull the children out of Indian society, while, on the other hand, the Indian elders would be clinging desperately to their young, trying to hold them within their traditional society. Indeed, this was exactly the picture drawn for us by a high Bureau of Indian Affairs (BIA) official on our first day on the reservation, except that, instead of the Indian elders, he blamed "grandma," who craftily lured her grandchildren "back to the blanket."

Our hypothesis about battlegrounds was to prove as inaccurate as his was about grandmas and blankets. Nevertheless, it turned out to be extremely advantageous, for it predisposed us to approach the Sioux pupils, their teachers, and the administration, as living members of social groups rather than as isolated respondents to questionnaires administered from a distance. Thus, we were obliged to sit for weeks and months in classrooms, watching what was going on and, in like manner, to talk not only to administrators and educational experts but also to Indian parents and to the children themselves. In due time we realized that the educators and Indian elders were not locked in battle for the soul of the Indian child, because the Sioux elders, faced with the power of the educational establishment, simply withdrew. In this tactic they were encouraged by the educational administrators who exhorted them: just send your children to school every day and we will educate them. The educators found the absence of the parents convenient and proper, since the parents would have had no background for understanding the operations of the school and could only have interfered. Yet, here, the educators were overconfident, for within the schoolrooms they were confronting children who were alien and who could elude their ministrations. Issuing from small local communities of kith and kin, and sharing a common set of values and understandings, as well as a language (Lakota) that was unknown to most teachers, the Sioux children could and did create within the formal structure of the educational institution, a highly cohesive society of their own. As the children matured, their society of peers became ever more solidary, and the teacher confronting them was reduced to operating at the level they would permit. Whereas an occasional teacher might gain the approval of this peer society, most teachers found themselves talking to a wall of apparent indifference and assumed incompetence. Interestingly, many teachers remarked that after the sixth or seventh grade their pupils became more "withdrawn" or "apathetic" every year, but not one realized that the wall was the outward manifestation of a subtle and highly organized rejection. The withdrawal remained a mystery to the educators.

In another respect, the design of our study differed from the more conventional ethnographic or social anthropological investigations, for we committed ourselves to a study of the Indian children *in the schools*. This meant that we were obliged to consider and try to understand not only Sioux society or culture but the reservation system (teachers and administrators), and how the Indians related generally to the agencies of the greater society as well. This commitment helped us to perceive very early that the administrators and most of the teachers looked upon the Sioux children not as members of a different or exotic culture but as members of an ethic and inferior caste. Their task, as they saw it, was to help their pupils become members of the superior caste.

The status of the Sioux as being lower caste was so conspicuously visible among the educators that we singled out one of its manifestations for analysis under the label of "The Vacuum Ideology." The reference is to the experiential background of the Sioux child, for the educators, especially the administrators, did not regard this child as participating in a distinctive culture and society but, instead, as lacking in those preschool experiences that distinguish the desirable kind of pupil. Judging by the experiences that were listed, the ideal pupil would have been of urban middle-class, Protestant (and White) background, and, insofar as the Sioux pupil lacked those particular experiences, it was not that he had others but that he was deficient. Since his parents had not read *Peter Rabbit* to him, he lacked familiarity with stories; and since they did not sing Anglo-Saxon lullabies to him, he lacked familiarity with music. The same ideology is also prevalent among educators confronting children of urban lower-class and ethnic backgrounds.

Subsequent experience has convinced us that many educators are passionately attached to the notion that their disprivileged or poor pupils come to them with empty minds that must be filled before they can compete with youngsters from "the usual middle-class home." Nevertheless, they withdraw in horror from the suggestion that a denial of experience constitutes a denial of socialization or human development. That a little child might not respond warmly to a teacher who sees him and his family as empty vessels does not occur to them.

Almost in spite of ourselves, we have been led to the conclusion that some of our most important general educational goals constitute ruthless attacks on the solidarity and self-respect of the ethnic and lower-class communities, and, indeed, on their very existence. The Vacuum Ideology is only one of the more recent tactical offenses. Another is the goal of individualistic achievement.

The modern school system is premised on the notion that its population is an aggregate of social atoms, among whom there are no significant or permanent linkages. In the ideology of the educators, these social atoms begin at the same starting line and then move onward in haphazard clumps, each atom achieving independently of the others and according to its own inner strength and motives. What an individual does in school, and later, in his vocation, is an achievement — his individual achievement — deriving from his own initiative and effort, and of benefit only to himself and his immediate family. Contrary to this ideology is the normative system of a folk community that confronts an alien society. For in this system the individual may excel only when his excellence enhances the position of his brethren. If this achievement were to derogate them before others, then it would be incumbent on him to conceal his talents. Thus, in the schools on Pine Ridge, our staff observed classrooms where, when the teacher called upon a pupil to recite, he would become the target of jibes and jokes whispered in Lakota and unperceived by the teacher, with the result that he would stand or sit paralyzed and unable to respond; meanwhile, the teacher, being oblivious to the secret life of the classroom, would be perplexed and distressed at her inability to secure responses indicating that she had covered the day's lesson. Similar observations were made by Harry Wolcott, who, for his doctoral dissertation, taught in a one-room school among Indians on an island off the West coast of Canada. Wolcott reports that, although he taught for a full year, living among the community, he was never able to learn just how much or how little most of his pupils knew, because, no matter what the nature of the classwork—whether test or seatwork or other areas—no student could be induced to work solely for himself.

The fact that the educators themselves seem unaware that individualistic achievement as they define it is considered grossly immoral behavior by the children they are trying to instruct is an obvious case of selective inattention. But the fact that social researchers are so often indifferent to this type of conflict and to its implications is more surprising and puzzling. This brings us to the second part of this paper: a consideration of the inadequacy of past and current research on schools and education.

## Pseudoempirical Research on Education

Because of the fundamental orientation of their research, most investigators have managed to avoid looking at what actually occurs within schools. Since they collect much data, their research appears to be empirical, but in actuality they have been selectively inattentive to important classes of phenomena. Educational psychologists, for example, convert the society of pupils into an aggregate of individual animals, each of whom must be trained to perform certain tasks established by the curriculum. Discovering what the pupils are actually engaged in doing and experiencing is irrelevant to the job that the psychologist has defined for himself, namely structuring the school situation so that each of the human animals is made to learn more and faster. The educational psychologist thus comes to function like the industrial psychologist whose role is to help increase production. For both, the fundamental tasks are established by the bureaucratically given structure, and the researcher accepts as his goal the devising of ways to accomplish those tasks most expeditiously. Whatever else may be going on within the school, or however else the child may be being educated, becomes relevant for the researcher only insofar as it clearly affects the performance of the curricularly given tasks.

In a like manner, structural-functionalists among sociologists have tended to orient themselves by defining their discipline as "the sociology of education" and by assuming that the school is that institution having education as its primary function. In effect, these plausible assumptions serve to transform the scientific problem of the *nature of the school* (and its relationship to other social activities) into the problem of evaluating the school in terms of the extent to which it performs a particular *educational function* (cf. Brotz, 1961). If further, the sociologist relies principally upon survey procedures, with rigid schedules administered to large numbers of pupils, then he has thoroughly inhibited himself from the observation of the school as a species of social organization. The pupils are perceived as social atoms, differing from each other only in terms of their ethnic-religious and social-class backgrounds, but the school is rarely studied as a society or social system that is more than an arena for the movement of these atoms.

Lest we be misunderstood, we should like to emphasize that the issue is not the learning theory of some psychologists nor the structural-functionalism of some sociologists. Either theory and discipline could be utilized in the empirical study of schools, but in fact they seldom have been, and the research that is done has a flavor that is tragicomic. For example, some investigators known to us are now engaged in elaborate investigations involving, on the one hand, the administration of large batteries of tests to hundreds of Indian and White pupils, and, on the other hand, the observation in detail of the relationships between Indian mothers and their children. The hypothesis informing the research is that the progressive "withdrawal" characteristic of Indian pupils in schools is the outcome of a psychic inadequacy related to their upbringing. Were these investigators to perform some elementary ethnography, inquiring as to how the Indians perceive their community situation and the role of the schools, and if they were then to observe classroom interactions, their comprehension of what they presume to be a psychic inadequacy might be thoroughly transformed. But for this to occur, they would have to be prepared to examine the school as a real institution affecting a real interethnic community of Indians and Whites, instead of reducing the school to an educational function and dissolving the Sioux child out of his community and his lower-caste situation.

On the other hand, research conducted along Community Study lines has often contributed a great deal to the understanding of the schools (whether or not the research has utilized a structural-functionalist or learning theory conceptualization). The major endeavors (Hollingshead, Havighurst, and Wylie), which have had the school as the focus of the community study, are well recognized, but it is important to note that almost any thorough study of a geographic community can contribute to our knowledge of the schools. In Whyte's study of Cornerville, it is necessary to read between the lines to learn about the schools, but in Gans's later study of an ethnically similar community, much can be gained from the brief pages on the topic (1965:129-136). Similar value can be found in the pages relating to the schools in the studies by Withers (1945), Vidich and Bensman (1960), the Lynds, Hughes (1963), Warner and associates (1949), and others of the better investigators of small American communities. Indeed, the fact that these studies are not focused on the schools has a certain advantage, for the educationally focused studies allow their research to be excessively oriented by the ideology of the schools, and so they spend too many pages in demonstrating that the schools do not provide equal opportunity for achievement and too few pages in describing what the schools actually are doing.

In contrast to these contemporaneous varieties of social research on education is a study so old as to be dated, having been published forty years ago. Yet this study, which, to our knowledge, has had no successor, is the only one that comes close to describing the school as an institution. We have in mind Waller's *The Sociology of Teaching*. Waller's research procedures appear to have been informal, and he seems to have relied mainly upon his own experiences and the reports and diaries of teachers who were students of his, yet, nonetheless, he systematically reviewed the major sorts of interactions associated with being a teacher. As compared with the several, methodologically sophisticated readers in the sociology of education on the market, Waller's has been the only book to discuss such significant topics as the elementary forms of collective behavior within the classroom or the role of ceremonies in the life of the school (the anthropologist, Burnett, revived the study of these ceremonies in 1966). In a sense, Waller viewed the school as a community, and its educators and pupils as social beings participating in the life of the community, and so he produced a monograph that can serve to suggest directions for research on contemporary schools. Stimulated by his book, we would like to advance several questions for research on the schools: What kinds of social roles emerge within the schools, among the teachers, the pupils, and the lay public associated with the schools? What social forms emerge within the context of the schools? Are there typical cycles of reform associated with the school system, similar, perhaps, to the reforming movements within the Catholic Church, of which some culminated in the founding of religious orders and others in the rise of new sects? What happens to children within the schools; how are children transformed into *pupils*?

A knowledgeable and shrewd anthropologist can advance a number of hypotheses in response to the questions we have just raised. He could, for instance, point to the differences between the kind of age-grading that occurs among the children of hunting peoples who roam in small bands and that which occurs within our public schools, where children are associated with a narrow stratum of other children of almost exactly the same chronological age. From there he could argue about the differences that would develop because the first kind of children would have the opportunity to associate with others much older than themselves and would have also the association with and responsibility for other children much younger than themselves; and, continuing the train of logic, he could argue as to the kinds of differences in personality that might ensue. Yet, much as we welcome such broad speculation, we do wish to insist that there is much about our schools that we don't know for certain because investigators have not been looking—they have administered tens of thousands of tests and conducted hundreds of interviews, but only a handful have looked systematically, diligently, and sympathetically at all phases of the school in relationship to pupils, educators, and parents.[1]

Just as we need to know more about how children are transformed into *pupils*, so must we know more about how young persons (usually college students) are transformed into *teachers*. The research in this area has been limited and is mostly represented by tests or other fixed schedules of questions that are administered to samples of teacher trainees and veteran teachers (cf. Guba, Jackson, and Bidwell in Charters and Gage 1963:271-286). In accounting for the attitudes and conduct of veteran teachers, most critics have stressed the relationship between the teacher and the school administration, the latter usually being bureaucratic, conservative, and timorous. However, we would also be inclined as to the effects upon a person of having to be on public display before — and in constant disciplinary control of — a large audience of alien children for many hours per day. It is not, we would guess, the school administration per se that develops the teacher type, but the administrative requirement of facing and controlling so large a body of youngsters. We are impressed by the fact that the problem of maintaining discipline in the classroom is foremost among the anxieties of the novice teacher, and also foremost among the demands made upon the teacher by his supervisors, and yet the literature of social research on the issue is so weak and so focused on individual children as "disciplinary problems." We are also impressed by the fact that most novices do manage to maintain discipline in their classes, and that critical attention is usually directed only to the conspicuous failures of discipline, but that few scholars ask how the stunt is performed. Yet the question of how discipline is maintained throughout a school is, we suggest, a paradigm for the question of how order is maintained in civil society.

## The School and the Great Tradition

To propose the foregoing questions — how do children become pupils? how do young people become teachers? how is discipline maintained within the schoolroom? — is to declare that the cross-cultural comparisons that anthropologists have conventionally attempted are limited in their relevance to formal education. By comparing the experiences of the contemporary schoolchild in the Bronx with that of a juvenile in New Guinea thirty years ago, we can say something significant about the personality development of the child, but we are in limbo so far as concerns much that is significant about formal education, as is evident in terms of the content of the readers and textbooks on anthropology and education produced but a generation ago. The authors of these works are well qualified, their essays are frequently of intrinsic interest, but their pertinence to the contemporary educational drama is negligible. For these anthropologists, trying to be culturally relativistic, defined "educational practices" in broad terms. Viewing cultures as separate and distinct entities that could be compared as independent individuals, they conceived of each as having its own system of child-rearing and, therefore, of education. Such a procedure did have and still has some uses, but it cannot hope to characterize the contemporary situation where *education* is of the order of an international mission activity, being exported from the United States and other Western societies. *Education* in this sense is avowedly intended to decease the isolation of other ("backward") societies and to alter drastically their cultural configurations. In its aggressive impact, this education is similar to the spread of Christianity, Islam, Communism, or capitalistic business practices.

Indeed, the traditional anthropological procedure was not even accurate for the history of Western society or of other civilized societies. For the Western system of formal education is rooted in its Great Tradition (Redfield, 1956 chap. 3; Singer, 1960) and can only be understood on that basis. Great Traditions, it will be recalled, are borne by a literate corps of disciples, and are in tension with the little traditions transmitted informally within the little community. Or, in the pithy language of Bharati (1963):

> What the missionary in a particular religion wants the less knowledgeable votaries to do, defines the "big tradition," and what he wants them to give up and to desist from in the future, defines the "little tradition" in any religious area.

Christianity has epitomized that tension, for, on the one hand, there have been its dedicated disciples, oriented toward the millennial creed of its scriptures, while, on the other hand, there have been the folk, who have required a religion, which, through its values and symbols, expressed the unity and morality of the little community. This tension has been clearly visible in the American churches, especially of the contemporary South: for, as its dedicated ministers affirm, the Christian message would require thorough desegregation, since all men are brothers in Christ; yet, to the members of the local White community, the local church embodies their moral unity and necessarily excludes the Negroes as alien and profane. The school stands in a similar situation, for, on the one hand, it, too, is a kind of local church, embodying the sacred values of the little community. Yet, on the other hand, the school is connected, organizationally and ideationally, with the greater society and with the Great Traditions of the West.

In their relationship to the contemporary and actual school systems, intellectual critics — such as ourselves — play somewhat the role of the fervent religious orders within the medieval church. The critics are painfully conscious of the true message; they are prepared to be tolerant of some of the little traditional beliefs, provided they can be incorporated within the body of dogma; but they are appalled at the heresy and corruption within the institutional church. They debate theories of education with their fellows, as if these were theological creeds, and they are perturbed that the school as a reality bears so little a resemblance to the school as the gateway to salvation.

If we may be permitted to continue this metaphor, we would suggest that what social scientists, especially anthropologists, could now accomplish in their research upon education is a purification of the dogma. The world of today is in the midst of a vast expansion and elaboration of the system of formal education: more peoples are sending their children to school, and more children are spending longer periods of their lives as students. This transformation is of such magnitude and abruptness as to deserve the label of *revolution*, and it appears quite comparable in scope to movements, such as the spread of Christianity in the ancient world, or to the Industrial Revolution. While both of these did become worldwide movements, in order to do so each has had to purify itself of much ideological dross. Christianity did not become really effective in Northern Europe until its populace had eliminated many of the peculiarities distinctive to the Mediterranean world from the dogma and had reformulated this dogma in terms of their own ethnic traditions. The Industrial Revolution did not begin to permeate many areas of the world, until its dogma of Manchester Liberalism was dismembered and replaced by local or nativistic creeds disguising themselves behind the flexible vocabularies of nationalism and socialism. Now, we should like to suggest that our United States educational system is similarly loaded with ideological irrelevancies that make it unsuited to other countries (cf. Thomas, 1966:72-74) and have made it clearly unsuited to our own ethnic and lower-class populations. We would hazard that the unsuitability of our system in other countries is, at present, disguised by the outpourings of financial and moral assistance from the West coupled with the native willingness of other nations to accept our institutional complexes in the dizzy hope of becoming as prosperous and powerful as the United States. In about a decade, the twin impetus should have disappeared, and anthropologists may then be in a position to observe some interesting attempts to reshape the educational structure. More than this, it should be possible for anthropologists to be of marked assistance in the reshaping and purification of education, provided that they are astute and critical and that they begin their work in the near future, and discard the restrictive blinders of irrelevant or system-biased research as we noted earlier.

Let us give an example of an ideological tenet that, as we have indicated, hampers the adjustment of some peoples to the Western system of formal education. United States and other Western schools have, generally, been organized about the notion of individual achievement with rewards of personal advancement and benefit. Looking historically and comparatively, we believe it can be argued that this tenet may not be essential and may even be somewhat of a hindrance, unless suitably modified. Great traditions, generally, and Western scholarship, specifically, have as we have noted been borne by associations of disciples, who have shared common goals and been subject to a common discipline. Anthropologists (or other social-scientists) would not accomplish what they do, wrestling with the hardships they must face, unless sustained by their association of compeers. There is individualistic competition, which does stimulate to achievement, but it is a competition that is regulated by formal norms against deceit and plagiarism and by informal norms of courtesy, fellowship, and camaraderie. Whenever the attempt has previously been made to widely disseminate great traditional knowledge throughout a population, it has been associated with a social movement having superpersonal goals. The Jews, who were among the first to do so, accomplished widespread literacy, and it was in a strictly religious context, in order to bring about the salvation of Israel and the participation of the individual in that joyous event. With Protestantism a similar movement for literacy developed, more individualistic perhaps, but nonetheless set in the context of a social movement and communal aspirations. Today, in the United States, we seem to be pushing the notion of individualistic competition within the framework of the school to an almost superhuman pitch. Yet, it is striking that real progress toward spreading literacy among lower-class or ethnic groups has so often occurred in the context of social movements: civil rights, the Black Muslims and Black Panthers, and, as always,the evangelistic churches.

Another example of an ideological tenet that has hampered the adjustment of some peoples to the system of formal education is, we believe, the notion that each child must be identified with a unique nuclear family and that the community encompassing the school is a community of nuclear families. As anthropologists, we are bound to ask whether as efficient an educational establishment could be fitted into a society with extended families and elaborate systems of kinship? Speaking from our observations among the Sioux (and our readings about other peoples, or even about the Hutterites and Amish), this is no idle question. So much of the procedures of the systems of schooling and welfare and public health are geared to the assumption that each child must be part of an intact family or else he is a neglected child, and the power of the state and the wealth of its agencies is thereby used to disrupt the extended family and cement the nuclear one. In the case of the American Indian, it is not yet too late to ask whether we should be doing this, and we may also bear in mind that many more peoples of the world are and will be increasingly involved with this issue.

## The School and the Little Tradition

Because researchers have focused on curricularly given tasks, and critics have focused on great traditional knowledge, no one has been looking systematically at the impact of formal educational institutions on little traditional processes of child rearing. Instead, there has been recourse to the concept of "cultural deprivation," which (like the vacuum ideology of Sioux educators) has enabled the theorists and administrators to ignore the culture of the impoverished and ethnic peoples, on the ground that it either scarcely exists or exists in such distorted form as best to be suppressed. Some social scientists have been arguing as if these peoples are lacking—linguistically, psychically, and culturally (Roach, 1965 and the retort by Hughes). Surely, here it is necessary to be concrete and ethnographic, and to ask in specific detail about the experiences of the child in various contests. Continuing our usage of the great/little traditional dichotomy and tension, we would suggest that the process of formal schooling is, to a large degree, the struggle to substitute one kind of tradition (or knowledge) for another within the mind of the child. Where, in a folk society, the child would have to master a great variety of particular bits of knowledge, concerning particular persons, topographic features, rites, skills, and so on, the archetypical urban school is oriented toward instilling a knowledge that is abstract, general, and in some sense, "rational," and, thereby, deracinated. In like manner, where in folk society there is a great stress on the function of language to promote consensus and maintain the integrity of the community (Wright), in the urban middle-class world and its schools the stress is on language as a vehicle for imparting "rational" knowledge to strangers. Within the hierarchy of schools, it is the elite university with its graduate education that has epitomized this type of knowledge and language dialect, but the demand now is being made that the elementary school system participate even more intimately in this effort.

But knowledge, or tradition, does not exist in a vacuum. It is borne by individual human beings. And the demand that is being made on the schools to rationalize their curricula even further is also a demand to produce a certain type of human being—abstract, theoretical, rational, and, hence, deracinated— the academic man writ large. But we are sufficiently disenchanted with our colleagues, and with the middle class of the United States, to ask that researchers and critics examine the issue. In making the school more efficient in its transmission of formal knowledge, to what extent will the reformers be helping to create human beings who are more thoroughly deracinated and dehuman- ized? Conversely, to what extent are the current, so-called "inefficiencies" and stupidities of the school system really a blessing or a source of hope, because it is in these interstices (and irrationalities) that the child still has some chance of developing as a human being? We can even ask about the little traditions of the school, the lore and experience that is transmitted informally among pupils, between teacher and pupils (and vice versa), within the school system. How much of what it means to be a man does a boy learn from his schoolmates (rather than from the curricular content of the school)? As reforms eat away the irrationalities and inefficiencies of the school, will they likewise reduce even further the opportunity to observe and experience the meaning of manliness? The skeptical reader may counter that we are here indulging in ethnographic nostalgia, and to be frank we are recalling the youthful Sioux, and their fine personal sensibility, the brilliance of their singing, the virility of their dancing, and their exuberant vitality. During one summer when we were examining Head Start programs operated for Indian children, there was one occasion in which we stepped from a powwow—distinguished by the most exciting singing and dancing—into a classroom where some well-meaning teacher was leading children through the familiar, dreary, off-key rendition of a nursery song. Later, members of this staff were to talk with us about what they were doing for these "culturally deprived" children.

As we look at the youth of the contemporary United States, we are not impressed by the success of our system of education and training. So many of our young men can perform well on the national test of achievement and yet they lack the pride and self-confidence in their manliness. We recognize full well that to an audience of anthropologists and intellectuals, these criticisms may seem overly familiar. Yet, we think someone has to raise these questions, as *research* questions, and we think that this is part of our task as intellectuals and anthropologists, because otherwise all of us tend to concentrate so exclusively on the issue of educational tasks—how the schools can teach better, faster, and more: how can kids be taught Russian at three, calculus at four, and nuclear physics at five—and neglect to ask a far more important question: what is happening to our children as human beings?

Let us summarize by using an economic model. Theoretically, it would be possible to isolate children in an environment free of all stimulation. Such environments, we would surmise, are fairly rare and would exist only in the most misguided and understaffed institutions. Given an actual environment, whether it be Harlem, Pine Ridge, or Summerfield, children will be experiencing and learning. If they are part of a folk society, they will be learning a folk culture. If they are part of the general middle-class of the United States, they will be learning its culture, and becoming better fitted for early achievement in school. For example, the child reared among the middle class may acquire a larger vocabulary than the child reared in the slum or the reservation. Yet, while the size of vocabulary is predictive of early scholastic achievement, it is not a statement of linguistic or social maturity; for, as but one illustration, consider that some people of a modest vocabulary can be far more eloquent than scholars whose vocabulary is huge. What the child experiences in home and school is but a selection from a vast possible range, so that, in economic terms, if the child is having one kind of experience, then he cannot be having another. If he is learning calculus, then he is not simultaneously learning to dance, powwow style. We are suggesting that most intellectuals, including anthropologists, are so sold on the value of children learning calculus that they have forgotten about the value of dancing, and that they are made so irate by the diction of incompetent educators who prate about the value of learning to play *with* others, that they have forgotten the intimate relationship between play and freedom.

# References

Bell, Robert R. 1962. *The Sociology of Education: A Sourcebook*. Homewood, IL: Dorsey Press.

Bharati, A. 1963. ''Eclectic patterns in Indian pilgrimage.'' Paper delivered at the annual meeting of the American Anthropological Association, San Francisco. Dittoed.

Brotz, Howard. 1961. ''Functionalism and dynamic analysis.'' *European Journal of Sociology*. (Archives Europeenes de Sociologie) 2:170-179.

Burnett, Jacquetta Hill. 1966. ''Ceremony, rites, and economy in the student system of a rural high school.'' Paper delivered at the annual meetings, American Anthropological Association, Pittsburgh.

Charters, W.W., Jr., and N.L. Gage. 1963. *Readings in the Social Psychology of Education*. Boston: Allyn & Bacon.

140

Friedenberg, Edgar Z. 1965. *Coming of Age in America: Growth and Acquiescence.* New York: Random House, Inc.

Gans, Herbert J. 1965. *The Urban Villagers: Group and Class in the Life of Italian-Americans.* New York: The Free Press.

Goffman, Erving. 1959. *The Presentation of Self in Everyday Life.* Garden City: Doubleday & Co.

Guba, Egon G., Philip W. Jackson, and Charles E. Bidwell. 1963. "Occupational choice and the teaching career." In *Readings in the Social Psychology of Education,* ed. W.W. Charters and N.L. Gage, pp. 271-286. Reprinted from Educational Research Bulletin 38 (1959):1-12, 27.

Halsey, A.H., Jean Floud, and C. Arnold Anderson. 1961. *Education, Economy, and Society.* New York: The Free Press.

Havighurst, Robert J. et al. 1962. *Growing Up in River City.* New York: John Wiley & Sons, Inc.

Henry, Jules. 1963. *Culture Against Man.* New York: Random House, Inc.

Hollingshead, A.B. 1949. *Elmtown's Youth.* New York: John Wiley & Sons, Inc.

Hughes, Everett Cherrington. 1963. *French Canada in Transition.* Chicago: University of Chicago Press, Phoenix Books, p. 139.

_____. 1965. "Comment on Sociological analysis and poverty" by J.L. Roach. *American Journal of Sociology* 71:75-76.

Redfield, Robert. 1956. *Peasant Society and Culture.* Chicago: University of Chicago Press, Phoenix Books, p. 53.

Roach, Jack L. 1965. "Sociological analysis and poverty." *American Journal of Sociology* 71:68-75, 76-77.

Singer, Milton. 1960. "The great tradition of Hinduism in the city of Madras." In *Anthropology of Folk Religions,* ed. by Charles Leslie. New York: Random House, Vintage Books (V 105). (Reprinted from *Journal of American Folklore* 71:347-388.)

Spindler, George D. 1963. *Education and Culture: Anthropological Approaches.* New York: Holt, Rinehart and Winston, Inc.

Thomas, Elizabeth Marshall. 1966. *Warrior Herdsmen.* London: Secker & Warburg.

Vidich, Arthur J. and Joseph Bensman. 1960. *Small Town in Mass Society.* New York: Doubleday & Co., Inc.

Vidich, Arthur J. and Maurice R. Stein. 1964. *Reflections on Community Studies.* New York: John Wiley & Sons, Inc.

Waller, Willard. 1932. *The Sociology of Teaching.* New York: John Wiley & Sons, Inc., Science Editions, 1965.

Warner, William Lloyd. 1949. *Democracy in Jonesville: A Study of Quality and Inequality.* New York: Harper & Row, Publishers, Inc.

Withers, Carl. 1945. *Plainville* by James West (pseud.). New York: Columbia University Press.

Wolcott, Harry F. 1967 (reissued with changes 1984). *A Kwakiutl Village and School.* Prospect Heights, IL: Waveland Press, Inc.

Wright, Rolland. 1964. *The Urban Man.* Detroit: Montieth College Readings.

Wylie, Laurence. 1964. *Village in the Vauclose.* New York: Harper & Row, Publishers, Inc., Colophon Books CN 24.

# Footnote

[1] After reading this essay in manuscript, Howard S. Becker commented that: We may have understated a little the difficulty of observing contemporary classrooms. It is not just the survey method of educational testing or any of those things that keeps people from seeing what is going on. I think, instead, that it is first and foremost a matter of it all being so familiar that it becomes almost impossible to single out events that occur in the classroom as things that have occurred, even then they happen right in front of you. I have not had the experience of observing in elementary and high school classrooms myself, but I have in college classrooms and it takes a tremendous effort of will and imagination to stop seeing only the things that are conventionally "there" to be seen. I have talked to a couple of teams of research people who have sat around in classrooms trying to observe and it is like pulling teeth to get them to see or write anything beyond what "everyone" knows.

# School and Peer Society
# within Indian Communities*

## Murray L. Wax

Informally and briefly I would like to report on some of the research we have been conducting within American Indian schools. I believe that it has relevance beyond the specialized area of Indian education. This report indicates some of the range of our researches in order that those readers who believe that the findings may be applicable to their own situation will find their minds stimulated and will know where to turn for further details. And, in order that I do not prejudge the matter of comparison and applicability, I will proceed by summarizing the course of our research among the Oglala Sioux of the Pine Ridge Reservation, South Dakota.

We chose this area and this people because they had been subjected for many years to a variety of education efforts from mission schools and schools operated by the federal government. Nonetheless, despite this prolonged exposure to the processes of formal education, the achievement level of the Sioux youngsters was quite low and the reservation as a whole was distinguished by poverty and social and cultural disadvantage. We wanted, then, to see where were the barriers or resistances that developed in a situation of this sort, where presumably some energetic and talented educators and reformers had been at work for so long a period in what must have been a very diligent fashion.

When we came to Pine Ridge, we found that the educational plant compared favorably with that designed for and serving impoverished and disadvantaged groups elsewhere in the United States. Many of the buildings were new additions; most of the teachers were provided with comfortable and modern quarters. In general, the facilities and equipment were reasonably adequate. Yet, the very adequacy of buildings and quarters made a most striking contrast between the school campuses and the dwellings of the people whose children were to attend the schools. The situation appeared almost ideally *colonial*. On the one side, there was a compound of schools and housing, sometimes even surrounded by fences or protected by other barriers; while, on the other side, there was the complete poverty and misery of the Sioux themselves. We found that this ecological portrait was symptomatic of the difficulties of the schools at the present juncture. For, indeed, the main problem of the school system could be laid to the caste barrier that existed between the Indian and the educator (whether non-Indian or not). This barrier, needless to say, was reinforced by the relative poverty and political impotence of the Sioux people.

* "School and Peer Society within Indian Communities" by Murray L. Wax first appeared in *Council on Anthropology and Education Newsletter*, Vol. 2, No. 3 (October 1971), pp. 1-4.

Within the schools the consequence of this barrier was that, by the intermediate grades, the Sioux children had begun to develop a closed and highly organized peer society inside the school walls and the classroom itself. The ease of organization of peer society was heightened by the distinctive language of the Sioux (which was, of course, other than English and so, impenetrable to the teacher), and by other distinctive cultural peculiarities of the children. As a result, the children could carry out within the classroom a very active and intensely satisfying social life, not only without the interference but without even the awareness of the teacher. It was not so much that the children were hostile to the teacher or to her educational procedures but that she stood outside and unable to influence the active life of this peer society. The separation of the teacher from the peer society was intensified, not only by the language, as we have noted, but also and even more strikingly by the caste barrier. The teacher did not mingle with the parents, and, indeed, parents rarely visited the school or entered the classrooms. Neither teacher nor parents communicated with each other easily and informally on the matters pertaining to the children, and the teachers mistakenly thought of this situation as a blessing. As some remarked to me, one of the satisfying things about teaching in a federal school for Indians was that parents did not interfere with their work. Yet, only the parents or other Indian adults would have been capable of perceiving the nature of the activities of the Indian peer society in the school and so of drastically affecting it and thereby directing the attention of children to the tasks of the schoolroom. In a sense, what we were observing in the schools was a culturally heightened form of the same antagonism and social distance that prevails in many urban situations, especially slums and ghettos.

It might naively be thought that since the conflict in the school pitted the teacher against the peer society that therefore the desirable and simplest remedy to the situation would be to destroy or disrupt the peer society of the Indian youngsters. In fact, many programs, whether consciously or not, are designed as to perform this disruption, and some theorists and observers of the Sioux have argued indeed that what is needed is a reinforcement of the nuclear family at the expense of the peer society. Dumont and I have taken the opposite view. We argue that the peer society can be turned very effectively toward the encouragement of formal learning and that, when this is done, the children proceed quickly and enthusiastically to the performance of educational tasks and that the learning that so results is dramatically effective. Both he and I observed — he more closely than I — classrooms in which the harnessing of the peer society to the educational tasks has been expertly performed by sympathetic and knowledgeable teachers. Some of these teachers have been Indian in their ancestry and others not, but in either case they have enlisted the enthusiastic cooperation of the peer society, so that the Indian children encourage each other in performing tasks and become expert at eliciting responses and inducing motivation among their peers. He and I have also argued that, if education is to be efficient, and if more teachers are to establish this satisfactory relationship with the Indian peer society, then the parents must be brought into the organization of the school system and in such a fashion that they were accepted by the teachers as being either peers or authorities. In short, we argue that it is very detrimental to the educational situations to have the teachers elevated to such a position that they can derogate the parents, because, when this is so, teachers have no real incentive to understand the cultural processes of either the parents or the children, and they are particularly likely to interpret difference in behavior as indicating inferiority.

We are inclined especially to stress the significance of our findings because of the recent emphasis upon programs for the pre-school children. Most of the programs have been justified by an argument that points out the inadequate performance of the disadvantaged child at the preadolescent and adolescent level, and the argument is usually made that this inadequacy can be traced to deficiencies in infantile and early-childhood training. We contend quite the contrary: that the deficiencies in scholastic performance of the older child reflect his contemporary situation and are not to be attributed to deprivations in his early childhood experience. In particular, we have repeatedly heard educators and experts derogate the child-rearing of the Sioux in terms that made us realize the superficiality and ethnocentrism of these critics. Our own observations are to the contrary and lead us to stress that, while the Sioux do not socialize their children in the same way as middle-class families, they are very expert in creating a particular type of child with some outstanding virtues and potentialities. Whether or not our argument on this point will be accepted by others, the fact is that the socialization and early childhood rearing processes of the Sioux, as of other disadvantaged peoples, deserve to be examined in their own right and not be speculated upon by those who have not been in a position to observe but who merely have hypothesized on the basis of the performance on children in class-rooms which are culturally and socially alien.

While we have not ourselves conducted research outside the continental United States among developing nations, we would hazard that the situation that we observed at Pine Ridge is much more frequent than people, including educators, usually care to acknowledge. Certainly, in large areas of Latin America where there are substantial populations of American Indians still speaking the native language and alienated from the Hispanicized society, we have every reason to surmise a kindred barrier in the educational process. As long as the teacher represents the antagonistic and superordinate Spanish culture and condemns and derogates the culture and social existence of the parents of the Indian pupils, the educational process will encounter a blockage as severe as the one in Pine Ridge. Moreover, in this regard we should like to remark that emphasis upon exceptional students and on the struggle to detach them, as individuals, from the community of their origin completely misses the point. If we are to accomplish anything in this situation, we should put our focus upon the education of peoples and communities, rather than merely affecting a few exceptional, and usually marginal, individuals. It is not too difficult to detach one, or several, exceptional individuals from a community, but what we are faced with in the process of development is the education of large masses of population. This can only be accomplished by a process that relates positively and equitably to the community as a whole, both parents and children.

# Bibliography

*Dropout of American Indians at the Secondary Level* by R.H. Wax amd M.L. Wax, 1964; mimeoed.

"The Warrior Dropout" by R.H. Wax. *TransAction*, IV, 1967, 40-46.

"Oglala Sioux Dropouts and their Problems with Educators" by R.H. Wax. *Education and School Crisis: Perspectives of Teaching Disadvantaged Youth*, ed. Everett T. Keach, et al. New York: Wiley, 1967, pp. 247-257.

"American Indian Education for What?" by M.L. Wax and R.H. Wax. *Midcontinent American Studies Journal*, VI, 1965, 164-170.

"Cultural Deprivation as an Educational Ideology," by M.L. Wax and R.H. Wax. *Journal of American Indian Education*, III, 1964, 15-18.

"American Indians and White People" by R.H. Wax and R.K. Thomas. *Phylon*, XXII, 1961, 305-317. Reprinted in *Education and School Crisis*, ed. E.K. Keach, et al.

"The Intercultural Classroom" by R.V. Dumont. Delivered at the Annual Meeting of the Society for Applied Anthropology, 1967; mimeoed.

"Indian Communities and Project Headstart" by M.L. Wax and R.H. Wax, Summary of a brief survey, mimeoed, 1965.